FIVE MINUTES

A JONELLE SWEET MYSTERY

R. LANIER CLEMONS

JOURNEY
WELL
BOOKS

Copyright © 2019 R. Lanier Clemons

Published in the United States by Journey Well Books

ISBN: 978-0-9967554-4-3 (ebook)
ISBN: 978-0-9967554-5-0 (Paperback)

Book design by ebooklaunch.com

JOURNEY
WELL
BOOKS

Books by R. Lanier Clemons

Burial Plot
(EBOOK ONLY)

Gone Missing

The Trickster

Five Minutes

Who's Riley?
A JSM Amazon Short Read: Book 1

CHAPTER 1

"They say the new boyfriend don't like kids," said the one in the yellow top. "They say he snatched that little girl."

"Boyfriend ain't got nuthin' to do with it. She didn't wanna be a mama no more," added the one bursting out of lime green pants. "You ask me. That girl took her own kid. Hid her someplace I bet."

Jonelle Sweet overheard the two women as she poured coffee from the convenience store's urn and tried not to think about when the container was last cleaned. What child were they talking about? It sounded as if they knew something about the mother which meant the incident probably happened nearby.

"So you say, Francie. So why didn't she let that child stay with her daddy if she didn't wanna be bothered?"

A child abducted. The mother accused.

She trailed close behind as Francie and friend went down the chip aisle, past the candy display and stopped in front of the pastries.

Francie picked up a box of donuts, peered through the cellophane, shook the container and placed it back on the shelf. "What I heard was that she didn't want to give the baby daddy the satisfaction of taking away the one thing left from the relationship."

"That little girl ain't property."

"True that."

When they looked her way, frowns plastered on their faces, Jonelle smiled. "Can never make up my mind when I come in here. Think I'll buy a lottery ticket. You never know."

With her cover blown, she walked away, aware of two pairs of eyes burning into her back. Their comments piqued her interest. Especially since new criminal cases at Shorter Investigative Services had slowed to a trickle. Nothing nearly as stimulating as last year's case of murdered twins came across her desk.

Instead, for the past month she'd served a summons on a deadbeat dad, photographed a woman cheating on her husband and confirmed the beloved Pug of a divorced couple was holed up with the husband in a Best Western off Interstate 95 near White Marsh.

This was the first time she'd heard of an abduction and her scalp tingled with excitement. With coffee in hand she grabbed the *Sun* newspaper from the rack near the door and took the publication over to the corner. She flipped through it searching for any news. Nothing. Leaving the paper on the shelf next to the chips display she walked over and stood in line behind three day laborers—two Hispanic, one African American. Dressed in hard hat, jeans and tee shirt, and smelling like the dirt that covered his clothes, the man closest to her juggled two pre-wrapped sandwiches, and a pint of chocolate milk.

She cleared her throat, but kept her voice low. "Say, what do you think about what happened to that poor child?"

He turned and looked directly into her eyes. They both had the same nut brown complexion, but his build was slim and hers was not. Jonelle figured he was probably around her age, somewhere in his mid-thirties.

She smiled and he smiled back. "Yeah. We all heard about that," he said. "Damn shame, you ask me. That young lady and her little girl come in here all the time. Looked like a good mother to me. Could 'a knocked me over when I heard what happened. 'Course some of the guys"—he indicated the two other laborers now standing by the door— "claim if she didn't do it herself, she probably paid somebody to do it for her. My opinion? Didn't nobody snatch that kid. You ask me . . ." Instead of finishing the sentence, he shrugged and placed his things on the counter.

"She live around here?"

"Sure. That there building across the street."

"I don't suppose you know her name?"

He paid for his items, and Jonelle set her coffee on the counter.

"Naw. Don't know her name. We never got friendly, though I wouldn't't've minded if you know what I mean?" He winked at her.

One of the Hispanic men yelled for him to hurry.

He tilted his head and smiled again. "Maybe I'll see you soon."

"Maybe so," she replied.

"You holdin' up the line, Miss," said the woman behind the register.

"Sorry. I'd, uh, also like a couple two dollar scratch-offs and, um, six dollars' worth of Mega Millions tickets."

Several people groaned.

As the cashier tore off the cards and printed out the tickets, Jonelle said, "I'm curious if you know the name of the young lady with the abducted daughter. Sounds like something I'd hate to go through."

"Only know first name. Tamora. Little girl real cute." Lines formed between her eyes. "Stuff like that doesn't happen 'round here."

Except it did, Jonelle thought as she placed money in the woman's hand. Standing outside, she stared at the building across the street. Jonelle checked her watch. Still early and she had nothing else on her schedule.

She sipped a little coffee, grimaced, and threw the cup in the trash. With only a first name to go on and no legitimate reason to pry, she squared her shoulders and headed to the mid-rise gray concrete building.

Structures often evoked emotions. While clean, the building lacked character. To Jonelle the apartment building seemed sad, even lonely. The absence of balconies meant tenants couldn't add personal touches to break up the plain façade. Bright-colored flowers might help add interest to the gloomy-looking evergreen bushes that adorned both sides of the uneven walkway. Glass doors in need of cleaning opened easily and faced directly in front of two banks of elevators.

The lack of furniture discouraged anyone from lounging around. If someone took the child from here, they'd have easy access in and out.

Raised voices erupted from an open door on the right. She smoothed her cotton skirt and made sure she hadn't spilled any coffee on her yellow tunic top. She noted the "Manager" sign on the door and entered to find a man, dressed in khaki pants and shirt, standing next to a desk. Behind the desk sat a large, light-skinned black woman. The name plate read "Mrs. Lorraine Watkins."

"When I tell you on Tuesday that I want the toilet fixed in 510, that means Tuesday. Not Wednesday and sure as hell you don't wait until today."

"I already told you Mrs. Spiller grabbed me and said she needed—"

"I don't care what she needed. She wasn't the one complainin' about the damn toilet. You got a problem you come to me and I'll handle the tenants. Now get upstairs and . . . help you, Miss?"

Engrossed in the exchange, Jonelle almost forgot why she was there. "Right. Yes. I was over at Marv's Mini Mart and heard some of the people talking about a child abduction. I'm a private investigator, and . . ." She dug in her purse for a business card and handed it to the woman. "And I thought maybe I could see if the mother needed any help with her case."

Mrs. Watkins' eyes narrowed. Without breaking eye contact, she said, "Go on up to 510 and don't come back until that toilet is fixed."

The man shuffled around Jonelle.

"And shut the door on your way out. Please."

Over the past few years Jonelle had learned to deal with all kinds of people and hadn't felt intimidated. Until now.

"You people go around drumming up business like this?"

"No. But the little I heard made me curious. I know her first name is Tamora, so if you'd give her my card, I'd like to help."

The manager leaned back in the chair, which protested loudly under her bulk. "Last I heard she was still in jail, though her sister told me she got an attorney. Court appointed."

"Jail? Somebody took the child from here, and the cops think she did it?"

The woman's voice rose. "I've known Tamora for almost five years. She's good people. She didn't do nothing to that girl. That damn child's daddy called the cops."

"Then, why—?"

"Because . . . they're claiming she lied. What she told the cops is not what they say the surveillance tape at the store shows."

CHAPTER 2

Apartment Manager Mrs. Watkins was unable—unwilling?—to give Jonelle any more details of Tamora's arrest. She dismissed Jonelle with a wave of the hand and "I'll pass your info on to Tamora . . . if I get the chance."

Jonelle made a beeline back to the minimart for her Jeep, now sandwiched between an Utz potato chip delivery truck and an HVAC service vehicle. She headed up Interstate 95 all the while drumming her fingers on the steering wheel, unable to get the child's kidnapping out of her mind.

She parked her Jeep in one of the agency's five reserved spots in the small, gravel lot on the corner. The only office building on the block wouldn't rate a second look. Small, blocky and beige, only the menu board outside the secured entrance provided any indication of what was inside. Jonelle punched in her code and made her way up the back stairs to the second floor.

At the end of the hall stood glass double doors. "Shorter Investigative Services" stenciled in large letters in the glass took up over half the space. Below that, in smaller script, "Private Investigations." She entered and waved a quick hello to secretary slash receptionist Rainey Gottzchek and said, on her way to her office, "Served the guy and now I'm gonna make a few calls." She punched in the number for Detective Thelonius Burton before her butt hit the chair.

Burt answered on the third ring, so she got right to the point. "Hey. It's Jonelle. What do you know about a recent abduction of a small child over in Maryland City?"

"And a good morning to you, too." His smile came through the line.

"Good morning. So what do you know? I was across the street from the mother's apartment and overheard some women talking. Do you have any information?"

He sighed. "All business this morning, huh? Okay. I think something popped up on an alert," Burt said, his deep voice echoing through the phone. "Hold on."

She opened her computer and checked emails while waiting for him to come back. Nothing interesting needed her immediate attention . . . big surprise. For a brief moment she thought about walking into her uncle Marvin's office to tell him about Tamora and the child. And quickly dismissed the idea. No sense telling him about the kidnapping before she knew any details.

"Called over to a detective I know in Anne Arundel County's western district," Burt said. "There's a recent abduction of a child named Lark Phelps, aged four, from her apartment. Of the people interviewed that night, no one saw or heard anything unusual."

Jonelle groaned. So young. "The mother is Tamora Phelps. Right?"

"Yep. They arrested her because her story didn't add up."

"She still in jail?"

"Yep." He cleared his throat. "By the way, how'd you wind up across the street?"

"Overheard people talking in Marv's Mini Mart when I stopped for a coffee." She hurried on before he could ask for specifics. "Do you have the attorney's name?"

"Why the interest? Kids go missing every day."

A knot in her stomach formed at his cavalier attitude. Not wanting to alienate the detective before she got more information, she pushed the feeling aside. "I want to talk to the lawyer, see if I can help."

"You didn't answer the 'why'".

"I'm not sure. Call it concern for a child's welfare, curiosity, or . . . truth is I love everything about my job, but what I'm doing now is grunt work. I hate that. Plus, everything I've heard so far, from different kinds of people, says Tamora was, is, a good mother."

Burt mumbled something.

"What'd you say?"

"Nothing. The attorney is Paul Langford. Don't have his number but I'm pretty sure you know how to find it."

"Thanks, Burt." She clicked off before he could ask any more questions. It only took a few minutes before she had Attorney Langford's telephone number in the Public Defender's office.

She punched in the numbers and immediately got voicemail. She left a message stating that if he needed investigative work she wanted to offer her services to him and his client Tamora Phelps. After leaving both her office and private cellphone numbers, she went around checking the plants to make sure they had enough water. She stopped in front of the large window and gazed over at the Johns Hopkins medical center complex. Her view was somewhat clouded, not by the sky—the day was filled with bright sunshine—but with the accumulation of dust and grime on the window. She made a mental note to ask Rainey about getting the windows washed.

Another circuit of the room landed her back in her chair. She jumped at the sound of the office intercom buzzing on her desk.

She stabbed the button. "Yes, Rainey?"

"Got a few more summonses for you to deliver."

"Damn!"

"Excuse me?"

"Sorry. Why don't the guys get these?" Jonelle asked, raising her voice.

"Stop complainin', Hon. Fact is, I already gave a few to Ben. Omar is still on that cyber security whatsit. You know the rules. You agents all handle whatever comes in. That's how your uncle keeps this business floatin'."

Jonelle lay her forehead on the desk. "Yeah, sure. I'll come out and grab them in a minute."

"They'll be waitin'."

She raked her fingers through her hair and glared at the phone, willing it to ring and praying for the attorney's voice to come through. Nothing happened. She moved the volume control back and forth, making sure the ringtone was set at its highest mark. That done, she trudged down the hall to retrieve the dreaded assignments.

Jonelle plastered a smile on her face as she came around to the desk. She held out her hand as the phone rang on the receptionist desk.

"Shorter Investigative Services." Rainey listened for a bit. "She just walked up. I'll put you on hold."

Jonelle lifted an eyebrow.

Rainey slapped the papers into her outstretched hand with more force than necessary. The stinging sensation, coupled with the scowl on the secretary's face, spoke volumes.

"Sorry for what I said earlier, Rainey. Feeling bummed is all. But I'll get over it, like I always do. Friends?"

The secretary's face softened. She nodded, which set two pencils—already lodged in her white-blond bouffant hair—dancing, and pointed to the blinking light on her phone. "That's for you. Guy says his name's Langford and he's returning your call."

"Thanks." She forced herself to walk casually back to her office when every bone in her body screamed *hurry and grab the phone as quickly as possible,* as if she were drowning and Langford held some kind of lifeline.

Before picking up, she breathed in for five counts and breathed out for five counts. "Hello? This is Jonelle Sweet."

"Langford here, returning your call," came the harried voice on the other end. Rustling papers and muffled voices made up the background noises, and for the briefest of moments Jonelle felt a little guilty.

"I know you're busy, but I've heard a little about the Tamora Phelps case and understand you're her attorney. I'd like to offer my services." She squeezed her eyes shut and plunged ahead, "To help in your case. Should you have need for a private investigator." Marvin won't like her going behind his back.

Several seconds passed without comment. Noises in the background continued. Although she wanted to sell herself to this man, she held her tongue.

"Tell you what," he said. "I always like a face-to-face meet, so come on over to my office. Gotta be today, though. In fact—hold a second." Langford made no attempt to hide his words to whoever was in the room. "Hey guys. What time are we needed in court?"

A female voice answered. "One o'clock. Sharp. Judge Connelly is on the bench, and he doesn't dick around."

"Guess you heard that, so if you wanna meet, it's gotta be in the next hour."

She agreed and promised to leave right away.

Caution came through the line. "Why're you interested? Are you a relative or something?"

"No. I've heard some things about the case, and it piqued my curiosity."

"Curiosity, huh?" He snorted. "Can't pay much, so if money means a lot to you, forget it."

"I don't know much at this point, and maybe when I learn more, it'll be a non-starter. But, well . . ."

"Well, indeed. See you in a few, Miss, uh, Sweet." He was gone before she could say good-bye.

Figuring she didn't need to get Marvin upset over something that might not happen anyway, she grabbed her bag and stuffed one of the Notices to Appear next to her .38 and headed out. Marvin's voice resounded through his open door. She tip-toed past.

"I'm off," she said.

Rainey squinted at her computer screen. That look told Jonelle that either Ben sent Rainey something she couldn't decipher, or Omar issued a report she had to rewrite before placing it in the closed file.

"Rainey?"

"Yes. You're off." She waved her hand. "If we need you I'll call."

She plugged the address of the Glen Burnie 7th District Court office in her GPS. Instead of taking the building's elevator, she climbed up to the second floor, her sandals clanging loudly on the metal stairs. A quick walk down a long hallway put her in front of the outer reception area of the public defender's office. "I called earlier and Mr. Langford said I could stop by."

The young clerk peered at her from the top of his glasses. "And you are?"

"Sorry. Jonelle Sweet."

He picked up the phone and announced her arrival. "Go on back. Third door on the right."

"Thanks."

She knocked softly and, after a loud "come in" opened the door . . . and stopped. The tiny, windowless office could barely contain the stocky man behind the L-shaped desk.

"Come in, come in." He pointed to the fabric-covered chair across from him, pockmarked with mysterious stains.

Her chest tightened. Her pulse raced as she took in the four-shelf wooden bookcase filled with law books and the black metal file cabinet crammed against the wall on his left. And the overflowing files taking up every available flat space.

"Give me a sec." Jonelle breathed in and out, slowly, deeply.

Langford cocked his head. "Problem?"

"Claustrophobic."

"Ah. Well, go ahead and leave the door open, but unless you wanna talk in the hall, this'll have to do."

"Is it okay with you if I move the chair closer to the open door?"

The corners of Langford's mouth curled up. "Whatever works. We don't have much time at any rate. What is it you want exactly?"

"I work for Shorter Investigative Services and we never, ever, seek out cases." Jonelle pulled out a business card and passed it over to the lawyer. She sat on the edge of the chair.

"I happened to be in the area when I heard several people talking about an abducted child. On the one hand, people said that Tamora—that was the name I heard—was a good mother. Yet, she was arrested—"

"She's out now. Got her released in her sister's custody."

"Great. See, I know the system is overburdened and, well . . ." She indicated the papers strewn around the small space. "I also know how busy you guys are, so I decided maybe I could help."

Langford flicked her business card back and forth between his fingers. "Think I've heard of you guys. Minority owned. Good reputation if I remember correctly." He leaned back in his chair. "Fact is Tamora hasn't been too open with us. Says she didn't do it but not much else. Plus, there's places where she's flat out lied about little stuff that she refuses to explain."

Jonelle jumped on the comment. "I'd heard that the police have proof of a lie. Can you share that with me?"

Langford folded his hands behind his head. Jonelle averted her eyes from the sweat stains under his armpits.

"Everything hinges on time," he said. "She admits she left the child alone to run across the street but insists she was only gone for five minutes. Surveillance tape shows her in the store a lot longer than that."

"Is she sticking to that time? Five minutes?"

"Yep. But getting information out of her is like pulling a tiny splinter from your hand. You gotta keep digging deeper and deeper. Truth is I thought at first she had a white people problem."

She frowned at the statement.

He held up his hands as if to ward off an imminent onslaught of verbal abuse. "Don't get upset. Some of these clients do. Will only talk to black lawyers 'cause they think white folks like me won't give them a fair shake. Offered to ask the judge to grant her another attorney, but she declined." He opened the top manila folder and flipped through a few sheets. "I'm thinking she might be honest with you. Something tells me you know how to get people to open up. Here's what I'll do. Let me run this by the boss, see what he thinks. If he says okay, and we agree to the terms, it's a go."

Now that she almost had what she wanted, she didn't know what to do next. The whole meeting went far easier than anticipated. Here she'd gone and sold herself to this guy and now had to face the fact that Marvin might not agree. What then? She'd put the name of the agency out there . . . an agency with his name and his reputation all wrapped up together.

"Thought you'd be a little happier than this. You having second thoughts?"

"No, no. Not at all. Thinking of next steps. Supposing your boss agrees and we go forward, I'm assuming I'll have access to all the documentation you have on the case so far. That right?"

"Of course. We're all working for the same team."

"Tell me something," Jonelle said. "Do you think she had anything to do with it?"

"Honestly? I don't know. Somethings off about her. Can't put my finger on what is it though."

"So. When can I expect to hear from you?"

Langford stood. Jonelle followed suit.

"We've got a staff meeting tomorrow, so it'll either be later that day or, more likely, on Monday."

"Monday works," she said quickly. That should give her time to prepare how to present what she'd say to Marvin. "Fact is I also have a staff meeting tomorrow."

"Good." He held out his hand and they shook. "You know. When you first called I was a little leery. You're not the first PI to come begging to help out on cases. No offense."

"Since I'm not 'begging,' none taken. Like I said, the agency doesn't go out looking for work. What little I heard about Tamora and her child affected me in a way I can't explain. Plus you know as well as I do that every day that goes by doesn't bode well for the child."

She turned to go. "Oh. One more thing. Who called the cops? Tamora?"

"Nope. The child's father stopped by. He said the door was open. Searched the apartment. Nothing. Thought maybe the kid was across the hall but she wasn't so he called the police. Good thing he did."

"Don't you believe Tamora would've called?"

Langford shot her a peculiar look. "You'd hope so, right?"

CHAPTER 3

*W*hy the hell wasn't the door locked? The door was supposed to be locked. At the very least she should have made it harder. I could've put marks on the door like in them crime shows. Give the cops something to think about.

Almost changed my mind. Once inside, I could've left the little one where she was—asleep on the one bed, curled up, warm and trusting—and gone away without anyone knowing anything. Her pretty pink pajamas with the butterflies looked almost too warm, yet when I picked her up, she wasn't sweating. Funny. Never held a child this size before. She smells like the powder my mama used to rub on me after a bath.

She shifts slightly in my arms and opens her eyes.

Uh-oh. If she gets upset I'll make some excuse, put her back down, and leave. But she didn't. The puzzled look changed to recognition as she gazed at my face. She yawned and closed her eyes again. Easy-peasy.

Everything I do in this apartment is for the best. Sure. The child is safe; she'll be fine. Keep telling that to yourself. That'll make everything better.

But I feel awful. Why'd the cops arrest the mother? That wasn't part of the plan.

CHAPTER 4

Unable to put it off any longer Jonelle approached Marvin's office. "Knock, knock," she said, tapping on the frame of his always open office door. He raised his head from the papers scattered across his desk and smiled.

"Come on in, Jonnie. Give me an excuse to stop looking at these. My eyes are starting to cross," he said.

She hurried over to the guest chair, sat, and immediately stood again. "Okay. Here's the deal. I—the agency—may be able to help in a case involving the abduction of a small child. The cops arrested the mother, but they let her go and its early days yet."

Marvin stared at her, mouth slightly open. He took off his reading glasses. "All I got from all that was help, abduction, and child." He pointed to the guest chair.

Jonelle sat as if the principal had asked her to explain why the teacher told her to leave class.

"Clarify. In a logical fashion if you don't mind."

She grasped the arms of the chair and took a deep breath. "Okay. After I served the summons this morning I stopped by a convenience store for coffee. While I was there, I overheard conversations about someone abducting a small child who lived in the building across the street, but I'm not one hundred percent certain that's where the kidnapper grabbed her. When I went over to talk to the apartment manager—"

"You did what?"

She swallowed. "I wanted to know more."

Marvin's face clouded.

"Um. Should I tell you the rest?"

"Might as well, considering your visit already happened."

She twirled her handcuff and pistol necklace round and round between her fingers. "Right. So. The manager, Lorraine Watkins, also said Tamora—that's the mother's name—was a good parent, but there was some discrepancy on what she initially told the police and what they later found out."

He raised his hand. "Bottom line it for me."

Somewhat chastened, she lowered her voice. "I've offered the agency's services to her court-appointed attorney Paul Langford. I told him I'd like to investigate what happened from the time his client left her apartment to the time the child went missing."

Marvin leaned back and stared at the ceiling. "Correct me if I'm wrong. All new cases go through me first. Is that your understanding?"

She nodded.

"So, on your own, you've gotten us a new case, without so much as a heads-up and no regard for what else this agency has on its plate. Is that also correct?"

She stared at her uncle without comment.

"We're not ambulance chasers. I've worked damn hard over the years to get us the good, no, if I'm honest, great reputation we have. And then you go and solicit—"

"No." Her tone made his eyebrows shoot up.

"I didn't *solicit*. I offered to help because it sounded like something we should do . . . help a poor mother who's probably frantic about what happened to her child." She fought to push down her anger.

"I'm sorry, but I want to be an investigator and investigators *investigate*. I know I have to do whatever the agency requires, and I accept that. But all I have on my plate now are a few lousy summonses to deliver. And then what? Yes, I get that we all have work to do, but things have slowed a bit." She pointed to the papers. "Even you can see that. All I want to do is help. And besides, the attorney doesn't even know if he can hire us. He has to speak to his supervisor first."

"You done?"

"Yes."

Their eyes locked and hardened.

A loud throat clearing turned their attention to the open door.

"You two okay? I only ask because your voices are carrying all the way out to the front." Rainey looked from one to the other, concern clouding her pale blue eyes.

"Sorry. Please close the door. We'll be done in a few minutes," Marvin said.

"I'll tell Ben and Omar the weekly meeting will begin a little late. It'll give Ben more donut eating time." With a quick glance at them both, she gently closed the door.

Marvin leaned back in his chair. "You did all this because you're bored. Does that sum it up?"

"Partly," she admitted. "I don't mind the grunt work . . . at least not much. But I'm starting to feel like one of those commercials where someone is pedaling like mad on a stationary bike, sweat pouring down their face, and going absolutely nowhere." There. She said it.

"In that scenario are you the person or the bike?"

He had her there. "Both," she said.

"Reputation is everything in this business, Jonelle—"

"I know that."

He slapped his hand on his desk and leaned forward.

Her eyes widened in alarm.

"Let me finish. If people think we're going around trolling for business by passing leaflets on the corner, or flipping a sign through the air, or even passing out business cards to whomever will take one, I've gone from top of the line to bottom of the barrel."

She loved her uncle. But his rigidity when it came to the agency got on her nerves. After silently counting to ten, she lowered her voice and continued. "Look at it this way. No matter how great a company is, if somebody comes along who does something better, reputation makes no difference. People want results. What's the difference if people find us through small print or digital ads, word of mouth, or active, uh, participation?"

"You went behind my back," he said, in a voice resembling a six-year-old boy instead of a sixty-plus-year-old man.

So that was it. "This was a spontaneous thing. I didn't go out seeking a client. If I hadn't gone in that place for coffee, I'd have never known about the child. Burt didn't even have any details."

Marvin laced his fingers together, placed them on top of his head, leaned back, and stared up at the ceiling.

"I called Burt to see if he knew anything about the kidnapping," she said. "He told me the district, and got the public defender's name."

He lowered his eyes and hands and stared at Jonelle for a bit, shaking his head over and over. "You don't waste any time, do you? Guess I should be proud you have initiative."

She breathed easier. "Thanks. It's entirely possible Langford will call and reject my offer."

"You want a yes though, right?"

"Of course."

He sighed deeply and stood. "I'm guessing that you probably impressed the guy so much that he'll sell your suggestion to his boss."

"We don't need to mention this in today's staff meeting, right?" she asked, rising to meet his eyes. "I mean, since there's nothing official yet." Plus, she didn't want the guys to pepper her with questions she couldn't answer.

"Next week. But before you agree to anything, I want to see the paperwork. If I think the price offered for our, that is, your service, is too low, I'll pass." He held her eyes. "And that'll end your involvement."

She hadn't thought about price. She only wanted to help a young mother prove she didn't have anything to do with her daughter's disappearance.

Jonelle eyed the clock on the wall. Only a few minutes until the one o'clock staff meeting. Normally the first to arrive, she lingered in her office, waiting for Langford's call. Though tempted, it wasn't in her DNA to keep her uncle waiting, even though other agents Omar Kamal and Ben Winfield didn't share that trait. Her phone rang as she stepped into the hall.

She recognized the number. "Mr. Langford, glad you called."

"Don't have much time. Wanted to let you know it's a go. Give me your fax number and I'll send the documents in about an hour or so. Return 'em ASAP." She recited the number and he disconnected.

Trying hard to keep from jumping for joy, Jonelle entered the conference room to find Omar already seated around the oval table. The agent's eyebrows rose in surprise. "My clock must be fast if I beat you here," he said. "That and the fact there's nothing to eat must mean bad Karma's on the way."

"Not necessarily," Jonelle said, sitting next to him. "Ben's not here yet."

"Oh, yes I am," Ben said, entering and sitting in a beige tweed-covered chair across from Jonelle. "I'd've been here earlier, but since there's nothing to eat," he shot Rainey a look, which she ignored, "I got myself a cup of coffee. You know. To keep the hunger pangs at bay."

"Like you need more food," Rainey shot back. "Your wife will thank me for helping you stick to your diet."

Marvin clapped his hands. "Okay, guys. Before we get started, Rainey can you close the blinds? While I love the wall of windows, the sunlight's a bit intense right now."

Rainey rose to comply.

"Thanks. Let's get started." His eyes darted over to Jonelle. "Instead of going in seniority, I can tell from the look on Jonelle's face that she has news so she can go first."

She took a deep breath. "I was gonna save this for next week but . . . Paul Langford from the public defender's office called to say they've accepted my offer to help on a missing child case. He's gonna fax me the documents."

The two senior agents looked from her to Marvin, who, after a slight pause, nodded.

Ben whistled. "I'm gonna call you Miss Velcro, 'cause crime seems to stick to you. Do we wanna know how you got involved?"

"I think not," Omar said. "That kinda stuff doesn't interest me anyway."

Jonelle stared into Omar's brown, almost black eyes until he glanced away. "That's not important now. I'll fill you guys in at the next meeting when I have more information."

The rest of the meeting passed without any further mention of Jonelle's case. After it was over she rushed to the supply room where the copier and fax machines stood in the center. While she waited, she tapped out a pencil on stapler rendition of Michael Jackson's "Beat It" until the papers from Langford slid through.

Gathering the items as soon as they left the machine, she skimmed each one. The top sheet contained a witness list, complete not only with names but also contact numbers and addresses. She pursed her lips to keep from shouting "whoo-hoo!" out loud. The majority of the people lived in Tamora's building which meant she didn't have to chase them down.

She entered Marvin's office without knocking, placed the papers on his desk, and sat. "The district attorney's office has given their approval to hiring the agency. The first few pages outline what they want me to do, and on page three is the price. The amount is a little low, but we've done work for less."

He waved her away. "Don't get comfortable. I want to look at these by myself, okay? I want my own thoughts on this. I'll call you when I'm done."

Back in her office she powered up her computer and searched for "pet supplies" for her new kitten. Several dollars poorer, and with no word from her uncle, she read through each summons and decided it was better to at least try and do something productive.

She was about to track down a failure to appear when Marvin's head peeked through her doorway.

"You going someplace?" he asked.

"Not anymore. What do you think?"

"What I want you to tell me is how much time you plan to devote to this case." He entered and dropped the documents on her desk. She glanced through them and smiled when she saw Marvin's signature on the bottom line.

"I got four summonses to deliver, and I'll serve them all." She leaned forward for emphasis. "I'll simply work longer, harder . . . whatever. I've gone over and over the possibilities of this case in my head."

The corners of his mouth turned up. He waved a hand for her to continue.

"Since the mother left the apartment that night, how did the kidnapper know the child was alone? For that matter, how did he, or she, get in?"

Marvin frowned. "Apartment, huh? What floor?"

"I guess that's somewhere in these documents. Does it matter?"

"Yes. Because if the mother lives higher than, say, the second floor, whoever did this took one helluva risk."

Jonelle filed that away in the back of her mind. "Good point. And why didn't she tell the police the whole truth? If she's protecting someone, I'll find out."

"What'll you do if you discover she had something to do with the child's disappearance?"

"I'll advise her attorney, and he'll take it from there."

"You promise me that's all you'll do?"

She laughed. He worried about her as if she were twelve instead of thirty-four. "I'm not going off the deep end if that's what you're worried about."

He studied her for a few moments. "Before you fax Langford our response, make sure Rainey opens a case file." He pointed at her. "And I want an update in every staff meeting from now on." With that he turned on his heel and left.

Advising the secretary was the second thing she did. She called Langford first and told him the signed contract was on the way. She also informed him she was going to Tamora's apartment building to talk to the residents.

CHAPTER 5

S till on a high from Langford's okay and Marvin's agreement to take the case, Jonelle drove to Tamora's building around nine on Monday morning and with the car radio tuned to an all news station, her ears straining for any news about a body found. So far, nothing. She pulled her Jeep into one of several empty spots in the front parking lot. Glancing to her right she noticed the maintenance man from the manager's office picking up trash with a long pole grabber. They locked eyes for a moment before he turned, ducked his head and hurried away.

"Excuse me," she called out.

He kept going in the opposite direction.

She rushed after him. "Hey!" He stopped and turned around. "Mind if I ask you a few questions?"

"You that lady from before. Who're you anyway?"

"I'm a private investigator." Jonelle showed him her ID.

He barely looked at it. "What if I say I do mind?"

She smiled. "I'll ask anyway."

He shrugged. "Don't know nothin'."

"Don't be so sure. I haven't asked anything yet."

"I got work to do." He moved away from her.

"How long you been working here?" she asked, matching his stride.

With eyes focused on the ground, he gripped candy wrappers, paper, and cigarette packs. "Few years."

"That means you know Tamora and her little girl. Right?"

"Maybe."

"Oh, come on. Listen. I'm trying to help. Her lawyer hired me to investigate her case, so I need to find out about what happened."

He stopped poking at the ground and looked up at her. "She didn't do nothin' to that child."

"Did you see her the day it happened?"

"Yeah. She left same time as usual that morning to take little Lark to her sister's daycare."

"Was it always the same? No deviations?"

"Uh-huh."

"And did she come home at about the same time on a regular basis?"

He gave her a peculiar look. "Sure."

So he knew her habits. "Go on."

He shrugged. "Nothin' else to say. When I was on my way outta here around five that afternoon, she was comin' in from her day job. Little Lark looked happy enough to me. I suppose she took the child to Miss Maxine. As usual. Miss Maxine looks after the little girl and a few others what parents have another job to go to."

"How'd she seem to you?"

"Who you mean? Tamora?"

Originally she meant the child but decided to hear what he had to say.

"Both."

He stared at a place in the distance. "Same as usual. Tamora said hi . . . and that's about it. Lark kept her thumb in her mouth. Sometimes she acts shy around people no matter how long she's known 'em."

"How well do you know Tamora?"

He glanced at her and just as quickly looked away. "What you implyin'?"

"Not a thing. But in your capacity as, uh, maintenance engineer, you must know the residents here pretty well."

His mouth dropped open. His long, narrow face broke into a wide grin. "Maintenance engineer. Ha! Been called lotsa things but engineer ain't one of 'em."

She tried a different approach. "I got the impression Tamora was quite attractive. Were you ever interested in her on a more personal level?"

Deep brown, almost black eyes, squinted at her. With a flick of the wrist the pole flipped upward, the end pointed near Jonelle's face. She stepped back quickly.

He opened his mouth to speak but instead stared at something behind her. He thrust the pole back at the ground, snatched up more trash, turned, and left her standing there.

"Hold on a minute. Where're you going? What's your name?"

He hustled to the far edge of the building where two green trash containers stood. He stopped, glanced back once, and disappeared behind the corner.

She turned to find out what caused the abrupt change in his demeanor, but saw no one. "Next time we meet, mister, you're gonna answer some real questions," she murmured to herself as she headed for the entrance. "Even if I have to follow you all around this place."

Although she'd kept her voice low to avoid anyone else hearing, a sideways glance from one of the tenants leaving told her otherwise. "Good morning," she managed.

"Mornin'," the woman replied.

Jonelle went directly to the manager's office and found Mrs. Watkins behind her desk, phone attached to her ear. The manager hung up and frowned. "You back here again, Miss, uh . . ."

"Jonelle Sweet. And I've been assigned to investigate Lark's abduction."

"Assigned, huh? By who?" she asked, a smirk on her round, cosmetic-laden face.

Jonelle's back stiffened at the amusement shining in the woman's eyes.

"Her attorney, Paul Langford."

The humor faded. The manager reached down and pulled up a canvas bag that looked like it could hold enough items for a weekend trip. "Don't have time for you now. I've got a doctor's appointment." She stood.

Jonelle didn't move.

Mrs. Watkins came from around the desk.

"Thought I'd let you know I'm here to ask the residents a few questions."

Mrs. Watkins stood outside her office, left hand on the doorknob. "I got to lock this."

Jonelle took her time leaving. "What if one of the tenants has a problem? Who watches this place when you're not here?"

"There's an emergency number they can call." Mrs. Watkins pulled the door closed and, after the click, fiddled with the knob as if to assure herself the lock had engaged.

Without another word the woman left as swiftly as her bulk would allow, leaving Jonelle standing in the lobby.

"Excuse me? Miss?"

Jonelle turned and faced three youngsters staring at her.

"Are you the one asking about Miss Tammy?" The question came from a pretty African American girl, standing tall and straight and a little separate from the other two.

"Miss Tammy? Is that what you call Tamora?"

All three nodded.

Did she need parental permission to question kids? How far could she push for information? "How old are you guys?"

"Twelve," all three said in unison.

Jonelle pulled out three business cards and gave one to each.

"Cool," said the young man in the group, a light-skinned African American.

The third youngster's white face displayed an array of freckles under hair so red that it could grace a "Visit Ireland" travel poster.

"Now that you guys know who I am, what are your names?"

"I'm Piper Enruth," said the young lady who'd spoken first. "And this is Grayson Watts and, uh, Fredricka Jace."

"Hey!" the redhead shouted.

"This lady here is on official business, so I had to give her your official name," Piper said, addressing her friend. She turned to Jonelle. "We call her Fred or Red Fred. She hates Fredricka."

Jonelle suppressed a smile. "Would you prefer I call you Fred? Red Fred?"

"Either. Just so long as it's not that other one."

Jonelle glanced at her watch. "Shouldn't you guys be in school?"

Eye rolls all around. "'Course not," Piper said. "Summer vacation started two weeks ago." She patted a small, lime-green clutch with cross straps laced around her chest. The gesture loosened a soft, flowery scent. "We got paid so we're gonna go take the bus to the IHOP and have us some pancakes."

"Paid? You guys have jobs?"

Grayson spoke up. "We got a pet-sitting service. Mostly we walk dogs 'cause some of the people have to go straight from one job to another. We also feed fish, hamsters . . . little critters like that. And clean up cat mess," he wrinkled his nose. "We make sure everybody's got fresh food and water."

Jonelle took in Grayson's loosely curled hair of such volume that he could probably hide a small kitten in there if he wanted. "Do you have a name for your business?"

"Yeah. We call ourselves 'Fidos, Felines and Friends'," Fred said, making a face. "It was Piper's idea. Not crazy about it, but I couldn't think of anything better."

The need to drill these kids made her body tingle. Jonelle knew children, or in this case, tweens, often saw and heard things adults didn't pay close attention to. She also knew as an adult she couldn't invite herself to join them for breakfast. Especially not after what happened.

"You guys might see me around here a lot as I try to help Tamora—Miss Tammy—prove her innocence."

"How d'you know she's innocent?" Grayson asked. "If you ask me—stop it!"

A swift elbow to the ribs from Piper prevented him from saying anything else.

She waited for the scene to play itself out.

All three kept their mouths shut, confirming Jonelle's original thought that Piper was the leader. The openness each had displayed earlier vanished, replaced by wariness in each of their eyes.

"Tell you what. When you see me around, if you remember anything that might be interesting, let me know. It doesn't matter if you think it's important or not. The great thing about being a detective is that we absorb information like a sponge. The more we hear, the better we like it. Enjoy your breakfast."

She strode over to the elevators. Langford's information stated Tamora and Lark lived on the seventh floor. Aware of three pairs of eyes on her back, she stepped inside the elevator and faced front. None of the group had moved. She waved before the doors closed.

A few seconds later Jonelle stood on the edge of a long hallway lit by weak overhead lights. A well-worn rug of indeterminate color ran down the length. She headed for apartment 707, stood outside, and pressed her ear against the door. Silence. Jonelle knocked and waited. When no one came to the door, she knocked again, harder this time.

"She ain't home."

Jonelle jumped at the sound. Across the hall an elderly woman regarded her suspiciously, one hand grasped around the collar of a faded blue cotton shift, white hair sticking out from her head like a halo.

"Yes. Well, I'd heard Tamora's staying with her sister, but I decided to take the chance she might've come back."

"Like I said, she ain't home."

Jonelle reached into her bag. The woman stepped back, her face tense with alarm. Jonelle froze, hand still inside and curled around a small black leather case.

"Sorry. Don't mean to scare you. I'm reaching for my private detective's identification. Okay to show it to you?"

Eyes still wide, the woman nodded once.

Jonelle removed the ID from her bag as slowly as if she were pulling a wad of gum from the bottom of her shoe. She inched toward the woman.

"Stay right there."

With her arm outstretched, Jonelle flipped open the case. On one side, the gold shield glowed dully. The other side included her picture and name.

The woman squinted at the ID and Jonelle wondered if she could actually see all the information.

"Hmm. What's your name then? Assuming that thing is real."

"Jonelle Sweet," she said, resisting the urge to point out it was written on the license. "I also have a business card if you'd like to see it. But that means I'll have to take it out of my bag. Is that okay?"

The woman nodded, this time with less reluctance.

After swiping the card from Jonelle's hand, she said, "Wait right there. I gotta go get my glasses." She turned and disappeared inside, leaving the door open.

Jonelle sighed and considered the woman probably should've put on the glasses before opening the door. With a smile firmly in place, she waited.

She didn't have to wait long.

"Fine," the woman said, large round glasses with dark green frames perched on the bridge of her nose. "You seem legit. What d'you want, anyway?"

She ignored the question. "What's your name?"

"Maxine."

The woman's attitude telegraphed no need for last names. "I'm working for Tamora's lawyer. You'll probably hear or see me around the building, asking questions about Tamora and the night Lark was taken. Can you spare a few minutes?"

Jonelle braced for the door to slam in her face. Instead, after a slight hesitation, Maxine moved aside and ushered her into the apartment.

Gold curtains were pulled back allowing bright sunlight to shine throughout. A slight antiseptic smell engulfed the room.

"I ain't got much to say about that night if that's what you want," Maxine said, sitting on a red-and-tan tweed sofa. A rectangular wooden coffee table held a tray with a mug and a half-eaten pastry.

"I'd still like to ask you a few questions. Mind if I sit down?"

Maxine nodded toward the matching chair, re-arranged her slight frame on the sofa, picked up the mug, and made a face. "Cold. I don't like my coffee cold."

"I can wait until you heat it up." Although she wouldn't mind a cup, the woman hadn't offered her any.

"No. Go on and ask your questions. I didn't see nothin' but go ahead. Don't want to seem rude."

Too late for that, Jonelle thought. "Um. Could you turn that down a bit?" She tilted her head at a flat screen TV.

Maxine grabbed the remote and turned down the sound.

"Thanks. What do you remember about that night?"

Maxine took a deep breath and said, as if by rote, "Tamora come in from her day job, same as always. That sometime boyfriend of hers stopped by . . . same as always. A bit later she brought little Lark to stay with me. I told the cops this, by the way. You guys should be coordinatin' all this stuff. Though I guess you're on opposite sides. Right?"

"You watched the child that night?" This must be the Miss Maxine she'd heard about.

"Of course. I watch some of the children in this building when their parents go on to their second jobs." She looked Jonelle up and down. "Most of 'em have to do that to make ends meet."

"How'd she get to work? Did the boyfriend take her?"

A shrug of the bony shoulders.

"What were the mother and daughter like?"

"Tamora is a good mama to that child. Lark's always clean and well-dressed; has enough food to eat. Tamora went across the street to buy milk. Did you know that?"

"I knew she went to the convenience store. Didn't know why."

Maxine huffed. "Now you do."

"What time did Tamora pick her up from your place?"

"About ten. Ten fifteen. Like always."

"So, the time all this took place was the same? No deviations?"

A slight hesitation. "That's what I said."

"The store is across the street. Why didn't she pick up the milk before she retrieved the child?"

Maxine shifted her weight. "I don't know. You gotta ask her."

"Who did she leave the child with when she went to the store?"

"Not me. That's for sure."

"She left the little one alone?"

Maxine studied the mug of cold coffee. "I . . . suppose so."

"Did she do that often?"

Maxine set the cup down, folded her arms across her chest, and didn't answer.

Jonelle waited. So did Maxine, with lips pressed tight.

"Going back to the boyfriend," Jonelle said, breaking the silence first. "Do you know who he is?"

"Of course."

Of course? "What's his name?"

"Jelani. Jelani Hill."

"How well do you know him?"

Maxine sat back against the sofa cushions. "About as well as everybody else that lives here. He works maintenance," she spit out the word, "if you can call it that, in this building."

Jonelle's mouth gaped open. "You mean the young man I've seen around here? He and Tamora are dating?"

A satisfied look crossed Maxine's face. "Suppose so."

"How long have they been together?" Wait until she saw him again. Jonelle hated when people lied to her.

"Don't know for sure. Wasn't too long after she got rid of that other one though." Maxine's eyes studied a spot on the ceiling. "Maybe two, three months. Something like that."

Jonelle wrote the name Jelani Hill on her notepad, underlining it three times. "Do you know the name of the boyfriend before Jelani?"

Maxine straightened her shift before answering. "Only know his first name. Reggie."

"That short for Reginald?"

Maxine glared at Jonelle as though she'd sprouted another nose.

"Never mind. What about the biological father? I understand he called the cops." That information was in Langford's notes, but she wanted to know how much of Tamora's private life Maxine was privy to.

"Sure do. Sometimes he'd stop by my place and pick up Lark if . . . well, if Tamora was going out on a date. Or something. His name's Vaughn. Vaughn Hanson. Nice young man. Got a good job and everything." Maxine picked up the pastry and nibbled.

"Don't know why these girls don't stick with a sure thing these days," she said, crumbs falling onto her shift.

Jonelle fought the urge to hand the woman a napkin. "Did you ever hear any arguing coming from her apartment? Not only the night the child was abducted but any night? Did you see or hear any fighting?"

Maxine regarded Jonelle again. "You mean from Vaughn? Nope."

"What about Jelani Hill?"

"No. Guy might be dumb as dirt, but he ain't violent. Least not that I know of. The only thing . . ." The arrogance displayed seconds ago was replaced by worry lines across her dark face.

"What else? Something bothers you about the relationship." Jonelle tried to keep the eagerness out of her voice.

As if noticing bits of pastry for the first time, Maxine brushed crumbs off of her dress. "Some of the kids don't like him."

"Why not?"

She shrugged. "He stares at 'em a little too long, tells raunchy jokes. Things like that."

"Anything else bother you about him?"

The worry lines deepened in Maxine's face. "That plus the fact Tamora had him look after Lark a few times when I 'specially asked her not to."

CHAPTER 6

*S*he *finally stopped crying for her mother. I calmed her a little by telling her that her mama got an important new job and had to go on a trip for a little while. We played her favorite games, and I promised to buy her a book about butterflies and try to find some butterfly toys. Butterflies are her favorite. I told her she'd talk to her mommy soon, although I have no idea if that's true or not.*

She kept running to the window, looking for her mommy. I told her for the millionth time that her mommy had to go out of town and that she missed her and would see her soon. That promise, along with the mind-numbing sameness of playing with her favorite bunny toy and putting oversized pieces in her butterfly puzzle calmed her down.

I'm getting nervous. I'm tired of watching her around the clock. They warned me not to let her look out the window again. What if someone notices? Damn it all.

Okay, what's next? So I've done what I'm supposed to do to keep her happy. But how long will that last?

It's a beautiful day today. I wanna go out but they warned me against it. The major news channels haven't picked up the story, so no pictures. Maybe I'll risk it and take her to the zoo. She'll love it . . . what kid doesn't? Afterwards we'll go someplace for lunch, and I'll get her some ice cream. We'll share. That should put her mind at ease . . . for a while at least. Mine too.

We had a good time at the zoo. But. Is it my imagination or are people giving me strange looks? Does what I've done show on my face? In the way I walk? The fact that we don't look that much alike?

Got a phone call today about some busybody woman going around asking questions. Told to keep my eyes and ears open on that one. Could turn into a problem somebody'll have to take care of.

Guess I'll go to the store tomorrow, pick up some frozen dinners and get ice cream.

Chocolate ice cream. That's her favorite.

CHAPTER 7

Although ticked off Jelani lied to her, before going in search of the maintenance man, Jonelle walked up and down the seventh floor hallway, knocking on doors. Most residents didn't answer, so she slotted her business card between the door and jamb. She reached out to insert her card in the door of the last apartment when a young African American man with fair skin and scraggly beard opened it. His unfocused eyes either meant she woke him up or his breakfast consisted of something other than cereal. After a few minutes of trying to get him to understand why she was asking about Tamora and her child, in the end all she got was his name—Randy—and all he said was that he hadn't heard or seen anything, and that maybe she should ask that "nosey old lady down the hall."

A quick trip down to the sixth floor yielded pretty much the same result. Since she'd run out of business cards, Jonelle boarded the elevator to go in search of the deceitful Jelani. She found him when the elevator doors opened on the fifth floor. His eyes widened in alarm at the sight of her. He stepped back.

Jonelle pressed the "open door" button. "Just the man I'm looking for. Come on in."

"I got work to do."

"So do I, but I'm sure we can find the time to chat a little."

The elevator's warning buzzer sounded.

"Better come in unless you want to fix this thing as well."

He slipped in and crammed his thin frame next to the control panel.

"So," she said. "I've been talking to a few of the residents."

He grunted.

"I heard you and Tamora are dating." She stared at the side of his face.

"So?"

"So that's a helluva lot different from what you told me before."

The doors opened on the main floor, and he hurried out, Jonelle matching him stride for stride.

They passed the manager's office, and Jonelle noted the closed door. At the end of the hall the red emergency exit sign glowed. He stopped as if confused about what to do next.

He turned and faced her. The concern displayed earlier in his eyes vanished, replaced by a hard stare. He clenched and unclenched his hands. She backed away a few feet.

"Listen," she said, raising both hands, palms out as if in surrender. "I'm working for Tamora's attorney to try and prove her alibi, so it's beyond me why you won't cooperate. Don't you care anything about her or that little girl?"

He paused as if weighing the pros and cons of her question. "I gotta vacuum and everythin's downstairs," he said. "We can talk there for a little bit." Jelani reversed course, took a left at the first opening, and at the end of a short corridor, went through an exit door. His footsteps clanked down metal stairs covered with cracked gray paint. Jonelle followed, skirting several stains of indeterminate origin. When they reached the bottom, Jelani shoved the door and let it swing behind him. Jonelle stopped it from closing with one hand.

They passed an empty laundry room, reverberating with the sound of dryers *thunka thunka-ing* round and round, the smell of hot air-heated clothes filling the hall. He continued past a closed door marked "Storage" and entered an opening. Inside the cramped space sat a battered metal desk, lopsided chair, and several containers of cleaning solvent. Various tools, mops, brooms, and filthy cloths were strewn haphazardly about. Without saying a word, he grabbed one of two old, dusty industrial-sized vacuum cleaners jammed next to several buckets and hauled it to the middle of the room.

That done, Jelani sat in the chair, which creaked under his slight frame. With no place else to sit, she perched on the edge of the desk. At first glance the young man looked as if a strong wind could blow him over. His clothes hung on him, and not because of the current style. His face, devoid of facial hair, regarded her with suspicion. Closer study revealed arms as sinewy as a tightly coiled rope. A tattoo of a wilted rose, with what looked like petals falling, decorated his right bicep.

"Tell me about your relationship with Tamora."

He picked up a set of pliers, opening and closing them over and over.

She waited.

"She ignored me at first," he said, staring at the tool in his hand. "Figured I was the help and didn't need to pay me no mind. But I kept speakin' to her every time we met, and she slowly warmed up. Started saying 'hello' first, stuff like that."

"This is a good-sized building. There must be a lot of single women living here. What attracted you to her?"

"She's real fine for one thing and built better than most. Those tits are . . . uh, never mind. 'Course there's lotsa good lookin' ladies, but . . . I dunno. Maybe it's the way she struts around like she's gonna *be* somebody."

"So the fact she had a kid didn't bother you?"

"Why should it? Wasn't mine."

Odd. So far everyone Jonelle talked to said more about Tamora than expressing concern about Lark.

"She ever tell you about her ambitions?"

"Said she wants to plan parties with her sister."

Jonelle made a mental note. The woman had goals. "She ever say how she intended on doing that?"

"Nah. But I guess she figures that since she likes to party all the time, that gives her all the experience she needs."

Uh-oh. "What do you mean by, 'all the time'?"

Jelani's eyes traveled up and down Jonelle's body. "I'm guessing you don't hang out a lot. That right?"

Her face warmed. "This is about Tamora."

He chuckled. "Right. We'd go out sometimes. And sometimes she wanted to hang by herself. Said she was doing research." He snorted.

"Who watched Lark while she partied?"

He hesitated. His tongue rolled over thin lips, a gesture Jonelle found somewhat disgusting. "Um, Miss Maxine I guess. Sometimes she got that snooty sister of hers to babysit the kid." He fiddled with the pliers again.

"I heard you also watched the child. That true?"

"Who told you that? Never mind. I can guess. What of it?"

"I also heard you said rude things to some of the kids in this building."

He dropped the pliers on the desk. "I never . . ." He squinted. "You got somethin' to say, say it."

She eased off the desk. "Why offer to babysit your girlfriend's child while she partied without you? Didn't you feel she was taking advantage?"

Jelani turned his head away from her. "She had a way . . . what I mean is, you knew she was usin' you, but somehow you didn't care. Whatever she wanted you to do, you did it. When she asked me to watch Lark, I said okay." He shrugged. "Kid wasn't a problem. Stayed pretty quiet. Played with her stuffed bunny, watched those stupid kiddie shows."

"Did you see Lark the night she was abducted?"

"No!"

"Okay, okay. No need to get upset."

"Look, lady. I already told the cops all I know. I wasn't nowhere near that apartment. Plus I got me an alibi."

"Which is?"

"None of your business."

Silence stretched for several seconds.

"Tell me this, then. Why do you think Tamora left Lark alone? I mean, if Maxine's right across the hall and you were willing—"

"Told you I wasn't there!"

"—to watch her, then why was Lark left by herself?"

"Tamora ain't perfect, okay?" he said through clenched teeth. "I mean, the kid's so freakin' quiet, it's like she ain't there half the time. So, if Tamora had to run out for a little while, she, um, left the kid by herself."

Jonelle's stomach tightened. "How many people know this?"

"Pretty much everybody who knows her." He stood. "I'm done talkin'. I got work to do."

"One more thing. Are you and Tamora still dating?"

His eyes flicked all around the cramped space. "Naw. She told me she and this guy at work hit it off. So . . ."

"Did that bother you?"

"Kinda, at first. But, hey, no biggie." Jelani maneuvered the vacuum in front of him.

"How long ago did you two split up?"

"'Bout a week or so." He stomped past Jonelle, leaving her alone among the caretaker's stuff.

She counted to ten, looked both ways down the hall, and, confident Jelani wasn't lurking about, proceeded to search the space.

The brown metal desk had two drawers on the right and two on the left. She opened the top right drawer and pored through mounds of paper. "Work Request" forms indicated which apartment needed what repaired, replaced, or installed. She flipped through several, searching for Tamora's name, and found a few. One request wanted a leaky faucet repaired, another a clogged toilet. Yet another notice demanded the screen on one of the windows be secured as "my child likes to sit next to the window, and I'm afraid she might fall."

Most of the papers had a large check mark across the top. A quick search of other drawers revealed blank forms, several three-subject notebooks, adult magazines, and a half-eaten box of Krispy Kreme's.

She peered into the hallway once more then headed to the locker in the far corner. A combination lock hung on the handle. She flipped it against the door a few times and pulled, but it still held. Damn. She fiddled with her handcuff and pistol necklace. Did Jelani lock it because he didn't want the residents poking through his things, or did he have something to hide?

Voices in the hallway, faint at first, grew louder and then stopped altogether. Jonelle poked her head around the doorframe and found the corridor empty. Figuring most buildings had more than one exit, she left the opposite way. Rotting food and waste assaulted her nostrils when she hurried past the trash room. She turned back.

Apartment buildings this size provided trash chutes on each floor for residents to dispose of their waste. Could a small child fit down a chute? She entered the room and gagged, the stench forcing her back into the hall. After several deep breaths she returned. Breathing through her mouth, she walked up to the chute opening into a large trash bin on wheels, approximately five feet high. Lined against one wall were several empty bins. One full bin stood next to a filthy, narrow corridor. Jonelle rushed out, grabbed a broom and an empty bucket from the maintenance room, and hurried back.

She turned the empty bucket over and placed it next to the full bin ready to be wheeled outside. Standing on top, she shifted her weight in an attempt to steady the bucket. Using the broom handle, she poked around inside, hunting for something she prayed she wouldn't find.

And she didn't.

With sweat pouring down her face she turned back to the container under the chute. A small four-year-old child could easily fit through the opening, but could the body slide all the way down or would she get stuck? "Wonder how often these things are cleaned?" Her nose answered, not often enough.

With the broom in one hand, Jonelle positioned the bucket next to the half-full bin. She stood on it, jabbing around like a woman possessed, and leaned too far over. The bucket gave way under her, toppling her inside the container.

"Shit, shit, shit."

She tried to stand but her feet slipped on the garbage bags and uncovered waste. She struggled to get upright, slipped, and fell again and again. Finally she wiped her soiled hands on her skirt, pressed them against the pimply sides of the bin, dug her fingers in the plastic, and, with feet thrashing about for purchase, reached up, grabbed the top, and lifted herself upright. She stood on several garbage bags, and, straining hard, pulled herself up, straddling the top edge. After catching her breath, she dropped down.

Covered in foul looking stains and smelling as though she'd bathed in fish heads, rotten eggs, and soiled diapers, Jonelle entered the hall. At the far end she encountered another exit sign and another set of stairs. She slowly ascended to the main level and peeked through the door.

No sign of anyone.

She hustled toward the lobby, noting the manager's closed door.

Disgusted and nauseated from the odor radiating from her body, Jonelle used her elbows to push open the entrance doors.

"Hey, detective lady."

Laser focused on how much she needed cleaning before getting inside her Jeep, Jonelle didn't notice three figures approaching.

She stopped and allowed the three kids she'd seen earlier to catch up.

"Hey," said Grayson. "You stink."

"And your clothes are funky," added Piper. The youngster wrinkled her nose. "What happened to you?"

Fred stepped back, hands waving through the air.

"Sorry, guys. I had to check something out, and, well, I need to wash my hands."

"And the rest of you. Plus, you better change clothes, 'cause you got some kinda gross lookin' crap all over your skirt and top," Piper said.

"Right. You guys know if that store over there would let me use the bathroom?"

All three shrugged.

"If my mom was home, I'd let you wash up in my place. But she's not, so . . . sorry," Piper said. At that moment two young men exited the building. Piper smiled at them and flipped one of her braids over her shoulder. Neither of the boys smiled back.

Grayson grunted. "Get over it, Piper."

Piper shot him a look that said she'd like to give *him* something to "get over."

"I understand your mom's concerns. You guys have a good breakfast?" Jonelle asked as Fred crept closer.

"Yeah. But that stink coming from you is making me forget. Real fast," Fred said, her freckled nose screwed up in disgust.

"Guess I better head out. But I'm coming back later this evening when more folks should be home. Will I see you guys again?"

Instead of answering the question, Grayson asked, "Did you go around questioning people? Like they do on TV?"

Piper groaned. "Of course she did. She's a detective, remember? So, who'd you talk to?"

Slightly amused that twelve year-olds were questioning her, Jonelle answered. "Well, let's see. There was Miss Maxine, and the maintenance man Jelani, and a young guy at the end of the hall on the seventh floor."

"Randy? He lives across from me," Fred said.

"Right. The light-skinned guy that looked like I woke him up. He said he didn't know anything."

"We think Randy's kinda weird," Piper said.

"Why weird?" Jonelle directed the question to Fred.

"Sometimes, late at night, he walks up and down the halls, mumbling to himself."

The kids snickered.

Jonelle no longer cared about protocol and talking to kids. "How do you know this, Fred?"

"'Cause . . . I've seen him. Most of the time my mom don't much care what I do, so sometimes I'll go across the street for a slushy. That's when I've seen him in the hall. No big deal."

Several more people left the building, staring at the three kids and one smelly adult.

"He ever say anything?"

"A couple times. Stupid stuff like, 'I'm gonna tell your mama on you.' Like she cares anyway."

An awkward silence hung in the air.

Piper spoke first. "That card you gave us. You know, about your business and all. It's got an address on it, right?"

Jonelle nodded.

"You near a bus route?"

"My office is in the city, so there are several buses that run within a block of where I work." Jonelle recited the route numbers of the MTA buses she knew offhand and suggested they check the MTA website to make sure.

"I'll probably be in my office around nine or ten tomorrow. Call me if you'd like to come visit."

Piper nodded. "Okay."

Jonelle waved good-bye and headed for the convenience store across the street.

"Hey, Miss."

She turned at the sound of Fred's voice.

"Randy sometimes does more than walk up and down the halls."

CHAPTER 8

The convenience store manager refused Jonelle's request to use their facilities. Rolling down all the windows in the Jeep helped but didn't wipe out the funky smell. She felt like a cartoon character where people could actually see wavy lines of stink coming from her body.

Even with the windows down, Jonelle turned the air conditioning on full blast. Before pulling out of the store's parking lot she checked her rearview mirror and picked up a dark blue sedan. She left the store's parking lot and turned left.

The sedan did the same.

The sun's glare, and the car's tinted windows, prevented her from getting a good look at the driver.

Who would follow her? Of the few apartment dwellers she talked to so far, only the caretaker Jelani seemed the most likely. But why would the maintenance man follow her? Especially since he tried to avoid her every chance he got. She kept driving and, about two miles from her home, thought about evading the tail when the sedan withdrew.

A half block from her condo she slowed to a crawl and checked up and down the tree-lined street in case the car had somehow managed to follow unnoticed. Nothing out of place caught her attention, so she pulled into her spot and let herself in the condo.

After a hot shower and change of clothes, and ten minutes playing with Gracie, she called Langford. To her surprise, he answered almost immediately. "Hi. Jonelle Sweet here. Wanted to let you know what I've done so far." After a quick recap, he whistled softly.

"That Jelani guy. We checked his alibi for that night," Langford said. "It holds up. But, this business of the two of them dating and him watching the kid." A huge sigh. "That's new. Neither one of them mentioned it. Could be something . . . or nothing."

"Do you know what kind of car Jelani drives?"

"No. Why?"

"Curious is all." She'd check it out herself later. "What about the sister?" Jonelle asked. "What was her name again?"

"Evelyn Clifton."

"Right. If Tamora is still with her, I can talk to them both."

"Ah. That's why I'm glad you called. Tamora is back in her own apartment, as of"— papers rustled in the background—"an hour or so ago. I've given her a heads-up that you'll stop by her place so it won't come as a surprise when you show up."

When she arrived back at the mid-rise, Jonelle headed straight for the elevators, pushed seven, and tapped her foot on the floor, willing the thing to go faster. She squeezed through the doors before they opened all the way. Jonelle glanced across the hall from Tamora's apartment and imagined Maxine staring at her through the peephole. She pushed aside the urge to wave and, instead, knocked three times on the door to apartment 707 before it opened.

Large, slightly bugged, red-rimmed eyes stared back at her. The young woman had a small waist and wide hips. Her large chest looked as if it was trying to escape the confines of a very tight, lemon yellow tank top. The jeans Tamora wore strained against skin struggling to hold it all in.

"You that detective lady?"

"Yes. Your attorney said it would be okay if I asked you a few questions. May I come in?"

Tamora shrugged and stepped aside. "Close the door."

Obeying the order without comment, Jonelle noted the pile of clothes in the middle of a well-worn hunter green sofa and the small tote bag resting on a sage-colored ottoman in front of the matching chair.

On the floor next to the sofa an open suitcase held more clothes. Scattered in the corner closest to the kitchen were several toys. Jonelle's heart ached for the little girl who played with them a few days earlier. Where was she now?

Down the narrow hallway a door closed with a soft *click*.

"My sister is staying with me for a while."

"I see. She owns a day care business, right?" Jonelle asked, eyes glued in the direction of the closed door.

"She's taking a few days off."

"Since she's here I'd like to ask her a few questions."

"You can't. She's taking a nap. Look, I'm kinda busy now, so if you wanna talk, get on with it." Tamora shoved the clothes aside and plopped down on the sofa, her mouth nibbling a cuticle.

Since Tamora hadn't invited her to sit, Jonelle said, "May I?" grabbed a chair from under the dining room table and carried it into the living room. She placed it close to the young woman and sat. "Jelani tells me you and your sister are going into business together, but he wasn't sure if you were joining her daycare business or something else."

The young woman took the finger out of her mouth and sat up straight. "What else did Jelani say about me? What I do, or don't do, is none of his damn business."

"Understood, but I've talked to a lot of people in this building, and he's one of them. Besides, you two dated and still see each other, right?"

Tamora stared off in the distance. "I can't believe this," she mumbled. "We don't hang out anymore. The guy's a freakin' janitor, for crissakes. No possibilities. No future. I want more for me . . . and my daughter."

Jonelle waited for Tamora to say more and, when she didn't, continued. "I know you're struggling with what happened, and I'm sorry I have to ask all these questions, but it can't be avoided since I'm helping your attorney." In fact, she wasn't the least bit sorry. The woman's attitude seemed odd for a grief-stricken mother.

"Where was Lark the last time you saw her?"

"Bedroom." Tamora cocked her head in the direction of the closed door and resumed chewing on a cuticle.

"Is that her room?"

"This is a one-bedroom apartment. We share. I'm working two jobs to get us a bigger place."

"What time was she taken?"

"Somewhere around ten-thirty or so last night."

"Or so?"

"What?"

"You said, 'Or so.' Aren't you sure?"

Tamora's eyes narrowed. "You can stop playing games, Detective. You know I was arrested, and you know why. Has anybody even considered that the surveillance camera over there could've been broken?"

Fine, Jonelle thought. No beating around the bush worked for her, too. "Why did you leave your four-year-old alone?"

Tamora sat back against the sofa and played with the red-and-gold braids intertwined through her black hair. "I . . . we needed milk, so I ran across the street to get some." Her voice hardened. "Are you accusing me of something?"

Jonelle spread her arms in a conciliatory fashion. "Look. We're on the same team here. I want to find out what happened to your little girl. Right now, the cops think you're involved somehow, so my job is to prove them wrong. In order to do that I need your help. So. You ran across the street for milk. Why didn't you ask Miss Maxine to watch Lark?"

"Because Lark was already asleep, and I didn't want to wake her."

"Miss Maxine could've come over here, couldn't she?"

No reply.

"Since you needed milk, why didn't you stop at the store before coming home?" Jonelle knew her questions were pushing the envelope, but she couldn't stop herself.

"Because I didn't know until I looked in the fridge when I got home, all right?" Tamora said through gritted teeth.

"How did you lock your door?"

"What do you mean 'how'?"

Jonelle walked to the door and checked the flimsy lock. She could pick the thing herself in under a minute. "Did you use a key?"

Tamora shifted her weight and turned her head toward the bedroom door before answering. "You don't need a key to unlock it from the inside. All you have to do is turn the latch. When you close the door, it locks automatically." The young woman crossed her arms.

"Okay. So it only locks when you twist the latch first." Jonelle turned the lever back and forth. "Before you left, do you remember engaging the lock?"

Eyes flashed in response.

"Did you take your key? You know, to get back inside?"

Silence filled the room. Jonelle waited.

Finally, "The door was open when I got back."

That wasn't the question. Jonelle let it pass. For now. "When you say 'open' do mean as in unlocked or ajar?"

"As in cracked open a little." Tamora's voice dripped with contempt.

Jonelle ignored the woman's tone. "What did you think when you saw that?"

"That some sonofabitch had robbed me," she said. As if illustrating that point, Tamora turned her head toward the flat screen television on the wall.

"Weren't you worried about your child?"

"What're you implying?" Tamora's hands balled into fists on her lap.

In a quiet voice, Jonelle said, "Your child was alone, and when you returned your door was open. It makes sense you'd be concerned for her safety."

"Of course I was. That's what I meant. Somebody could've robbed me of my child. Look. I'm tired. I can't talk to you anymore right now."

She sprung up from the couch and stomped to the door.

Jonelle repeated the question she'd asked before. "Did you take your key with you when you left?"

"I . . . yeah. Probably. Stuck it in my jeans along with the money when I went to the store."

Jonelle doubted Tamora could stick anything into those jeans.

"Did you meet anyone at the store?" The store's surveillance camera had picked up Tamora talking to a young man.

"Lotsa people go there all the time. Reggie's one of 'em. We used to go out, and we're still friends so we always speak, shoot the breeze, that kinda thing. So what? I got a lot of friends."

I'll bet you do, Jonelle thought. "I'd like to come back tomorrow. After you've rested a bit. If your sister's still here, I'll talk to her as well."

Tamora opened the door without comment.

Before she left, Jonelle held the young woman's eyes. "Listen. I'm not the enemy. I want to do everything I can to help find your little girl and bring her home safe."

Tamora's eyes filled with tears. "Fine," she murmured.

"One more thing. How long was it from the time you left to the time you returned to your apartment?"

"I don't care what the cops' so-called evidence shows, I was only gone five minutes."

CHAPTER 9

*M*ama *always told me if you want somethin' done right, you gotta do it yourself.*

I done my part. No problem. Since the jackass didn't show, I had to get in and out of that apartment like a horney sailor with a half hour pass. So what do I get for all the risk I took? I get a call. Last night. Told me some people was having second thoughts. Second thoughts? What the fuck? Seems like they wanted to see an older kid. How the hell can somebody go through all this crap and not mention how old she is?

Not happy about this. Not. At. All. No way I'm gonna let them stick me with this kid the whole time. She likes where she is now, so I say let her stay there. But no. Following the plan means keep moving her around. I'm sick and tired of being stuck in . . . this place. Got my own life to live. My own responsibilities.

Told 'em I'll take my turn but I'll keep her only 'til the end of the week or else pay me more money. A lot more. If that don't happen, I'm gonna take matters into my own hands. Plan or no plan.

CHAPTER 10

Adrienne sat at one end of the couch with Gracie on the arm at the other end. Both eyed each other suspiciously.

"This is what happens when I leave you alone for a few weeks." She pointed to the calico kitten across from her. "You turn into a crazy old cat lady."

Jonelle placed a tray of nachos and wine on the coffee table. "I object to that. First, I'm not old, and second, one cat doesn't make a person crazy. Besides, you can't ignore the fact that she's the cutest thing ever. Why, only this morning, she—"

"That's what I mean," Adrienne said. "That's how it starts. You begin telling everyone who'll listen what cute thing Fuzzy did and—"

"Her name's Gracie."

"Fine. Whatever. The point is that's how it starts. Next comes all the pictures and YouTube videos. And the smell. Honestly. The next time I go on vacation, am I gonna have to demand you report in before this place is overflowing with critters?"

As if to solidify her status, Gracie jumped from the arm of the sofa and deposited herself on Jonelle's lap, nearly spilling the glass of wine. "Oops. Careful, little one."

Adrienne pointed an accusatory, manicured nail at Jonelle. "And you're talking to her as if she were a person. When was the last time you went out on a date?"

Careful not to dislodge the kitten, Jonelle positioned herself in such a way as to provide maximum comfort for Gracie and still grab a few nachos. "I don't want to get into an argument about her," she said, ignoring the last question. "She's staying and that's that. Besides, you didn't smell a thing when you came in, right? Now, do you want to hear my news or not?"

Adrienne sniffed the air. "Point taken," she said, still giving Gracie the stink eye.

Jonelle often confided in her best friend on her PI cases. Adrienne acted as a sounding board and gave good advice. "Mmm. Think I should've put a few more jalapenos on these. They don't have quite the kick they usually do."

"You gonna tell me the news?" Adrienne asked.

"Have you heard anything about a little girl abducted in Maryland City?"

The wine glass stopped before Adrienne's lips made contact. "You involved with that?"

"I found out the name of the mother's court-appointed attorney and offered my services. He accepted."

Through narrowed eyes Adrienne said, "You went out and got a case on your own. And Marvin's okay with that? I bet he had a few choice words to say."

Outside of immediate family, Adrienne Roth knew Marvin Shorter very well.

"He said more than a few words, but I convinced him I could do my work at the agency as well as this case. Langford, that's her lawyer, seemed to think, and I agree, that as a black woman, the mother might open up to me. Still working on that."

The sound of crunching chips filled the air for several seconds.

"Don't tell me there aren't any black folks in the public defender's office, 'cause I know there are. If she didn't want to answer questions from the white guy, they could've assigned somebody black."

Jonelle nodded before Adrienne finished. "Tamora didn't want to change attorneys."

"That her name?"

"Yes. And I've already had my first interview with her. Didn't learn much because she's still upset. There is one thing I need to run by Langford, though. There's nothing in her file about how the kidnapper got in, except there was no sign of forced entry. Tamora didn't answer whether or not she took her key with her when she left the building that night."

"She left that child alone? What the hell for?"

Jonelle sighed. "I know. She said she ran across the street to get milk for Lark's breakfast and that she only stayed in the convenience store for five minutes. Anyway, my point is, if she didn't take her key that meant she left the door unlocked. Who does that in an apartment building? I don't care how long you think you'll be."

Gracie yawned, hopped off Jonelle's lap, and trotted to the cat bed in the corner next to the bookcase. Adrienne's eyes followed the feline's every movement. "You better watch she doesn't try to eat those fish in that aquarium."

Jonelle rolled her eyes. "She doesn't bother the fish. Back to Tamora. The maintenance guy in the building said he and Tamora dated and he babysat Lark a few times. In spite of the fact that right across the hall is an older woman who regularly babysat while Tamora worked her second job."

"Nobody saw or heard anything, right?"

"Not a peep. It's amazing how many people go blind and deaf when something happens where they live, yet they pull out the phones and start the video when they're someplace public. More?" Jonelle wiggled the half -empty wine bottle.

Adrienne held out the glass. "I'm serious about that dating thing. When was the last time you saw Burt?"

Jonelle groaned. "Oh, give it a rest why don't you? He's a friend, that's all."

"All I meant was he could probably help you with this new case."

"I don't need his help," she said, a little too loudly. "I know what I have to do. I need to prod Miss Maxine about what she really saw that night and check out the convenience store. If I'm right, the same people tend to hang out at the same time. So, the plan for this evening is to go back there at around ten and ask a few questions."

Adrienne sat up straighter. "By yourself? What's Furr Ball gonna think, you leaving her alone and all."

"For the last time, her name's Gracie, and she'll be fine."

"What time do you want me to pick you up? And don't argue. I don't want . . . Gracie here to become an orphan so soon."

As a way of not showing too much enthusiasm for Adrienne's suggestion, she gave a flippant, "Nine thirty is good."

Three young men slouched next to the store's "No Loitering" sign, laughing and smoking, illuminated by the bright interior lighting spilling outside.

A police car approached.

The young men's heads followed the vehicle as it drove slowly past without stopping.

Jonelle checked her watch. "It's a little after ten. That's about when Tamora arrived." She indicated for Adrienne to follow as she entered the store.

"Should we buy something?" Adrienne asked.

Jonelle scanned the aisles. Men outnumbered women in the store. "Good idea." She headed toward the heated compartment. "I wanna check something out."

A young man in his twenties, dressed in a blue security guard uniform, stood next to a rotating container that held slices of pizza.

"You're not gonna buy that, are you?" Adrienne asked in a shocked voice.

The young man turned at the sound of her voice. Jonelle waited a few beats for him to take in Adrienne's blue lace top, dark blue capris and, sure enough, he smiled indicating he liked what he saw.

"Hi," Jonelle said, interrupting his assessment of her friend. "We—my friend here and I—were wondering about something we heard."

Adrienne chimed in. "Right. We both work for the community newspaper and wanted to know if we could ask you a few questions about the little girl taken from the building across the street."

Community newspaper? Jonelle scowled. That wasn't what they discussed on the way over.

The smile on his face faded.

"Off the record, of course," Jonelle added quickly. "We won't mention names. We only want to print a story that proves what a good mother Tamora was, is, I mean. How about it?"

"How come I never seen y'all in here before?"

"Because 'y'all' don't live near here," Adrienne replied, a slight edge to her voice.

Jonelle jumped in before her friend's attitude spoiled everything.

"What she means is, our beat includes this area, but the office is on the other side of town. Fact is I'm new at this. Trying to make a name for myself as a journalist, if you know what I mean. So. What, if anything, do you know about that night? Were you here when Tamora came in for milk?"

The man's shoulders relaxed a little. "Yeah. I'm usually here around that time to get a couple Red Bulls. I work night shift, so I come in on the way to work."

"Did you speak to her?" Jonelle asked.

He shifted from one foot to the other.

"Bet you guys are friends, right?" Adrienne asked.

Jonelle's eyes flashed a "knock it off."

Adrienne ignored the look and smiled. "I mean, you guys probably hooked up a time or two. You being good-looking and all."

Without answering he turned and walked to the far end of the store. Jonelle and Adrienne followed.

After grabbing his drinks from the refrigerated case, he faced the two women.

"You keep asking questions in here, you're prob'ly gonna find out anyway. Yeah me and Tam dated a while back. We see each other, we speak. Hi, what's up, that kinda thing." Stitched in white above the pocket of his shirt was the name "Reggie" followed by "Alpha and Omega Security Company."

"That short for Reginald?" Jonelle asked. "What's your last name?"

He hesitated.

"I'll keep it out of the article."

He looked from one to the other.

"One thing you should know about her," Adrienne said, pointing at Jonelle. "She promises something, she doesn't go back on that promise. Your name's not gonna appear in the paper."

Good ole Adrienne.

"No biggie, I guess. So, yeah. Name's Reginald. Reginald Tobias."

There was no mention of him in the notes Langford sent.

"So, Reginald. Why'd you guys break up?"

"You can call me Reggie. Ask her. She's the one who said we didn't have no future. What the hell does that mean, anyway? Future? All she wants to do is go out and have a good time. Didn't look to me like she was lookin' for any kind of 'future.' Tam is definitely a minute-by-minute girl, you ask me."

"What do you know about her relationship with her daughter, Lark?"

He averted his eyes. "Kid had plenty to eat, clean clothes to wear. Tam's a good mom. Don't let nobody tell you different."

Adrienne stepped in closer to Reggie. "So, tell me something, Reg. You ever been alone with her in the apartment? Or was the little one there all the time?"

Reggie scowled and backed away a few feet.

Jonelle cleared her throat. Adrienne's "get to the bottom of things now" attitude kept getting in the way.

Before she could apologize for her friend's question, Reggie piped up.

"Sometimes the kid was there, and sometimes she was at that old lady's place across the hall."

"How did you and Lark get along?" Jonelle rushed in, a warning to Adrienne to stay out of the questioning.

He shrugged. "The kid's only four. Most times she didn't say nothin' to me and I didn't say nothin' to her. Crawlin' around on the floor playin' with toys ain't my style."

"What do you know about the other men Tamora might've dated?"

"How the hell would I know anything?"

"I'm not saying you knew for sure, but I imagine you heard rumors about who she went out with after you two broke up."

Reggie headed up to the cashier with two Red Bulls and a long tube of potato crisps.

No one spoke until they left the store.

"Listen, I didn't keep tabs on her or anything, all right? I heard stuff."

"Like what?" Adrienne asked, garnering another angry look from Jonelle.

He sighed deeply. "Like, she tended to go for the guy who could do the most for her. Give her the most money, take her to the best places to eat, drive around in the fanciest car. I mean, she's got the looks for it, but most guys around here don't have that kinda dough. Hell, I've gotta work nights just so's I can keep up with the rent."

Yet she still went out with you, Jonelle thought. She pointed to the company name on the shirt. "Where does Alpha and Omega send you?"

"Different places."

"Around here?"

"Why you wanna know that?" he asked, an edge in his voice.

"Curious is all."

Reggie pressed his lips together and turned his head, gazing at the other cars in the lot.

Jonelle changed the subject. "Who else was she talking to that night? Was there anybody inside you'd never seen before?"

He took one of the drinks out of the bag and popped the top. After a large swallow, he looked first at Adrienne then back at Jonelle.

"Look. She's friendly. I don't pay much attention to who else she talks to." He looked at his watch. "I gotta get to work."

"Hold on a minute."

Reggie stopped and turned around.

Jonelle reached in her bag and handed him a business card. "I'd like you to contact me if you happen to hear anything that would help her case."

He squinted at the card. "I thought you said you worked for the local newspaper. Says here you're a private investigator. What gives?"

Damn.

"You're right. Sorry for the deception but I needed information." She shot a scathing look at Adrienne who shrugged.

He pocketed the card in his shirt. "Yeah. Well." He turned to go. "I'm guessing you talked to Lark's daddy since he's the one called the cops," he said over his shoulder as he opened his car door.

Reggie entered a dark sedan, but Jonelle couldn't swear it was the one that had followed her.

"Anybody have a reason to snatch that child, well, I'd start with him. He coulda called the cops to throw everybody off and get Tam into trouble."

"Why do you say that? Have you met him?"

Reggie shrugged. "Only know what Tam said. Guy is some kinda control freak."

"He's on my list. Before you go, I'd like to ask if you can clear up a major discrepancy. How long would you say Tamora was here in the store?"

He shrugged. "I dunno. Didn't time it but since she was already here running her mouth with some dude when I walked in, and I know we shot the breeze for fifteen or so, I guess it was about twenty minutes, maybe more."

CHAPTER 11

"So that five-minute thing is a definite no-go. Wonder why she lied about something so simple?"Adrienne asked as the two rode in Adrienne's Saab on their way across the street to Tamora's building.

"Hard to say. Maybe she didn't want anybody to think she'd leave her child alone for so long and, once she started that line, had to stick with it." Jonelle suggested Adrienne wait in the car while she went and talked to a few people, but her friend would have none of it. Adrienne promised to keep her mouth shut and let Jonelle do the talking.

"So. Who're you talking to first?"

"Miss Maxine. There's something going on with that lady. You know how some older people have a sharp edge to them that only gets sharper the older they get? Well, she's one of them. She was guarded from the beginning, and I'm curious to find out why."

A minute later the two of them stood outside the apartment building's double glass doors. Jonelle pulled at the handle. "What the? I just walked in before. Wonder why it's locked now?" She pulled again as if thinking maybe the door was just stuck.

A sticker with a drawing of a video camera hung low in one corner.

Adrienne stepped back and looked up. "How many floors in this thing?"

"Ten," Jonelle replied, trying to figure out which button on the security pad to push.

"So there's probably a resident manager, right? Those buttons are somewhere on the bottom. Push all those. See what happens."

"The only manager they've got lives elsewhere. When she's gone the residents call an off-site emergency service. Damnit. I should've anticipated this and gotten a few phone numbers when I was here before."

Adrienne started laughing. "When did you become a 'woulda-shoulda' kind of person?"

"Oh, be quiet. Guess we'll have to wait until someone either walks in or goes out."

A short while later, as they stood on the sidewalk, staring into the empty lobby, the elevator doors opened and three people exited. The two men and one woman approached, and Jonelle and Adrienne stood aside to let them pass. One of the trio held the door open without so much as a backward look.

"So much for security," Jonelle muttered under her breath. Once inside the elevator, Jonelle's fingers lingered over the sixth- and seventh-floor indicator buttons.

"You forget where we're going?" Adrienne asked.

Jonelle shook her head. "Trying to decide where to start."

Knocking on more doors resulted in more people and more answers that no one saw or heard anything the night Lark disappeared. On the seventh floor Jonelle's face broke into a smile as the door was answered by Red Fred.

"Well, hi there. Is your mom or dad available? I'd like to ask a few questions."

Fred peered around Jonelle.

"This is my friend Adrienne. She's along as a, um, silent partner as it were."

"My mom's not home. And if she was, she didn't hear nothing. Or see nothing, either. Never does."

Adrienne shifted behind Jonelle, but Jonelle kept her eyes focused on Fred. "Are you here alone? It's almost eleven."

"I'm not a child," Fred said loudly.

"Of course not. Do you know if Randy's in or . . ."

"Nope. Haven't seen him much. Maybe you scared him off."

"Me? How?"

Fred shrugged.

"We're on our way to talk to Miss Maxine again. Did she ever keep an eye out on you and your friends?"

Fred crossed her arms. "Are you kidding me? I'm twelve, not a baby. Besides, she doesn't like people in her place unless they're payin' her. Been in there a couple times when my mom needed somethin', but the place freaked me out. Everything's always so closed up. One day I opened a closet, and all these different kids' clothes were in there. I mean, all types and sizes and stuff. So why'd she need all those clothes, huh? Parents got their own."

"Who're you talkin' to?" yelled a harsh voice from somewhere in the apartment.

"I gotta go." Fred slammed the door in her face.

"You're not doing so well tonight," Adrienne said.

"Wonder what that's all about? I mean, why say she's alone when she wasn't?"

Adrienne headed for the elevator. "I don't know. What I do know is I'm getting bored hanging around this place of no-nothing and see-nothing people. I wanna go home."

"In a little while. I have to ask Maxine something. Once you get her going, she likes to talk."

"Fine. Am I still the silent partner?"

Jonelle almost said yes. "Actually, she's a tough bird, so a little input from you might not hurt."

Spreading her arms out for emphasis, Adrienne said, "Finally!"

Before heading down to Maxine's, Jonelle crossed the hall and knocked on Randy's door. No answer. Next they walked to Maxine's apartment and only had to wait a few seconds until the door opened. Jonelle wondered if someone gave the woman a heads-up she'd stop by.

"Come in. Come in." A big smile spread across Maxine's face. In the middle of the coffee table sat a coffeepot and three cups, confirmation Maxine expected their visit.

Jonelle sat on the sofa and waved away the offer of coffee. "This is my friend, Adrienne Roth. I hope you don't mind if she sits here while I ask a few questions."

Maxine beamed at Adrienne, who also declined the coffee.

Jonelle zeroed in on the change in Maxine's mood. "I know it's late, so I'll get right to the point. I'd like your opinion on something. Who do you think took Lark?"

Maxine's hand shook as she poured herself a large mug of strong, thick coffee. The acrid smell hovered in the air while she added four teaspoons of sugar and some milk. She took several sips.

Adrienne gave Jonelle an "are you thinking what I'm thinking" look.

"No idea," Maxine replied.

"How often would you say Tamora left Lark by herself?"

Maxine shrugged and brought the cup to her mouth.

"I'll bet you know every time somebody entered and left that apartment. Isn't that right?" Adrienne asked.

"What're you trying to say?" Maxine stared at Adrienne.

"What my friend means is that noises from the hallway are probably evident and that when someone closed a door— especially one from across the hall—or even knocked, the sound probably traveled. So you'd check the peephole. Right?"

"Sometimes. That night my favorite program was on so . . ." Her voice faded. "Listen, this is a good building. The people here are friendly and I always feel safe here. Plus, I got a couple friends that give me extra security."

"Who?"

"Mister Smith and Mister Wesson sleep right next to my bed." Something in the woman's tone rankled.

"That's fine for you, except a small child is missing and no one I've talked to saw or heard anything. Did you hear Tamora leave that night?"

"I already told—"

"So tell me again. Please."

Maxine sat up straighter. "I heard Tamora leave. She was talking to someone, and before you ask, like I told the police, I don't know who or what they were saying. I heard her door close and that's that."

"You didn't look?"

"No. Told you my favorite program was on."

"Do you have a key to her apartment?" Jonelle asked.

"I, uh, well yes. But only when she leaves to go to her night job. She gives it to me in case I need something in the apartment for Lark. I give it back when she picks up the child."

"You give it back that night?"

"Yes."

"You sure about that?" Adrienne asked.

"Don't think I like your attitude, Miss."

Jonelle shot Adrienne a warning look. "How many children are under your care at night?"

"They aren't under my care. I'm mostly a babysitter."

"Doesn't matter to me if you're licensed or not. I'm not a lawyer. How many other kids do you watch and for how long?"

"Four including Lark. And anywhere from two to five hours every night during the week."

"What are their ages?" Jonelle asked.

Maxine cleared her throat before answering, "A three-year-old boy and two five-year-old girls."

"What are their names?"

"You don't need to know that," Maxine said sharply.

"Who was the last to be picked up?"

Maxine shifted on the sofa. "It varied. Most times it was Lark. But that's because Tamora knew she was safe with me."

"Were you close to the other parents?" Adrienne asked.

A puzzled look crossed her face. "Close?"

Jonelle clarified. "Someone mentioned seeing a lot of children's clothes in here. Since you only babysit children in this building, why the extra clothes?"

Maxine reached for her cup, her eyes drifting over to a small table that held two bottles, one containing a clear liquid, the other amber. Although Jonelle couldn't read the labels, she assumed the first was either vodka or gin and the other whiskey of some sort.

"Maxine?"

"What? Oh, right. Well, in case they spill juice or food, they'll have something clean to put on."

"You don't have keys like you do for Tamora's place?"

Maxine's eyes wandered again to the liquor. "I don't go around visiting too many people. I got Tamora's key 'cause she lives across the hall, so it's easy."

"Are these their own clothes, or do you keep stuff on hand just in case?" Jonelle asked. "That's going above and beyond if you ask me."

"Ain't nobody asking you," Maxine shot back. "We're done here." She folded her arms across her chest.

Jonelle mentally counted to five. Talking to Maxine was like trying to get information out of a guilty eight-year-old. "We're leaving. Since you're one of the few people around most of the time, I'm only trying to find out as much as I can in order to figure out how a child can vanish under everyone's nose."

"And I said everything I'm gonna say. See yourselves out."

"In a sec. When I was here before, you said some of the kids indicated that Jelani made them nervous."

"Oh, that." She waved her hand dismissively. "Well, mostly he would stare at Fred. I mean . . . you've met her, right? Well, there's nothing wrong with it, mind you, but, um . . ."

This time Maxine looked over at Adrienne as if wanting her to help out with what she wanted to say. Adrienne's gaze shifted to Jonelle.

"You've lost me, Maxine. What about Fred?"

Maxine leaned forward. "I think she's gay," she whispered.

"Is that all?" The thought hadn't occurred to her. "Why do you say that?"

"She don't hide it. Dresses like a boy all the time. Real rough around the edges. The only reason she wears her hair long is that no-good mother of hers is too stoned most of the time to care about getting it cut. Don't get me wrong, I like Fred. She's real sweet under that hard shell, but, well, most people don't want her associatin' with their kids." Maxine shrugged. "I guess they're afraid of them catching the gay thing."

Adrienne snorted. She opened her mouth to say something, but Jonelle cut her off.

"Did Fred or the other two, Piper and Grayson, have any contact with Lark?"

"Naw. They got that pet-sitting business and Tamora don't have no pets. The only thing Lark likes is butterflies. A body can't have a butterfly as a pet."

"You know what's curious? No one, including yourself seems all that concerned about Lark's welfare."

"What—"

"Everybody expresses their belief in Tamora's innocence but no one seems worried about what happened to Lark? Why?"

Maxine's eyes lingered on the liquor bottles.

The silence stretched for several seconds.

Something else nagged at Jonelle, but she couldn't pinpoint what it was. "Well, thanks for the information."

Jonelle nodded for Adrienne to precede her to the door. She turned back to face Maxine. "If I think of anything else, I'll be back."

Maxine grunted her reply.

Next to the elevator, Adrienne said, "Nice lady," in a voice laced with sarcasm.

"She's a piece of work, that one. And here's something else odd. According to the police report, the child's father called the cops when he arrived at the apartment and found the door open and his child gone. So if Maxine heard the door close, how'd the abductor get inside?"

They rode the elevator in silence. On the main floor, Jonelle's hand paused before opening the glass doors. "Now I know what else's been gnawing at my brain. I've been focusing on the wrong thing."

"What do you mean?"

"I've been concentrating on how the child was taken. You know, when, who heard what. That kinda thing."

"So?"

"There are a lot of kids in this building, all ages, mostly black, but some white and Asian." Jonelle paused.

"And your point is . . ."

"So the real question isn't so much how Lark disappeared. The main issue is why her."

CHAPTER 12

I'm goin' crazy lookin' at these four walls. A quick walk to the park won't hurt anything. Problem is the kid is takin' a nap and I don't wanna wake her. If that happens she'll want to play, eat, or worse, come with me. What'll be the harm if I leave for a little while? Wouldn't it be a hoot if the kid wandered off? I hum a little at the very idea.

I check on her one more time before I ease out the door. I forget to lock it.

It's so freakin' hot out here. With sunglasses on I pretend I'm a spy with a huge secret. I almost laugh out loud at how close to the truth that is. I pass a few women whose joggin' clothes are so new, they probably just took the tags off this morning. When I do laugh out loud, they give me an odd look and hurry past. I head for a bench under a large tree before the old geezer coming from the opposite direction can get there. I ignore the dirty look he gives me.

The leaves block out the sun and I swear it feels a good ten degrees cooler. I take a few deep breaths. This is what the difference is between jail and freedom. I close my eyes and wonder about my possibilities. What if . . .

Somethin' squeaks and I open my eyes. Here comes a lady pushin' a kid in a stroller. The kid kickin' his chubby legs and suckin' on a thumb is almost as big as the child that I left sleepin' on the couch.

When I get back I don't need the key to open the door. And damn it all, the kids still there sleepin'. I pour myself a cold one and check messages. I stop drinking and listen. I hit play again. Someone originally balked at the kid's age, but, according to my contact, after seein' a picture of her, like the fact she's light-skinned and tall for her age. They say she might be a good fit after all.

CHAPTER 13

Instead of exiting through the glass doors, Jonelle pivoted and bumped into Adrienne standing directly behind. "Hey, watchit," Adrienne complained. "Where're you going?"

"I wanna check something out," she said. "You stay here."

Jonelle took the elevator up to the sixth floor, scooted around the back and walked up the stairs to seven. She tip-toed to Tamora's door, knocked, and moved out of sight of Maxine's peephole. A few seconds later she knocked again, louder this time, and slipped to one side. After the count of five, Maxine opened her door and looked out. Her eyes widened in alarm at the sight of Jonelle staring back at her.

"See, here's the thing," Jonelle said. "I don't think you're being totally honest with me. I think you make a habit of knowing who comes and goes on this floor." Her hand knocked once more on Tamora's door.

"And here's the second thing. She's not home. Maybe she's not home a lot. And you probably have a pretty good idea about that as well."

The surprise in Maxine's eyes evaporated into a cold, hard stare. "Tamora is a good mother," she said.

"Define good."

"That child was always well-fed, well-dressed and—"

"And she left her alone frequently," Jonelle interrupted. "How the hell is that 'good'?"

Two doors down a door opened, and a young face peeked out. Piper stepped into the hall. "Oh, hi. Are you coming to see me? Hey there, Miss Maxine." Piper scowled. "You okay?"

"Everything's fine." Maxine slammed the door.

"Miss Tammy ain't home."

"I see that," Jonelle said. "Do you happen to know where she went?"

Piper shrugged. "Naw. Don't see her much at all, 'specially these days."

"I'd like to meet your mother. It's a little late, though, you think it'd be okay?"

As if in answer to the question, a woman appeared. The woman's height and slight build gave no doubt she was Piper's mother.

Jonelle held out her hand. "I'm Jonelle Sweet. I've been hired by Tamora Phelps' attorney to help on the case. I can show you my private investigator's shield."

"No need." She shook Jonelle's hand. "Name's Alexis Enruth. Piper said she met some PI lady. In fact, you were here the other day, right?"

"Right. I should've introduced myself, but at the time it didn't seem appropriate."

"And now it does? At this time of night?" After a slight hesitation, Mrs. Enruth invited Jonelle inside.

"Take a seat." They sat in a semi-circle facing a large television screen. "I'd offer you something to drink, but frankly all I have is ginger ale and it's too late to make coffee."

Jonelle smiled at Mrs. Enruth's no-nonsense attitude.

"Something funny?"

Jonelle shook her head. "No. I'm thinking that you're the first person who seems to take the direct approach to things. Considering all the people I've talked to so far, I find that refreshing."

Mrs. Enruth folded her legs under her on the well-worn couch. "I appreciate that, Miss. But it's getting late, and this one"—she indicated Piper—"should be in bed. I'm smart enough to know that won't happen as long as you're here. So. Go on and ask me whatever questions you want."

Jonelle hid a smile behind her hand. "Did you hear or see anything near Tamora's apartment around ten or so the night Lark was taken?"

"Nope. Told the cops I got home around six thirty, the kids ordered pizza, and after a few beers I watched TVOne until around eleven and—"

"You fell asleep on the sofa, and I had to wake you up. As usual," Piper said, rolling her eyes at her mother.

"Is it okay if I ask Piper questions as well?"

"Go ahead. Hard to keep her quiet anyway."

The youngster poked her mother, who tickled her before returning the poke.

A slight twinge in her gut pulled at her. Jonelle ignored the feeling, wondering where it came from.

Jonelle addressed Piper. "Did you happen to notice the time when you woke your mom?"

"No, but it's always the same. Right when the late news goes off."

She looked from mother to child. "Can you both give me your impressions of Tamora and Lark? You first, Piper."

Piper sat up straighter.

"Well. Miss Tammy is really nice. Dresses real flash. There's always guys hanging around her apartment. Even Jelani." She made a face at the name. "Though I guess he's okay since they're dating and stuff."

Mrs. Enruth stared at her daughter. "And you know all this, how?"

"I see stuff in my business, you know."

"Right," Jonelle said. "I remember you guys telling me about your pet-sitting business when we first met."

"Fidos, Felines, and Friends," Piper answered with pride. "We're gonna expand to include finding lost pets. Fred claims she knows of a cool way we could do that."

"Back to Tamora, Miss Tammy," Jonelle said, afraid of losing focus. "Can you tell me more about the relationship with Jelani?"

Piper glanced at her mother, who nodded slightly.

"We don't know why she's going out with him. He's creepy."

"Creepy how?"

"Once we went across the street for a slushy and, when we came back, caught him putting dog poo on the swings behind the building. Grayson yelled at him, and when he turned around he laughed and gave us the finger."

"You never told me that," Mrs. Enruth said. "Wait 'til I tell Lorraine. As the manager she needs to know these things."

"Has he ever done anything to you guys?"

"Not really. He stares a lot. Especially at Fred. I guess he thinks she's . . ." Piper shrugged and glanced sideways at her mother, who stayed quiet. "One time I thought I heard him call Gray a half-breed."

"Have you ever seen him with Lark?"

Piper scrunched her face in concentration. "I've been thinking about that. Once when I went to the trash chute, I looked down the hall and saw him go into Miss Tammy's apartment when she was at her second job."

Jonelle leaned forward. "Do you know if Lark was home or with Miss Maxine?"

A slight shrug.

"When was this?"

"Not sure. But it wasn't the first time. Once, mom told me to return a CD to Miss Tammy, and when I knocked on her door, he answered. I wanted to give it to her directly, but he said she wasn't there. So I gave it to him."

Jonelle frowned. "How did he get in?"

Mrs. Enruth answered. "He's maintenance so he probably has a master key."

"Right." She turned back to Piper. "Did you see Lark?"

"Nope."

"What about strangers? Anybody hanging around here that you two haven't seen before?"

Both shook their heads.

"What about delivery people? Did you see any of them hanging around?"

Mrs. Enruth opened her mouth to speak, but Piper beat her to it. "They're not allowed to come on the floors. They have to stop in the manager's office."

"Right," Mrs. Enruth added, looking at her daughter with humor in her eyes.

Although Jonelle wanted to concentrate only on facts, she wanted Piper's input on something else.

"I don't normally speculate when I'm investigating a case, but I'm curious as to what Piper thinks might have happened the night Lark was taken."

Piper began picking at her yellow cotton pajama bottoms. "Well . . . we kinda argued about that at the IHOP. You know, that day we met you. And. Well. Gray thinks somebody let a stranger in the building that wasn't supposed to be here. Fred thinks Jelani has something to do with snatchin' Lark and I, um . . . well, I really like Miss Tammy. Honest. But I think she dates too many men, too fast. And, well, she coulda, by mistake you know, have pissed one of them off, and he came back to get even."

Jonelle jotted down another note. Proceed with caution. "Do you or your mom have any, um, idea as to how many men we may be talking about here?"

Mother and daughter looked at each other.

"Well," Mrs. Enruth began. "I don't really *know* this for sure, but, well, you hear things, don't you? I mean, people gossip and all. But . . ."

Another glance at her daughter. "Well, Tamora tends to date multiple men at the same time. At least that's what I heard. And I also heard that her second job isn't something a respectable person would do."

"Plus," Piper chimed, "they say that's why Lark's daddy left."

"What about that second job?"

Langford's file stated Tamora worked for some kind of medical company during the day. The only mention about the second job was that it was on call.

"That's not what I heard. I heard something about . . . Only rumor. I shouldn't even repeat it. Sorry." Mrs. Enruth stifled a yawn.

She decided not to press the point. "Back to Lark's daddy. I plan on talking to him. Have you met him?" she asked.

"A few times," Mrs. Enruth said. "Nice guy. Shocked the heck outta me when I first learned they broke up. Now he's got his life together and she's, well . . ."

"Is it possible the daddy saw what was going on with Tamora and didn't want his daughter living like that?"

"Naw," Piper said. "'Cause why? I mean. He picks her up all the time, so he coulda just kept her. He wouldn't do all this sneakin' around."

Out of the mouths of babes. "Good point," Jonelle said. "Still. Maybe something triggered his extreme action, which is why I'm trying to reconstruct all of Tamora's movements that day. I've already talked to Miss Maxine. And I want to talk to Tamora's sister. Anybody else you guys can think of?"

Mrs. Enruth stretched and Piper yawned loudly.

"I like Lorraine but be sure and check her out," Mrs. Enruth said, shaking her shoulders. "She don't just sit behind that desk. Knows all and sees all, if you catch my drift."

CHAPTER 14

Too late to stop by the apartment manager's office, Adrienne drove Jonelle home through a blinding rainstorm. "So I guess that means you're done for the night, right?"

Instead of answering her friend directly, Jonelle said, "Pull up next to my Jeep. I've gotta check something out."

"Why do I get the feeling Gracie's not gonna see her mama yet. Where else do you need to go at this time of night? In this weather?"

"Curious about something and too antsy to rest now."

"What? Do you need backup?"

Backup, indeed. "I'm not even getting out of the car. I'll fill you in tomorrow." She hopped out and into her own vehicle.

Jonelle reviewed everything she'd heard that evening. The warmth of her condo called to her, but instead of succumbing, she pulled out of her parking space, bothered by the fact that Tamora wasn't home. In her glove compartment on a list of interviewees and their addresses was Tamora's sister, Evelyn Clifton, the owner of "Evie's Little Tykes" daycare. She plugged in the address on her GPS.

Less than forty-five minutes later, Jonelle turned onto a street illuminated by sodium street lights and lined with cars on both sides. As ordered by the digitalized voice, she pulled up in front of a fenced-in bungalow. Unable to see the actual address, the street lights reflected off of several plastic toys scattered about behind the chain link. A small multi-colored sign announced Evie's Lil Tykes daycare.

All the windows were dark. Jonelle found a place to park and pulled her Jeep into a spot two houses down and across the street and cut off the engine. She stared at the darkened structure, unsure of what to do next. If she knocked on the door at this hour, everyone inside would think it was some sort of emergency, and since Jonelle didn't have a ready excuse for stopping by, all she'd end up with is very pissed-off people.

The rain slowed to a slight drizzle. She peered out at the other houses, all similar in style and all tidy from what she could tell in the semi-darkness. Loud voices, followed by laughter, came from somewhere down the block.

Under a large umbrella a couple walked down the street, arm in arm, leaning into each other. The taller one laughed, and the other joined in. As they strolled by, a slight pang inside reminded her here she was, sitting in a dark car, dampness all around. Alone. As usual. She shook off the feeling and suppressed a yawn. The hell with this, she thought. I'll come back later. She leaned forward, hand on the ignition key.

One more glance at the house and . . . the porch light flared. She sat up. The light went out again.

Puzzled, she peered into the darkness around the house, her eyes straining to catch movement.

The light went on and off again.

The sound of a motor forced her attention away from the house. A small car, headlights off, crept up the street. As she turned to get a better look, her arm hit the steering wheel, setting off the car horn.

The blare sounded as loud as a foghorn from a lighthouse. The car stopped. The porch light stayed off. A moment later the vehicle flew down the street, tires squealing as it took the corner too fast.

"Damn!"

With her cover blown, instead of following the speeding vehicle, she pulled out of the parking spot and stopped in front of the house. She caught a faint movement of curtains from the one large window. Fine. It wouldn't hurt for Tamora to get the message she took finding out the truth very seriously.

She racked her brain to come up with a reason someone in that house should signal another car, but her tired mind wouldn't cooperate. Yawning once more, she placed her car in gear. Not only did she wonder who the person was in that car, but what, if anything, did their presence have to do with the missing child?

CHAPTER 15

*G*ot *that detective lady's business card with two phone numbers, address, and email. With her throwin' these things around all over the place, I wonder how many crank calls and emails she gets. The contact keeps tellin' me not to pay no attention to her. That she's not learnin' anything that the police haven't already found out. Still.*

I nearly peed my pants when some old bitty caught me stuffin' kid's clothes in the washer. Since she only had on pajamas, I had to dress her in some of the stuff out of this big box they gimme. A couple cotton tops and shorts fit. But she's a messy eater and keeps spillin' stuff and wipin' her hands all over her clothes.

Some nosey pants wanted to know if I had relatives staying with me. Told her I was doin' a favor for a friend of mine whose washing machine broke. Not sure if she believed me, but I need to keep my eye on that one. At the bottom of the box was a cute little handbag— pink, of course—shaped like a butterfly. Butterflies are her favorite. Boy was she happy. Her little face had the biggest smile.

Later on I told 'em I was drawing attention to myself by washing children's clothes. They said don't do that no more. They also changed the rules.

I was supposed to take my turn until they were ready to move her someplace else, and that was it. Now, on top of all that, they want me to check out that detective lady. That Jonelle Sweet.

Reminded 'em with more responsibilities come more money.

Me and the little one are gonna sneak out and go for a ride. She's gettin' real good at our own special game of hide-and-seek.

When I yell "hide!" she ducks down and stays there until I say, "gotcha!" Then she pops up and giggles, like when I tickle her over and over.

The game never varies. One thing I'm learnin' about kids is you can do the same thing a million times and still get the same result.

We got a visitor today. About time too. The kid perked up a little. Gettin' the new toys helped.

After the visit, she got a little upset, but calmed down after I told her that everybody would get together real soon. I made mac and cheese with cut up hot dogs, and chocolate milk, and that made her happy.

Pretty soon we should make the transfer and then I can get back to leadin' my own life. I'm never doin' this again, even though the money's great. At least not with kids this young. Older might work better; somebody around eight, nine, ten can be kept quiet without botherin' too much about how fragile they are.

Of course, older kids give you different kinda problems.

I look over at her, snorin' a little after eatin' everythin' on her plate. Such a sweet little face. My butterfly princess. I'm trying to ignore the tiny pangs of guilt formin' in my gut. They warned me not to get too attached.

Gotta think of somethin' else. That PI. That Jonelle Sweet. Maybe I'll do a little investigatin' on my own.

Had to wait until the coast was clear for the little one and me to leave. Have to admit she's a smart one. Catches on quick to any new "game" I teach her. Today it was "now you see me, now you don't." Keep your head down, walk fast, and no one will see you. She loved it. All I had to do was tell her not to keep giggling.

Made it to the car with no problems. At this time of day, I don't think of the few people around that anybody noticed us, which is why *we picked this area. Nearly everybody had a job to go to. Whatever fool claimed that all poor black people liked to do was sit around watching television never met anybody around here.*

Once she was buckled in, I handed her the white-framed sunglasses and floppy straw hat. Bought both at the store. They sell everything in that place. Told her that'll help her stay invisible.

Think I'll pass by where that detective lady works. I'm gettin' goosebumps thinkin' 'bout it.

CHAPTER 16

U nable to sleep, Jonelle woke at six thirty, made coffee, poured herself a bowl of Cheerios, and added sliced banana and milk. She cleaned and refilled all of Gracie's food and water dishes—the kitten had a bowl for dry food and separate bowls for wet food and water. After a few minutes of playing bat the ball the kitten yawned and headed for her nest. Feeling a little better, Jonelle poured coffee in a travel mug and headed to the office.

"And to what do I owe this pre-dawn pleasure?" Rainey asked.

"Oh come on. I'm not that early."

Rainey bit into her brownie and sipped from her can of Coke. "Yes. Yes, you are. Not that I'm complaining, mind you. By the way, I left two messages on your desk. I didn't call you because he said it could wait."

"Messages so soon this morning?"

Mouth full of chocolate, the receptionist nodded.

The memos sat in the middle of the desk. Written on both, in Rainey's flowery hand, was the name Vaughn Hanson, Lark's father. Both stated he'd like her to call him and were time-stamped thirty minutes apart. She called the number listed, and he answered on the second ring.

He cut her off when she attempted to explain her role in Lark's abduction.

"I know who you are and what you're doing. We need to talk, and I don't want to do this over the phone."

Somewhat put off by the abrupt tone of his voice, she suggested they meet that morning. "You choose the place and time. I'm flexible," she said.

"Your office," Hanson replied. "It's only three blocks from where I work. Ten works for me. You?"

"Sounds good." Jonelle told him to press the button to the outside security system and they'd buzz him in. After he'd agreed and disconnected, she pulled up Tamora's file and read the information about him. Everything consisted of one page and contained little more than his name, age, and place of work. No indication that he and Tamora were ever married but . . . Jonelle read the line again—Hanson wanted full custody of Lark. Further on, Langford's notes stated Hanson called the police to report his daughter missing and had an alibi for the entire night Lark was abducted.

Jonelle studied the picture of Lark and her mother. Taken at a department store studio, both had large smiles, although Jonelle could see a slight sadness around the child's wide, round eyes. She scribbled some questions she wanted to make sure to ask and waited.

Right at ten, not a minute earlier or later, Rainey buzzed her to say she had a visitor. Jonelle instructed the secretary to send him back.

As soon as he entered she knew he was the child's father. Of the two parents, Lark favored him. The same milk chocolate skin color and large soulful eyes. He had what could best be described as a kind face—not handsome, but certainly not unpleasant. His dark gray suit wasn't tailored, but he wore it well. Standing to greet him, she had to look up to meet his eyes.

He sat across from her, arms draped loosely over the chair's arms.

"Thanks for meeting me so soon," he said.

"I was going to call you anyway, so this works fine."

"What have you found out?"

"Let's not beat around the bush," she said, trying to lighten the mood.

He didn't smile back.

"Okay, then. I've talked to a few people, including Tamora, but they were initial interviews. The first time I like to get a feel for the person and, depending on what they say, build on that in subsequent interviews."

"I don't care about all that. Where's my daughter?"

She sighed inwardly. "I don't work like the police. Paul Langford is my client, and my job is to find out as much as I can from everyone who had any contact whatsoever with either the child or Tamora that night, so he can use that in her defense."

Hanson's jaw tightened.

She waited for him to say more and, when he didn't, continued. "I know you told the police you stopped by unannounced and discovered Lark missing. Where were you the rest of the night?"

The muscles in his jaw looked as if they were waging some kind of war. For a moment Jonelle wondered if the man had anger issues.

As if reading her thoughts, he responded in a calm, measured way. "I'd gone from my job straight to my attorney's office. I'm sure you already know I'm petitioning for sole custody. Anyway, I left her office around seven that night. I knew Lark was at Miss Maxine's so—"

"How'd you know that?"

"Because that's where she stayed when Tamora went to her night job."

"That was the routine, yes. But did you call to check?"

He frowned. "No. If there was a problem, Maxine would've called. She has my number."

Jonelle motioned for him to continue.

"After the lawyer's, I stopped by and picked up Chinese for the two of us."

"The two of you?"

"Me and Cheryl. My fiancée. Once I get custody, I'm . . ." He stopped. He closed his eyes for a moment, and when he opened them again, Jonelle could see the pain written there.

"How long were you with Cheryl?"

"All night. Until I stopped by the apartment."

She leaned forward, arms folded on the desk. "Why stop by that particular evening?"

A crooked smile formed on his thin lips. "Not only women have hunches. Can't explain it any other way. All of a sudden I got an urge to check on my daughter in person."

Hanson went on to recount everything in the copy of the police report.

"After they arrived that night to take your initial statement, did they follow-up?" She needed to know how seriously the cops were taking the report.

"Yeah. Around eight thirty the next morning. At work. Wish they hadn't done that. Imagine the look on my supervisor's face when the detectives strolled in wanting to talk to me."

"Wonder what Tamora was doing all this time?" Jonelle murmured.

"What?"

"Oh, sorry. Thinking out loud. What did you think when you realized Lark was missing?"

"That Tamora, considering only herself, let it happen . . . somehow. To get even with me or something. Maybe got one of her boyfriends to help."

Jonelle knew of two men who'd dated Tamora recently. Maxine hadn't mentioned anyone else, and no one she'd talked to in the apartment building shed light on any other men.

"Do you know who those boyfriends are?"

He shrugged. "Only know that maintenance guy. And some dude she met at that minimart across the street. Somebody from her day job. Those are the ones offhand."

"What's the name of the guy at her job?" Jonelle flipped through Tamora's file. She couldn't find a reference to him.

"I don't know."

"Then how do you know she went out with him?"

"'Cause every time she complained about me and Cheryl, she'd throw up the fact that she could get anyone she wanted and that the 'guy at work',"—he used air quotes—"took her out and bought her nice things." He turned and looked toward the windows. "My lawyer wants names, too. I'm working on it."

And so would she. "So tell me. What do you really think happened to Lark that night?"

He gripped the chair's arms and leaned forward, eyes blazing. "I think she's hidden Lark somewhere to screw with me."

Jonelle leaned back in her chair and considered what he said. On the surface, based on what little she knew of Tamora, it kind of made sense. Except the woman's selfishness didn't jibe with getting herself in trouble. "You know she was arrested, right?"

He nodded.

"You know Tamora. Do you really think she'd risk jail to screw you?"

Henson leaned forward, elbows on her desk. He put his head in his hands. "I don't know." He raised his head. "Please do whatever you can to find my child."

"I'll do my best, Mr. Hanson. Promise."

He stood to leave.

"Hold on a sec. How'd you get inside? Do you have a key?"

"That's the other thing. She refused to give me my own key. Claimed the manager wouldn't let her for security reasons. Yeah, right. What really pisses me off is the door was already open when I got there."

Jonelle escorted Vaughn Hanson out of her office with the words, "I'd like to stop by your place this evening, if that's all right."

"Why?"

They stopped at the receptionists' desk.

"To meet your fiancée and maybe ask her a few questions. That's not a problem, is it?"

Hanson fiddled with his gray and white-striped tie. "Well . . . I need to clear it with Cheryl first. I'll call and let you know."

"I promise not to stay long. Less than an hour."

"As I said, I'll let you know." He nodded at Rainey as he left the agency.

"Interesting man," Rainey said. "I got a feeling you're gonna stop by, not waitin' for permission. Am I right?"

"You know me too well. I mean, so what if he slams the door in my face? That'll tell me a lot."

CHAPTER 17

J onelle paced around the reception area, too full of energy to go
back to her office and sit behind her desk. After the fourth
circuit, Rainey cleared her throat. "You're makin' me nervous
movin' around like that. Go back to your office or get outta
here."

"Hmm. Think I'll head over to Tamora's job. See if I can
talk to a few of her co-workers."

"Is she back at work?"

"Don't think so. She's not in her apartment, or at least she
wasn't last night. I figure she's at her sister's place, so after
checking out where she works, I'll stop by there." Jonelle
swallowed the word "again."

Several surface streets and one interstate exit later, Jonelle
pulled up in a parking lot surrounding a large red brick medical
arts building. She studied the directory and headed to the office
on the main floor. She entered the large reception area and stood
in front of the nearest of several smiling young women located
behind a long, low counter.

"Hello. Which doctor are you seeing today?"

In answer, Jonelle pulled out her PI license. "I'd like to speak
to Tamora Phelps' supervisor if they're available."

The smile faded. "Take a seat while I call to the back."

"Thanks, but I'll stand."

A mixture of young and old and representative of about every
racial and ethnic group she could identify occupied nearly all of

the brown fabric-covered chairs. Bright-colored posters advertised "Hematology and Oncology" as the specialties. When called, each person stood without comment and obediently followed a technician, both disappearing behind a wooden door.

"May I help you?"

Jonelle turned and faced a middle-aged woman in a white smock.

"Yes. I'm here to ask a few questions about Tamora Phelps. I'm working for—"

"Follow me."

Without another word, the woman led Jonelle past the reception area and down a narrow hallway. After an abrupt right turn, she entered a large office and asked Jonelle to close the door.

"Please sit."

"Thanks." Jonelle pulled out her PI license and showed it to the woman, who hadn't yet identified herself. "I'll get right to it. I'm here on her lawyer's authority. I understand she works here."

"Worked. She's been dismissed."

Jonelle tried to read the woman's face and came up with nothing. The nameplate on the desk read, "Susan Mahoney, RN, Administrator."

"Fired?"

A quick nod.

"For what reason?"

The bland expression was replaced by a bitter smile. "We don't like it when our employees end up in jail."

"She's out. And, I might add, hasn't been convicted of anything. What happened to 'innocent until proven guilty'?"

Mahoney leaned back against the leather chair. After a slight hesitation, she continued in a softer voice. "Her arrest was the last straw. I'd given her several warnings. After each one she promised to do better, and she never did. Fact is, until about six months ago, she was a good employee. Not great, but . . ." She shrugged.

"Warnings about what?"

"Attendance. Always attendance. I can forgive someone coming in a little late now and then, but there were days when she wouldn't show up at all. A few times she'd call in sick or say her daughter didn't feel well and she had to stay home. Even then, I tried to give her the benefit of the doubt. These last few months she didn't even bother checking in. I'd ring and leave messages. Nothing. A few days later, she'd waltz in as if nothing happened."

Mahoney stood, walked to a wooden file cabinet, found what she was looking for and sat. "The day after Memorial Day I told her if she didn't come in as scheduled and on time, I was letting her go." Her eyes met Jonelle's. "For a whole week she was great. And then, nothing."

Jonelle understood the woman's feelings. "If everything was getting better, well, how could she know she was going to be arrested?"

"I know when she went to jail. She stopped coming to work about four days before that happened."

"So what did she do here?"

"Front desk. Checked people in. Made appointments. That kind of thing."

She didn't know what to think. Everyone she talked to insisted Tamora followed the same routine. If she wasn't going to work, where was she going? "How did you notify her that she'd been terminated?"

"Left messages on her phone and also sent a registered letter."

Hanson said Tamora had a boyfriend at work. Mahoney struck her as the type who'd know. "Did Tamora have any friends here?"

Another shrug. "She was friendly to everyone. No problems at all with her getting along."

"I'd like to speak to anyone she was especially close to."

"Why?"

"Maybe they'd know where she was during the time she was supposed to be at work."

Mahoney swiveled back and forth as if weighing how much to tell. "I asked everyone, and no one admitted to knowing what was going on with her. But it's possible they simply weren't telling me the truth. Frankly, I didn't press it because at that point I no longer cared." She glanced at a spot behind Jonelle. "I'll see if Shawn is available. Those two seemed real friendly. Wait right here."

In a few minutes, a tall man with a medium build, in blue medical garb, entered, and Mahoney directed him to sit in her chair. He paused, a quizzical look on his face. "Um. You sure? I mean, where're you gonna sit?"

The high-pitched voice coming from the man didn't fit his size.

"I think Miss Sweet wants to talk to you alone. Come get me when you're done." She glanced once at Jonelle before closing the door.

She waited until Shawn sat before beginning with her credentials and why she needed to speak to him.

"You a detective, huh? Cool." His eyes smiled as if he knew a secret.

"Private. I work for an agency assigned to help in Tamora's case."

"Oh. Still . . ." He grinned, exposing a large gap between his front teeth.

"Right. Shawn is it? What's your last name?" Jonelle took out her pad, pen poised to write.

"Don't I need to swear to tell the truth or something?" He looked around as if expecting to find a bible somewhere.

She made a mental note to keep the interview simple. "No. No bible needed. Last name?"

"Mowerby. Spelled like it sounds." He grinned again.

"Thanks. I understand you and Tamora knew each other well when she worked here. That right?"

The grin faded. "What you mean by that? I don't know what happened to that little girl."

"I'm not saying you did. What I'm interested in is your relationship with Tamora."

"Friends. 'Cause, you know, she's a real friendly kinda person." There was that grin again.

Her next words wiped that smirk off his face. "Did you see her the night the child was taken?"

He sat up, back straight as a two by four.

"No way. I ain't never been to her place. We only hung out . . . around here. That's all."

She didn't believe him for a minute. "Where?"

He narrowed his already small eyes at her. "Happy hour. Went out for a bite. That's it."

"I understood she had a second job. Where did she find the time for the two of you to go out after working here?"

Things weren't adding up. Tamora's so-called routine kept unraveling.

"Oh that. That job was part-time—some kinda on-call thing. She didn't have to go there every night. Least that's what she told me."

"She tell you anything else about this other job?"

His eyes roamed around the office.

"Shawn?"

He shrugged.

"Anyone else you guys hung out with? Either here, or maybe meet up with someone from her other job?"

"Naw. Only us together. Some of the girls who work here were kinda jealous of her. And I don't know nobody from her other job."

"Were the two of you a couple?"

His eyes widened. "What? No. Tamora didn't want nothing serious, which was okey-doke with me. Know what I mean? Guys always gave her the once over, and she was kinda flirty, but that wasn't no problem."

"You sure you didn't mind her toying with guys when you two went out? Most men wouldn't like that at all." Unless. She studied him a bit more closely.

"Like I said. It didn't bother me."

She let it pass. "Anyone else here she hung out with?"

"Not really."

Jonelle thanked him and handed him her card, requesting that he contact her if he thought of anything else.

The two parted company in the hallway. Jonelle looked around for Mahoney, didn't see the administrator anywhere, and left.

Although not included in the day's plans, she opened the browser on her phone and pulled up the website for Tamora's second job at a medical supplies company. While they were open twenty-four hours, Jonelle was anxious to get as much information as she could when she spoke to Tamora again. She wanted to confront the young woman with all the lies that were beginning to build.

She drove by the address the first time and had to go around again and again before she found it on the third try. The low brown building was so nondescript it looked as if someone had put it there by mistake. The address only appeared on a small sign situated on the ground along with several others, and its pale letters on a white background almost guaranteed it couldn't be read from a distance.

Annoyed at having to leave her car and slog around looking for the entrance, Jonelle pushed through the double doors on the one-floor building and stepped in a place filled with walkers, canes, orthopedic wraps, and various other items she hoped she wouldn't have to use for many years, if at all. She didn't have to worry about wasting time on pleasantries since she was the only person in the space.

"Hello? Anybody here?"

A few minutes later a young man with dark pants and white shirt hurried out from somewhere in the back. "How'd you get in here?"

"Through the door. How'd you think?"

He slipped past her and tried the door, which opened easily. "That's supposed to be locked." He ran his fingers through his short sandy-colored hair. "You're supposed to ring the bell, and someone is supposed to let you in. This is a secure location. You're not supposed to be able to walk right in and—"

"Yeah, well I did. So if you'll stop obsessing and 'supposing' about the obvious for a minute, I'll tell you who I am and why I'm here. Okay?"

He paused before giving her a quick nod.

She handed him her card. A quick explanation of who she was and why she was there was met by worry lines on his forehead. "I never heard of the woman. You sure she works here?"

"Positive. But she works on-call at night. Who's in charge in the evenings?" Not seeing any chairs around, Jonelle wandered over and sat in one of several wheelchairs lined up against a wall.

He opened his mouth to object.

She held up her hand. "Unless you got someplace else for me to sit, I'm staying put. I'll ask again. If you're not here, say after five or so, who is?"

"Wait right there." He headed toward the back, turned once to look over his shoulder, and disappeared through a revolving door.

Jonelle released the brakes on the chair, grabbed the large wheels, and eased forward and back, forward and back. Feeling a little silly, but unable to stop herself, she wheeled the chair up to the door, turned around, and slid back to the original spot. Curious as to the turning radius, she tried to manipulate the chair in the tightest circle she could. Someone clearing their throat stopped her from completing a second circuit.

"Excuse me. But how—"

"Oh, Jesus, Mary, and Joseph, let's not go through that again. Didn't Sparky over there explain all that to you?" Jonelle indicated the young man standing partially hidden behind a white woman dressed in a dark skirt and blue, short-sleeve blouse. She set the brakes and stood. Reaching into her bag she held out her PI identification.

"Follow me," she said, after studying Jonelle's ID. "We can sit in my office."

The room reminded Jonelle of her first office at the agency. She'd had to use a former storage space until the renovations were complete. This area was no bigger, and she felt a familiar tightness form in her chest. "Um. Don't close the door, if you don't mind. I've got a touch of claustrophobia, so I'll make this quick." There was no nameplate on the tiny desk. "Can I get your name for my records?"

"Lillian. Lillian Comer." The woman's pale eyes regarded her with suspicion.

"Thanks. I'm interested in finding out whatever information you have about Tamora Phelps. My understanding is she works part-time in the evenings."

"Not every evening. We call her, along with about ten or so others, when we start to get swamped with orders."

"She took orders? What kind?"

"Small items and she didn't take the orders, our day crew does that. She took the order sheets, found the items from the warehouse in the back and packed them for mailing."

"How often did she work last week?"

"Hold on." Comer reached behind the desk to a metal bookcase and pulled out a red binder. She flipped through pages and placed a finger on her lips. "According to this, she didn't work at all last week." Comer rifled through a few more pages. "Looks like the others did, but not her."

"You sure? Are you here nights?"

"No, I'm not, but the night supervisor always puts the names of all those working every night." She flipped through several more sheets and frowned. "Tamora's name isn't listed for the week prior to that, either."

CHAPTER 18

*T*he kid's gonna stay with somebody else for a while so I can focus on that PI. Keep an eye on her to see how close she's gettin' and to take matters into my own hands if necessary. I'm praying I won't have to do anything . . . complicated. That's way above my head. All I've had to do so far, is keep the kid out of sight. I've depended on the cops chasing their tails and haven't been disappointed.

Wonder what time she leaves the office? Who's paying her? Know she ain't doing all this investigating for the fun of it. When I told everybody I could make her stop snooping around, they all laughed. Claimed I could barely take care of myself. Then why, I pointed out, did they trust me with the child.

Said it didn't have anything to do with trust. Convenience. That's what they keep telling me.

I'm involved because it's convenient.

CHAPTER 19

After learning from Comer that Tamora's last evening of work was two weeks prior to Lark's abduction, Jonelle called and left a message for Langford, updating him on the case. She hated informing him his client seemed allergic to the truth.

Still too early to check out Vaughn Hanson at home, she pulled into the drive-thru of Burger Palace and ordered a burger with the works, fries, and diet soda. She ate in her car, relishing the total silence while figuring out what to do about Tamora.

Nothing added up.

The woman kept to the routine of leaving the child with her sister in the mornings supposedly to go to a job she didn't have any more. Afterward, Tamora picked Lark up to take her to Maxine's before leaving again.

To go where? Not to work, based on what she'd found out from the manager.

Time to check out Evelyn Clifton. If Tamora didn't go to either job, did she visit her sister to work on their so-called party planning business?

Arriving at the daycare, Jonelle slid her Jeep in a spot directly across the street. A small multicolored sign in an array of topsy-turvy letters announced, "Evie's Little Tykes Daycare For Ages 2 Through 6." Although the plastic toys from the night before still cluttered the ground, no children played in the front.

She unlatched the gate to the chain-link fence and strode up to the porch. Squeals of laughter erupted from the other side of a high security enclosure behind the house. Instead of knocking on the front door, Jonelle went around to the side. She looked for a gate, found none, and headed for the opposite side. No gate there, either. It looked as if the only way to access the rear yard was through the house.

The curtains on the one large window were drawn back. Before she could knock, the door opened, and she faced a woman about Tamora's height but at least twenty pounds heavier and about thirty-years-old whereas Tamora was twenty-three.

"Help you?"

"Yes. I'm Jonelle Sweet. I'm working with Tamora's lawyer as a private investigator. I've been assigned to gather as much information as I can about the night Lark was taken. Are you Evelyn Clifton?"

"That's right."

"May I come in and ask you a few questions?"

Instead of answering right away, Evelyn pulled the door closer, preventing Jonelle from seeing inside the house. "Now's not a good time," she said.

"In your line of work, finding a time when a child doesn't need something might be an issue. But . . . I can come back later, if you prefer. Want to set up an appointment?"

"Appointment? How much time are you talking about?"

Jonelle answered with a smile and a shrug.

Evelyn looked behind her shoulder as if wanting permission to continue talking. After another moment of indecision, Evelyn moved aside. "C'mon in. They just ate lunch and are playing for a while before I put them down for a nap. You can have a few minutes."

Jonelle stepped inside. The soft whirr of a window air conditioning unit and a large ticking clock on one wall were strangely comforting, almost hypnotic.

Framed photographs occupied tables, shelves, and mantle of a bricked-up fireplace. Most were of smiling children, and a few were attired in mini caps and gowns.

"How many children are in your care?" Jonelle sat in an overstuffed chair with Evelyn across from her in a matching chair.

"Since school's out right now, I have five. In the fall that'll increase to around eight or so."

"Why does the school year affect your business? Parents still have to go to work, right?"

"Yes, but some have older children who can watch the younger ones, so rather than pay me, the siblings take care of them. I don't worry about it. I have a waiting list as it is."

An adult voice cut through childish giggling.

"Is Tamora here?" Jonelle asked, twisting in the direction of the sound.

"That's my assistant, Vickie. She's been with me since I opened the business."

Evelyn hadn't answered the question. "I've been trying to locate Tamora. She's not answering the door at her apartment, and both her employers tell me they haven't seen her in a while. The day job supervisor dismissed her about a week before Lark was taken. A supervisor at the part-time on call job at the medical supplies company, a Lillian Comer, told me Tamora stopped coming to work about two weeks before Lark was taken. Did you know that?"

Evelyn's lips pressed tighter and tighter with each of Jonelle's words.

Jonelle waited, hoping for some kind of response. When none came, she continued.

"I started out thinking there was no way a young mother would have anything to do with her own child's abduction. Everyone I talked to went on and on about what a good mother Tamora is. Now I find out she hasn't been going to work in spite of keeping to her same routine." Jonelle leaned forward. "I follow information wherever it leads, good or bad. I'm going to do whatever it takes to find out as much as I can about Tamora's whereabouts before and during the time Lark went missing. You're her sister. I'm asking again. Did you know she hadn't been going to work after she dropped Lark off here and at Miss Maxine's?"

The hum of the AC unit and the ticking of the clock grew louder for each second Evelyn didn't answer.

"It wasn't anything bad," Evelyn finally said, her voice low. "She and I are thinking about going into business together, and she needed time to . . . research some things. I knew she'd stopped going to her day job, we argued about that, but she said she didn't worry about the money, she still had another job. I didn't know it'd been that long."

"The evening job isn't every night. She's on call and hasn't showed up there most of the time. What kind of job requires 'research' all day and all night?"

A satisfied look crossed Evelyn's face. "Party planning. Parties go on all day and night, you know."

"Agreed. And I also know it's not rocket science, so how much do you need to study?"

Something large crashed somewhere in the house. Young voices shouted, followed by angry words from an adult. Evelyn stood. "I have to go. I'll see you to the door."

"Where's Tamora?"

With one hand on the open door, Evelyn waited until Jonelle stood outside on the porch. "She's . . . I'll tell her you need to speak to her."

"Is she staying with you?"

"No." The answer came a little too quickly.

"You sure?"

"I don't think I like your attitude, Ms. Sweet."

"And I don't like being lied to. Especially when it involves the health and well-being of a child. Instead of covering for your sister, you might want to consider Lark in all this and what that poor little girl may be going through." Jonelle turned on her heel.

"My sister would never—"

She whirled back. "Save it. I'm tired of hearing how great a mother she is. So far I haven't seen much evidence of that. Tamora has until ten this evening to contact me. If I don't hear from her, I have a detective friend who would be very interested in what I've found out about her—and her friends and family— so far."

The door slammed behind her. Jonelle didn't bother to turn around, afraid her middle finger would take on a life of its own. She headed to the office, intent on doing grunt work until she could stop by Vaughn Hanson's place.

She walked into an empty reception area, opened her mouth to call out to Rainey, then thought better of it. Shooting the breeze with the secretary might calm her down, but she wanted her anger to continue bubbling. Whenever she allowed that to happen, it cleared up her thinking.

Once inside her office, she picked up two messages—both from Langford. She called him back and was put through right away. "I planned to call you today," she said when he answered. "Though I'm not sure you're gonna be happy about it."

He sighed deeply. "Can't say I'm surprised at this point. The DA is pressing charges against her. Right now they're not charging her with the actual kidnapping, but they believe she's involved. While I've kept her out of jail for now, she's treating me like a pariah rather than someone who's trying to help, and, frankly, I'm getting sick and tired of it. I hope you got better results."

Jonelle gave him a quick run through. Except for several expletives, the lawyer asked no questions. "Here's the thing," she said. "I'm not happy with how she's treating me, either. And she's not the wonderful, innocent mother I've been led to believe from the people in her apartment. I'm not one hundred percent convinced she knows who took Lark. Have you considered the biological father in all this?"

The sound of shuffling papers came through the line. "Yeah. Uh, oh here it is. Guy's name is Vaughn Hanson. We talked to him. He called the cops about his missing daughter."

"Right. And I'm sure he told you about suing for custody, but I want to get a better feel of how deep his feelings were about Tamora's social life. If he was obsessed about his daughter's welfare, he might not want to wait for the courts to decide."

"True." Langford chuckled. "I gotta say, though. The one bright spot in all this so far is that you're certainly giving me my money's worth. Keep me informed."

As soon as she disconnected, Jonelle picked up the last summons. A quick good-bye to Rainey, now seated behind the desk, and she was off. The "Failure to Appear" worked at an auto parts store and had evaded service previously because his co-workers covered for him. Not this time.

She knew what the man looked like, so when she arrived at the store, she marched up to the front counter, smiled brightly at the manager behind the desk, and without comment headed through the service door.

"Hey!"

She ignored his protests, strode up to a skinny brown-haired man wiping oil from his hands with a filthy rag, and shoved the papers at him. "Robert Spencer, you're served. Have a nice day."

The manager caught up to her. "Listen, Miss. You can't come in here and—"

"I just did." She slammed the door on the rest of his words. Sitting in her Jeep, she felt the tension from earlier fade away. "One more creep about to get his due."

Jonelle drove to Centennial Park and slid her Jeep into a space nearest the start of the walking path. She cut the engine, and grabbed walking shoes from a cloth storage container stowed behind the driver's seat.

She set out, determined to circle the lake twice, which should make it almost five miles. Even though she'd managed only once around, the solitary movement gave her time to mull things over.

Obviously there were two different Tamoras. To those where she lived, she was conscientious and put her daughter first. However, Tamora's employers described an undependable woman. One of the things she wanted to address with Hanson was whether or not he could shed light on the different impressions about his ex.

Two hours later she pulled up to the curb of his townhouse and parked in a visitor's space.

The robin's-egg blue with white trim structure looked new, but Jonelle had seen many of these go up fast in the area. A garage on the side was closed. She pulled up on the pad in front and parked. A quick trip up three steps and she pushed a bell not audible from the outside. Wondering if the thing worked, she pressed again, harder.

"Hold on, hold on." The door opened, and Jonelle found herself staring up at Hanson, still dressed in the same suit from earlier. "Oh. It's you. What're you doing here?"

"Told you I'd stop by."

"Yeah, but you didn't say it'd be this soon."

"Problem?"

He looked behind his shoulder. "Guess not. Dinner's almost ready, though, and I hate cold food."

"I won't stay long. Is your fiancée here?"

"Yeah." He ushered Jonelle into a tiny foyer where a set of steps led directly up to the second level.

At the top of the gray carpeted stairs, a small woman stood stirring something in a pan on the stove.

"Hey, Cheryl, we got company."

Cheryl turned, quickly replacing the smile with a slight frown. "We're getting ready to eat."

"I know. This is Jonelle Sweet, that private investigator I told you about. She stopped by to ask questions about Tamora."

"I don't know the woman," Cheryl said.

"That's all right," Jonelle said. "I really wanted to clarify a few things with Mr. Hanson. Specifically about Lark."

The smile returned. "Sweet child. We love having her here," Cheryl said. "I wish . . ."

"Yes?"

"Nothing. Dinner will be ready in about fifteen minutes." She shot Hanson a look before turning back to the stove.

Opposite the kitchen and dining room was a spacious living area, complete with buff colored leather couch and two matching chairs. "Nice place," Jonelle said.

"We like it. And so does Lark. There's space that I use as an office now that I'll convert into a room for her," he said.

Assuming she's safe, Jonelle thought. "You sound convinced you'll get custody."

"Why not? I mean, think about my life as compared to Tamora's. No contest. Especially since she let somebody kidnap my child."

"Wait a minute. You don't know that for a fact."

Hanson slouched into one of the chairs. Jonelle sat on the couch to his right.

"Earlier today you hinted one of Tamora's boyfriends might have something to do with what happened. Why?"

He gripped the armrests. "You're a detective. You must've learned by now that she's got crap taste in men."

"Oh, I don't know. You seem okay to me."

"She's got you there," Cheryl called from the kitchen.

Hanson glared at his fiancée who began setting the table.

The sharp aroma of Mexican spices and fried meat hung in the air. Cheryl placed what looked like taco fixings on the table.

Jonelle ignored the rumblings in her stomach. "Do you consider any of the boyfriends dangerous?"

He grunted. "Everybody's dangerous if you give them a reason."

"What kind of reason?"

"Leading them on. Getting them to buy you stuff and then turning around and hanging out with other guys. You know what I mean."

"She ever do that to you?"

Another glance at Cheryl, who kept her head down.

"This isn't about me. I want my kid back. That's all. Every day I call the cops, and every day they claim they're working on it. Yeah, right. Meanwhile my kid is somewhere, probably scared out of her mind. Or worse."

His eyes filled. He turned away.

Jonelle tore several sheets of paper from her notebook and handed him her pen. "Write down every name of the men Tamora hung out with. Include stuff like addresses, phone numbers, places where they work—"

"I don't know all that stuff."

"Write whatever you do know. A description of them, what kinda car they drive. Do they live in her building. Anything and everything."

"Hey," Cheryl piped up. "What about that guy who works in her building? She dates him. Or dated, anyway."

"Jelani Hill? I've talked to him a few times, and he's definitely on my radar. I know enough to give her lawyer a definite heads-up about the guy," Jonelle said.

Cheryl walked over to where they were seated. "And did you know he was around when another kid went missing in that building?"

CHAPTER 20

Hanson shook his head over and over. "I was living in that building with Tamora when that whole thing broke. Mrs. Watkins told us what happened. She said the Jamaican couple always fought, and one of them—think it was the wife—got pissed and disappeared with both kids. Police found everybody safe and sound in the Bronx a few days later."

He handed one piece of paper back to Jonelle. On it he'd written four names. Not much to go on, but she folded the sheet in her bag.

"How long were you living in the apartment?"

"I left when Lark was about a year old." Again that hangdog look. "Never should've done that. Never should've left my baby with . . ." He put his head in his hands.

Cheryl hovered around the dining room table. Now that Hanson opened up, Jonelle didn't want him to stop. "Can you give me a feel for Tamora as a person? People at the apartment building generally had good things to say about her. Her supervisors at work indicated she wasn't reliable. She's more mysterious than I originally thought."

He looked up. "Mysterious? Ha! She's a whack job. Only thinks about herself."

"If that's how she is, what attracted you to her in the first place?"

Jonelle gazed over at Cheryl, who returned to the stove. Hanson's fiancée seemed the polar opposite of Tamora. Thin, where Tamora was curvy, short hair worn in small curls framing her face, whereas wild was the best way to describe Tamora's hairstyle. Viewed side by side, Tamora was the one a man would look at twice.

Hanson leaned forward, took off his suit coat, and removed his tie. "I'm not the same guy I was five years ago. I was twenty-four. She was eighteen but seemed older. A lot older. Back then, the hotter looking a woman was, the better. Didn't much matter what was going on inside her head. What was important was what all the dudes thought. You wanted their approval. You wanted them to envy your woman. Stupid."

He paused for several seconds. "Not long after we hooked up she got pregnant. Also stupid."

"What kind of mother was she?"

He hesitated. When he spoke he measured his words carefully. "If I'm honest, she was very attentive and took good care of the baby. Lark barely got out a cry before Tamora would rush over and pick her up. And all the baby clothes. She couldn't pass a store without checking to see if they had an 'infants and toddlers' section. Have you seen the prices on those things? Had to put my foot down." He sighed. "Guess I shoulda been happy that for once she lavished money on someone other than herself." He looked down at the carpet. "I really thought we could make a family."

"What changed?"

"A few months after she got that job at the doctor's office, she wanted to hang out with her new friends. That wasn't so bad, at first. Heck, I went out a few times myself."

"Who watched Lark when you both went out?"

"Her sister Evelyn or Maxine."

"Go on."

"Anyway, sometimes when I'd get home she'd go out again. After a while, instead of going out once every now and then, she started hanging out on a regular basis. Got tired of arguing with her, so I left."

Jonelle bit her tongue. His walking out didn't help his child. "Do you know why Tamora started missing work?"

He looked up. Jonelle followed his gaze to where Cheryl now stood motionless next to the dining room table.

"Go on and tell her everything," Cheryl said. "No point in holding back now."

"When I decided to petition for custody, I followed Tamora a few times. After she left her day job and picked Lark up from her sister's, she went back to the apartment. I knew she left Lark with Maxine. So I'd wait until she came back out again, to go to her night job. A few times she went straight there. But the third time . . ."

Again, he looked at Cheryl, who nodded for him to continue.

"She went to work, but instead of going inside, she parked and got in another car. I couldn't see who was driving, but I do know it was a man. I followed them and ended up in a shitty part of west Baltimore. The building looked abandoned, yet occupied. Know what I mean?"

She thought about Luther. "Sure. Go on."

"Anyway, she and this guy park in front of one of the doors with iron bars top to bottom. No sign on the front. They get out and bang on the door. A little while later it opens, and they both go inside. I waited about an hour, but they never came back out. So I left, went to pick up Lark, and told Maxine that if Tamora wondered where Lark was, to tell her my daughter was with me. At about two in the morning, she arrived pissed that Lark was with me, but I didn't care."

She carefully studied Hanson. "Is the guy you saw her leave with one of the names on this list?"

He shook his head.

"Would you recognize him if you saw him again?"

"Not sure. It was dark. I didn't get a good look."

"You're a smart man. What kind of place did you think that was?"

His hands gripped the chair again as his eyes bored into hers. "I went back there a few nights later. I saw the same car parked out front. I got out and walked up to the door. This time, I noticed a small decal, the words, 'adults only,' printed in red. I'd heard about places like that before. That's where they shoot porno films."

Jonelle felt as if someone punched her in the stomach. "You sure?"

"Pretty sure."

That wasn't good enough for her. "Did you try to get inside to confirm your suspicions?"

"Naw. I was so disgusted that I went out and got me a lawyer to get custody of my kid. Nobody should have a whore for a mother."

"Vaughn," Cheryl said, concern in her voice.

"Well, that's what she is, and you know it as well as I do."

Hanson's words gave whole new meaning to the phrase "party planner." Jonelle scribbled the words "porn star??" on her notepad. "Do you remember the address?"

"Like it was yesterday." Hanson recited a location not far from where Luther stayed with his community of fellow indigents. Though he could be prickly, Luther had helped on a few of her cases. She'd search him out—find out what he knew, if anything, about what went on behind those barred warehouse doors.

CHAPTER 21

*D*amn! What the hell's he doing here? This is not good. Wait 'til I tell everybody Hanson visited that PI at her office.

Speaking of which, you'd think she'd work in a fancier building than this. Granted, it looks clean from the outside, and nobody's hanging around, but I woulda thought that she'd work in some kinda fancy high-rise near the harbor or something.

Waited to make sure Hanson was out of sight before I approached. It took a minute to find the PI's office. Checking the names outside, the only one that comes close is Shorter Investigative Services. Shorter? Thought her last name was Sweet. No matter. Now I know for sure where she works and I already know the kinda vehicle she drives. Wonder how many brownie points I'd get if I follow her and give everyone her home address?

The transfer of the child went smooth. The idea is to keep moving the kid so if the heat went on one of us, somebody else could take over. It helps that she's seen us all at least once. I make everything like a game, and I'm getting the feeling she's starting to like the back and forth. The only complaint now is when I tell her to eat different food. Even so, another butterfly toy usually does the trick to calm her down.

Also . . . them kids. They put up "Lark Missing" signs. Who told 'em to do that? Bet it was the pretty one's idea. She looks smart. Or maybe that weird redhead. She wanders around all over the place, day and night. She ain't careful, somebody's gonna snatch her . . .

CHAPTER 22

J onelle needed to speak to Luther. The sun hung low on the
horizon, which meant his community of friends might start to
straggle in at his camp in the abandoned warehouse on the
outskirts of the city. The site had a hierarchy with Luther at the
top, so the other occupants treated her with as much respect as an
outsider could receive.

She drove quickly to the east side Baltimore neighborhood
lined with decrepit warehouses and boarded up row homes. No
longer wary of the occupants, she still kept an eye out for
anything suspicious as the police had long given up on even a
cursory patrol of the area. She parked at the curb across from a
gaping hole in the chain link fence, grabbed a large paper bag
filled with groceries, and, as an added precaution, locked and
engaged the alarm on her Jeep. Not out of concern from the
people who called this place home, but in case a wandering addict
stumbled upon the building.

Once she slid the bag through the hole, squeezing through
the fence was easy—the opening had expanded in size from
constant use. She turned on the penlight to guide her through the
clumps of dead grass, weeds and dirt and into the huge side
opening. A few points of light glowed in the distance but weren't
enough to cut through the darkness. She stood outside and called
out before going any further. "Luther!"

No response.

"Luther, it's me, Jonelle Sweet. You here?" The answer came from shuffling sounds all around. She remembered his private patch was on the next level but knew she couldn't go further inside until given permission to do so. She tried to remember a name she'd heard in the past. Was it TJ? "Hey. If Luther's not here, is there someone named TJ around? We met last year, remember?"

"Lady, will you please shut up? I'm tryin' to sleep. Luther knows you're here—hell, people up in Canada know you're here yellin' like that."

She had no choice but to wait. She let out a frustrated sigh and pulled out her cellphone, and right in the middle of checking emails a slight shuffle, pause, shuffle, pause, made its way to her across the warehouse floor. A voice up close said, "Ain't seen you in a while. Why you here?"

She shone her penlight at the voice.

Without waiting for an answer, he motioned for her to follow him. Once her eyes had adjusted to the dimness, she was able to make out several shapes across the floor. At first glance, disorder seemed the rule. But as Jonelle followed Luther deep inside the immense space, a type of order emerged. Those with the most belongings gathered along the periphery, as well as something she hadn't seen before—a woman with a small child. Jonelle's heart sank.

"Why are children in here, Luther? This is awful. You can't—"

"Relax. It's only one and it's only temp'ry. Anita's gonna have a place tomorrow for her and the little one. She only needed a spot for tonight, and this place is safer than most. 'Course, you already know that." He chuckled deep in his chest.

She did know. Past experience proved the protection the group provided to each other. He sat on a wooden crate, reached down, and turned on an LED lamp. Jonelle had presented him with several of the lights as a Christmas gift last year. The hope was that the group would use the lights for illumination instead of the much more dangerous barrel fire and candles.

"So," she said. "How've you been?"

He squinted at her. "You come all this way and at this time 'a night to see if I'm healthy? Girl, you gots to be kiddin' me. What you really want?"

She wasted no time relating the story of the abduction of four-year-old Lark Phelps and her assignment to find out as much as she could about the child's mother.

"Everyone in her building kept saying what a good mom she was and I believed it at first. Still do, in a way. Except she missed so much work, she lost her full-time job. Yet, she kept up the routine of taking her daughter to her sister's place in the morning, picked her up again around five or so, and had a neighbor watch the little girl while she left for her second job. Problem is the second job was on call, so she wasn't required to be there every night. Even so, she was absent there several times and lost that job as well."

"So you're gonna find out where she been going? You think that's got somethin' to do with the kidnapping?"

"Not sure yet. The biological father says one time he followed her to a warehouse district not far from here. He thinks one of the buildings produces pornography videos."

Luther slapped his leg. A wide grin spread across his dark face. His scraggly beard had grown whiter since she last saw him six months ago. "So, she's hot, huh?"

Jonelle held her anger in check. "This isn't funny, Luther. A child is missing."

"Yeah. You right. What you want me to do?"

"Do you know if there are places around here that produce films like that?"

"Sure. More'n you think. And you can't walk right in them places. You gotta ring a bell 'cause the doors are always locked.

I know on account of I got shooed away a hunnert times. And they got them big metal bars on the door and windows out back."

"How do you know what's out back?"

He cocked his head. "How d'ya think?"

Not one to judge anyone's morality, Jonelle needed proof to give to Langford. The information about Tamora's other life might be devastating to her case if the prosecution knew something her lawyer didn't.

"If I show you a picture, could you tell me if you've seen her go inside one of those places?"

"Mebbe. Lemme see it first."

One of the things Jonelle had Langford do was send her recent photos of Lark and Tamora. She pulled up Tamora, expanded the picture to fill the screen, and showed it to Luther. "Pretty girl," he said. "Do she sometimes wear her hair piled on top of her head and wound 'round and 'round like a snake?"

"Not sure."

He handed the phone back to Jonelle. "Kinda looks familiar. But when them girls come and go, I ain't really lookin' at their face. Know what I mean?" He winked at her. "What's the problem? You're real good at followin' people."

"She knows what I look like." She stared off in the distance.

"If you're thinkin' of havin' me sneak inside, that won't do. Hell, I couldn't get past the damn door."

"No. Not you. However, I have a friend . . ." Adrienne was game for just about anything and could pull off the look, except for the bra size and there were ways to get around that.

"What? What you thinkin'?"

"I've got to witness Tamora enter that place and for Adrienne to get inside and make sure they're filming what we think they are. Trick is how to get her inside? Gotta think more about this."

"You thought about this other thing?"

"What other thing?"

"That little girl. You think the reason that little girl was snatched got somethin' to do with what her mama is doin'? Mebbe they gettin' a two for one?"

"Jesus, Mary, and Joseph, she's only four."

"All kindsa pervs out there. Not just ones that like lookin' at naked people goin' at it."

She tried to shake the image out of her mind. "It might be related . . . somehow. But I don't believe she'd do that to her child. I'm concentrating on what Tamora's up to. Once I figure that out, maybe it'll lead me to Lark."

She drove back to her condo with an idea of how to prove what Tamora did all day forming in her mind. She parked in her assigned space. She entered the building to the soothing, deep bass of Hamilton Yee's cello floating from his condo above. No sooner had she entered her apartment when someone knocked softly on her door. The only other occupant was Sheila and her work day was beginning when others ended. And no one would describe Mathilda's knock as "soft."

"What's wrong Franklin? Is it Mathilda?" she asked, opening the door to the elderly man rubbing his hands over and over.

"She's acting . . . peculiar," he said, panic in his voice, "and I don't know what to do."

Jonelle put her arm around his shoulder. "Let's get you back inside."

Franklin allowed himself to be escorted inside his apartment.

She hadn't been around much lately, so she'd assumed that Mathilda's new habit of repeating words and actions was simply a case of advancing age. Franklin nodded to the sofa where a slight figure sat immobile, eyes glued to the television screen.

"Mathilda?" Jonelle advanced slowly.

The vacant stare from Mathilda's pale blue eyes was gut-wrenching. The worry lines between her eyes faded as the fog lifted and recognition dawned. "Oh, hi Jonnie." She looked around as if seeing the living room for the first time. "Um. Where's Franklin?"

"I'm right here, Mattie." He shot Jonelle a "see what I mean?" look. When she had more time, she and Franklin needed to have a long conversation.

Mathilda rose unsteadily to her feet. "I've gotta get dinner ready," she said.

"No way," Jonelle said. "Franklin said he's treating you tonight. He's gonna order takeout from your favorite Chinese place. Right, Franklin?"

"Yes. Yes. Kung Pao chicken Mattie. Your favorite. Plus they deliver fast."

Mattie smiled and snuggled her small body deeper into the overstuffed sofa.

Jonelle motioned for Franklin to follow her to the door.

"Keep an eye on her at all times, understand?"

"You see what I mean, though, right? She's not the same Mattie as before." His eyes began to water.

She patted his arm. "You might have to prepare yourself for a new normal."

He nodded, and with a slight wave good-bye, closed his door.

Once inside her own condo, Jonelle wanted to drop where she stood and not move for hours. Several small meows and gentle fur against her ankles kept her upright. She reached down and picked up the kitten, planting a soft kiss on top of her head and stroking the soft multi-colored fur. "Too tired to play now, kiddo. How about a treat? What say I let you play awhile with catnip Clara and when you get tired of that, have at your bat the ball toy." With Jonelle's hours, maybe Gracie would like a brother or sister. She smiled wondering what Adrienne would think.

Jonelle set the kitten down and checked the food and water dishes. That done, and with Gracie madly chasing "Clara" around the living room, Jonelle poured a generous amount of chilled white wine in an oversized wine glass.

"Here's looking at you, kid," she said, raising the glass in a mock salute toward a frantic Gracie now rolling over and over on top of a drug-infused toy mouse. Jonelle staggered to the sofa, kicked off her shoes and leaned back against the cushions. She couldn't remember the last time she was this tired.

Instead of turning on the television, she used the remote to turn on the stereo, adjusted her cellphone to mute, swallowed a generous amount of wine, and lay back against the sofa. The tightness in her shoulders eased. She breathed evenly and deeply and settled the wine on the coffee table.

When she awoke, everything was dark, and a small lump lay on her chest. She moved the sleeping kitten and sat up slowly, trying to clear the confusion from her brain. "Ugh. Nothing worse than going to sleep with only wine in your system." She checked her phone and moaned when the display read almost eleven. She trudged into the kitchen and made herself scrambled eggs with onion and cheese and stuck a k-cup in the new coffee maker.

The plan swirling in her head on how to get inside the studio depended on Adrienne, but was she ready to get her best friend involved in who knew what kind of situation?

CHAPTER 23

Jonelle punched Tamora's number for the fourth time. Once again the call went directly to voicemail. She glared at the phone as if it was the instrument's fault the woman didn't answer and turned to Adrienne. "If you don't stop fiddling with the top, all that padding's gonna pop out," she said.

Adrienne sighed dramatically. "Can't help it. This stuff keeps shifting around. I still don't understand why I need all this foam rubber. No way I'm taking my clothes off for these people."

"Don't want you to. That is, if you even get the chance. I gave Luther a burner phone and told him to hang around the area. When I see Tamora, I'll give him a call. We wait until he comes and grabs their attention, and then you hop out and act like you wanna see somebody about a job. You know, you're an actress and you don't wanna be a waitress any more, yada, yada. You get the drift."

She pulled her mini binoculars up to her eyes and scanned the area. The only thing they noticed in the forty-five minutes they sat at the far end of the block behind two abandoned cars was the arrival of three men—two white and one black—laughing and talking as one pulled out a key and they entered. So far, no sign of any women.

"You sure you got the right night?" Adrienne asked, still poking at her chest.

"No idea what night they shoot." She looked at the time readout on her phone. Nearly ten. "I figure the so-called talent waits until dark before they show up, which is fine with me. We're pretty safe from notice out here since the only working street light is on the other corner."

Adrienne turned around in her seat. They elected to take her Saab as Jonelle's Jeep was too conspicuous. "So what're you thinking about the mother? She have something to do with the kidnapping?"

Jonelle leaned back in the passenger seat. "I've been going over and over that. Hard to believe she had anything to do with it. However, she's lied to just about everybody connected with this case, so you have to ask yourself, why?"

"Okay. Why?"

"She can't help herself. Her first reaction is to come off looking good no matter what and damn the facts. If she is a porn actress—and I use the term actress loosely—these people are most likely self-absorbed in order to do this kind of thing."

"How much d'you think she makes taking her clothes off?"

Jonelle's eyebrows shot up.

Adrienne wore a tight red leather mini skirt and tight black low-cut sequined blouse enhanced by something called a bomber bra purchased at a high-end lingerie store. A few additional pieces of foam were added for maximum effect.

"You thinking about making a career change?"

"Don't be ridiculous. I'm only curious."

"No idea what the money's like," Jonelle said. "Probably more than working for a medical supply company."

Silence hung in the air until a car drove by. The dark sedan slid next to the curb in front of the building. A woman emerged, carrying a small case.

"That's her," Jonelle said. She alerted Luther.

"Okay," Adrienne said. "What do we do?"

Jonelle raised her binoculars. A dark figure approached from the opposite direction, moving as fast as his pronounced limp would allow.

"Here he comes. Hop out before she goes inside. Run up to the door. Hurry!"

Adrienne bounded out of the car and hightailed it toward the building. "Hey, Tamora," Adrienne called. "You are Tamora, right?"

"Hey, good-looking," Luther called. "You two fine ladies got any change for an ole man?"

The driver of the car got out, and Jonelle recognized him as Shawn from Tamora's day job. He stood between the two women and Luther and gestured at the homeless man. Luther stepped back, arms raised to ward off whatever came next.

Ready to run to Luther's aid if need be, she was relieved when both women were let inside the building. Once Luther witnessed that, he turned and hobbled off the way he came. Shawn watched him for a few seconds, got back in the car, and drove off.

Now for the hard part. Waiting for Adrienne to return. She worked out the time at the condo. If Adrienne didn't make some excuse and return to the car in an hour, she'd attempt to get inside by telling them she was Adrienne's sister and demand to speak to her. The two friends looked nothing alike, but that was beside the point. If Tamora objected, well . . . she'd figure out what to say.

Rather than sit and watch the time, Jonelle decided to go in search of Luther. It was never pitch black in the city, so she found him around the back, poking through the trash bins. He hadn't heard her walk up and jumped when she called his name.

"Damn. You wanna give me some kinda heart attack or what?"

"Sorry. Didn't wanna wait in the car. Heard anything about the missing four-year-old?"

Without stopping his search through the trash, Luther answered the question. "Not much. And you know why as much as me. It's 'cause her mama's black and ain't got no money."

Jonelle believed that was only part of the reason. "Lark's picture's been on the news, so somebody must know something."

He paused what he was doing and peered at her through the dim light coming from a weak security fixture high on the building. "Mebbe. But I ain't seen no fliers or nothin' around, have you? You should ask yourself how come that is. How come no relatives or nobody goin' around demandin' somethin' be done, huh? Don't know how much you know about that woman inside, but she don't look so broke up to me."

Luther was right, yet she wasn't ready to concede that Tamora had something to do with her child's abduction. "I'd like to ask another favor."

He stopped digging around. "Was waitin' for you to go there. What you want?"

She ignored the dig. "Keep your eyes and ears open. Ask around. If I was going to snatch a kid, I'd want a damn good reason to take the risk. I'm ruling out money because Tamora's not wealthy. Her sister owns her own business, but from what I've seen, her daycare isn't making her rich. The only other options are that someone wants to use the child in some way. That's why I need to find her."

Luther shook his head over and over. "You don't need to find her. That's the cops' job. Bein' who you are, you *want* to find her. Can't leave well enough alone, can you? Always gotta go and get involved."

He had her there. Still. "Will you help me?"

Luther shuffled over to another bin. "Don't I always?"

"True. I'm guessing they have Lark stashed away some place, but it's also possible she's been out in public, however briefly. Ask if anyone's seen a little girl with a short, light-skinned man, or a skinny one about my complexion."

"How you know it's a man?"

"Don't know. Only a feeling."

"Feeling, huh? Girl, you got any idea how many people that could be?"

"I've got a photo of Lark here in my purse." Jonelle dug around and pulled out the picture she photocopied. "Take this and show it around, and I'll get posters made. You know as well as I do that most kids that age are usually seen with their mothers. A man might stand out." She handed the picture to Luther who shoved it in his pocket. She wanted to tell him to be careful with it but knew he didn't want anyone telling him what to do.

He moved to go and then turned slowly around. "Hate to bring this up, but you thought about the uh, other thing, right?"

"What other thing?"

"The possibility that she ain't alive."

CHAPTER 24

Too many people. Why the hell're there so many people involved? Lark's getting anxious. Nobody else sees it, but it's obvious to me. Every time we find a good place that damn woman comes nosing around and people start freakin' out. Everyone but me votes to take Lark to a place I know she hates. I tell them someone will see because it's too open, but I'm overruled. They claim it's a genius idea. Genius my ass. It's stupid, and I'm against it.

But nobody pays attention to me. It's like I have no say. Keep your eyes on the prize and your mouth shut, they tell me.

Well, the prize is changing. Things are different now. I gotta start thinking about my future. I see how valuable the little one is. Be even more valuable if the money wasn't spread over all these damn people.

Stared at her long and hard the other day. Startin' to see her in a brighter light. We get along, her and me. What'll be the harm if we start gettin' along even better?

CHAPTER 25

A little over an hour later the door to the so-called studio opened and Adrienne staggered out of the building. Jonelle grabbed her gun from where she'd stashed the lockbox under the passenger seat. The unmistakable titter of Adrienne's high-pitched giggle cut through the night.

"What the hell?"

Adrienne teetered over to the car, wide grin spread across her face.

"Hey there," she said. Her hand reached for the car door handle and missed. She tried and missed again.

"Ohmigod," Jonelle said as her friend succeeded in opening the door on the third try. "Are you loaded?"

"Hmm. Could be. Define loaded." She giggled again and reached for the ignition.

"Oh, no you don't. Change places with me." She returned her gun to the box.

After steering a wobbly Adrienne around the car and into the seat, Jonelle stared at the lopsided grin covering her friend's face.

"What happened?"

"Got a touch of the,"—Adrienne mimed smoking a joint— "wacky tobaccy." Another extended giggle.

Their college days taught Jonelle it was no use trying to communicate with Adrienne at this point. She'd have to wait until the effects wore off, which also meant she couldn't trust her friend to drive home by herself until completely sober.

"Okay. We're going to my house until you're fit to drive," Jonelle said.

Adrienne shook her pink-highlighted hair. "Nope. I wanna go home."

Not wanting to waste valuable time taking her friend home and waiting for a call to find out what happened inside the studio, Jonelle ignored Adrienne's request and drove them to her condo. Before entering, she glanced next door. She'd check on the couple in the morning.

Footsteps sounded on the hall stairs. A pair of black-and-white saddle shoes appeared followed by white knee socks and a gray and red pleated skirt. Sheila's blond hair was done up in pigtails. Jonelle's upstairs neighbor worked when most people retired for the day.

"Hey, lookit you," Adrienne said.

"Back at you," Sheila replied, her eyes questioning.

"Had a late assignment and this one here took it to another level," Jonelle said.

"So I see. Anything you need help with?"

"I've got this," Jonelle answered.

"She's got this," Adrienne mimicked with a giggle.

Jonelle rolled her eyes at her best friend. "Guess the theme for tonight is naughty schoolgirl?"

Sheila's very lucrative job required she respond to the needs of men's sexual idiosyncrasies at a time and place when their wives were not around.

"Always one of my most popular costumes," Sheila said, twirling around for effect. "Makes you wonder if they've got kids, though."

"You stay safe," Jonelle said. She always worried that her friend's profession would someday land her into a hinky situation with the wrong guy.

"I'll do my best with the help of my little friend here." Sheila grinned and patted the small red shoulder bag, big enough to hold her Ruger LC9s, waved and pushed open the lobby doors.

"See ya!" Adrienne yelled to the closed doors.

Jonelle ushered a still loopy Adrienne into the spare room where she had her office and a sleep loveseat. She settled Adrienne in a chair and proceeded to make up the bed. That done, she eased her friend between the covers. A compliant Adrienne made no objections, so Jonelle turned out the lights and closed the door.

Gracie followed Jonelle into the kitchen. She reached down and picked the calico up, grateful for the soft purring as she cuddled the kitten in her arms. "Heck of a day today, Gracie, and I'm still not sure how this will bring me closer to finding Lark." Saying those words out loud reminded her that finding the child wasn't her concern. Yet she couldn't help herself.

Jonelle went into the kitchen, and before she placed the kitten on the floor, Gracie jumped onto her shoulder. "Okay then. Hold on and don't you dare fall off." With kitten neck warmer firmly in place, Jonelle poured herself a glass of Cabernet. She turned on the stereo, kicked off her shoes and sat on the sofa. Gracie hopped from her shoulders and onto her lap. With the kitten curled in a tight ball, Jonelle snuggled against the sofa cushions to the sounds of Boney James playing, "Stop, Look, Listen."

Her mind wandered. The case was missing something.

Breathing in and out deeply, she tried to allow the facts to intrude rather than forcing them inside her mind. Jonelle believed Lark's abductor knew both mother and child. Okay, then, not a stranger.

Fact: Tamora left the door unlocked. Even given Tamora's insistence she went out for only a few minutes, the convenience store surveillance tape inside showed her wandering around, talking to several young men, including Reggie, for at least twenty minutes. Did Vaughn Hanson's unannounced visit spoil some kind of plan?

And why didn't anyone see or hear anything? The fog in her mind lifted. Jonelle assumed Maxine knew everything that happened on the seventh floor. Yet what reason would the elderly woman have for keeping Lark's kidnapping a secret?

She sat up and drained her glass. Why would someone take a child from a single, working mother? Hefting her bag off of the floor, she pulled out a pad and jotted down some notes. At the top of the page she underlined the name "Shawn"and wrote, "What's the deal with him?" Was he the one who turned Tamora on to the adult porn studio? If not him, who?

With pen in hand, in addition to Shawn, she listed all the people she'd questioned so far. Before their names she placed a number in order of their importance. Jelani came in at number two because he had a propensity for lying and, as maintenance man for the building, knew everyone's comings and goings. Even though he claimed to have an alibi, he could've had help from someone. Next number belonged to Randy.

Randy was interesting. A guy who roamed the halls at night would have a window of opportunity. She shook her head and scratched out his name. A stoner like that couldn't get in and out that fast with a child without alarming someone.

What about the father? While she believed Vaughn Hanson, it was possible he became so upset when he found out about Tamora's other life he decided to take matters into his own hands. But why call the cops?

What about Miss Maxine? Jonelle tapped the pen against her teeth. What motive would the elderly woman have for taking the child from her mother? She shook her head and went back over the list. Once again, she deliberated about Randy, and then put him back on the list. Something was off about the young man, and it had nothing to do with drugs.

Tilting her head against the sofa cushion, she struggled with whether or not another name deserved a place on the list. Decision made, she sat up and wrote the name "Red Fred."

CHAPTER 26

The pressure on her shoulder wouldn't let up. She tried shrugging it off but couldn't. "Leave me alone," she said.

"Get up already. I wanna go home, and I can't find my keys."

Jonelle opened her eyes. The blurry vision above her looked familiar. "What?"

"I said, get up."

The fog cleared as Adrienne came into focus.

"What time is it?"

"After nine in the morning. I can't believe you let me sleep so long. I've got things to do today."

"And I don't? Damn. I must've dozed off." She stretched and grimaced at the pain in her shoulder. "I need to stand in a hot shower. I've got a million muscles all complaining at once."

Adrienne held out her hand. "Keys. Now."

"What's your damn hurry? Usually you want coffee. Besides, I need to know what happened inside that building."

Adrienne removed her hand from in front of Jonelle's face. "Oh, right. I've still got a head full of mush, so maybe a shower and coffee is what I need. No way can I put dirty clothes on this body, so the faster I can get outta here, the faster I can come back. Besides, she,"—Adrienne cocked her head at Gracie who posed on the coffee table staring at the two friends—"looks like she's waiting for breakfast."

After promising to return without delay, Adrienne left.

Jonelle took care of Gracie and, after unkinking her muscles under water as hot as she could stand, fixed a quick breakfast, and stepped into the hallway. Sounds from Hamilton Yee's cello filled the small space. Jonelle stood outside the Brobishes door, enjoying the deep bass. After a few moments she raised her hand and knocked.

Almost immediately, Franklin opened the door, a slight smile on his face. "She's better today," he said. "I think maybe yesterday was a fluke. She seems like her old self."

"Who is it, Franklin?"

"It's me, Mattie. Jonelle."

The tiny woman appeared, white hair combed. A pale yellow cotton blouse and brown polyester pants covered her thin frame. "Come in, dear. Franklin, don't be rude."

Oh, yes, Mathilda definitely seemed like her old self.

"No time to visit. Going to the store later. You guys need anything?" Her eyes looked into Franklin's own. She inclined her head, and he joined her in the hallway.

"I think we're good until maybe the middle of the week." He lowered his voice. "I'll let you know."

Jonelle leaned in close. "Make sure you do, 'cause if you don't, I'll remind you."

"What're you two whispering about?" Mathilda called.

Franklin winked at Jonelle, who winked back. "I should go put on my walking shoes," he said, voice slightly raised. "Mathilda and I are going for a walk."

"Sounds like a good idea. You guys have fun."

Back inside her condo, she studied the notes she'd taken last night. She tried to remember why the interest in Randy, but the thought had evaporated. Shawn piqued her curiosity. She mulled over Fred's name, thought about crossing it out, yet left it on the list.

Several minutes later, Jonelle's security buzzer sounded. "Yes?"

"Me."

Jonelle buzzed Adrienne in and unlocked the door.

Adrienne entered dressed in pink shorts, white camisole, and multi-colored, bead-covered flip-flops. She pulled out a small plastic ball with bells inside and shook the toy. "Where's the fur ball?"

On cue, Gracie padded into the living room. Adrienne threw the ball into the kitchen, and the kitten flew after it, bells tinkling as kitty baseball commenced, making both women laugh.

"Okay. Down to business," Jonelle said. "What did you find out last night? That's if you can remember. Gotta say I'm a little disappointed you let yourself get stoned."

Adrienne pointed. "Don't lecture. How would it have looked if everyone toked up and I'm like little Miss Priss sayin' 'thanks but no thanks,' huh? They'd have thrown me out faster than a major leaguer pitching at an old folk's game."

"Good point. So. What'd you find out?"

"First, Tamora's definitely one of their top stars." Adrienne used air quotes around "stars." "They refer to the so-called talent as models. Did you know that? Anyway, as soon as we entered the place, everyone assumed we were friends. When she said she didn't know who I was, they almost kicked me out. Told them I needed the work. Said I had a kid I needed to support and I just lost my job and would do anything they wanted. Professionally, that is. Told Tamora I was sad to hear about what happened to her kid—"

"How'd she react?"

"She said, 'Thanks', and that was it."

"Strange."

"You're tellin' me. She acted like it was no big deal. After that little exchange, Tamora went through this black curtain to change, or unchange as the case may be."

"You get a look at what was behind there?"

"Nope."

Jonelle sighed. "I don't like that she's not acting like the good mother everyone said she was, but continue. What else did you find out?"

"This big, buff white guy came out from behind another black curtain on the opposite side. Tight jeans, cowboy hat, no shirt, ripped abs. Think I could've bounced a whole boatload of change off his chest and stomach."

She smiled at the image of Adrienne throwing coins at the man's upper body.

"Needless to say I wanted to hang around for the shoot, but instead this weaselly-looking guy named Jasper herded me into this dump he called an office, offered me a joint, and started asking a lot of questions."

Jonelle tried to keep the humor out of her voice. "Did you, uh . . ." She motioned with her hands at Adrienne's clothes.

"I did not," Adrienne said, disgust dripping from each word. "He wanted to know about my acting experience, vital statistics, and, yeah, he wanted a peek, but I said nope. Told him I wanted the job first. He and I went around and around on that. He claimed he couldn't offer anything to me without checking out the merchandise. The more we argued, the more we smoked, and I almost gave in, until I remembered the, um, enhancements I had on. So I told him I couldn't oblige since I had to pick up my kid. I promised to reveal all tonight."

"So, are you telling me you didn't see Tamora doing her porn thing?"

Adrienne smiled slyly. "I didn't say that. On my way out I got a peek at her and Mister Buck Nekkid, in their birthday suits and rubbing some kinda oil all over each other."

"Good. I can use that when I see her again. Thanks. I owe you."

"You do. But that's not all."

Adrienne reached for her purse and pulled out a piece of paper, folded twice. "I snatched this. It's an advertisement for the latest film."

Jonelle studied the grainy black-and-white photograph in the center. While a male torso covered a third of a woman's face, Tamora's large eyes and full lips left no doubt about the identity of the female. The photo featured the name "Tammy Tickle." The words, "Next Month Tammy's Little Surprise," was written in black marker.

She tapped the paper. "I've gotta fax this to Langford. This is great ammo for Lark's father, but I'm not sure how this helps me find out what happened to the child. What it does is tell me where she went when she was supposed to be going to her regular jobs. Wonder if Miss Maxine knows about Tammy Tickle. Everything rests on motive. No one's said anything about a ransom, so money's not the issue. The only other reason I can think of is that someone wants to use the child for a particular purpose. Hence, 'Tammy's Little Surprise.' Have to face facts—someone might want to use Lark for . . . perverted reasons."

"Child porn, you mean."

"Yeah."

"You think mother of the year here is involved?" Adrienne asked.

"Possibly. While Tamora lied about the amount of time she spent in the minimart, in a perverse way that actually gives her an alibi. The store's video clearly shows her entering the store and not leaving until almost a half hour later. My guess is, going with the theory she's involved, that she got help from someone. That whole 'she's a good mother' train has left the station. When I really think about it, the one time we talked, Tamora never brought out any pictures of the child or expressed fear about her welfare."

"So what're we gonna do?"

Jonelle swallowed a snarky retort at the word "we." Adrienne risked a lot in the past twenty-four hours. Jonelle's phone chimed before she could respond.

"Hey, Rainey. On my way. Won't miss the staff meeting."

"No problem. You got a call from a young lady named Piper who said she tried calling you but your phone went directly to voicemail. I tried that, too, and it did. That's why I called your personal line."

"Oh, damn. Forgot I turned the phone off when I left last night. I gave some kids my card with the office number and address. What's the message?"

"They want to come by and see you. Told them to call back in fifteen minutes to see if that was okay. What do I tell them?"

She glanced at Adrienne. "Tell them I'll be in the office in an hour." Jonelle disconnected. "The kids want to see me. They may have news, so I'll need to pick more of your brain later, okay?"

"Kids? What kids?" Adrienne cocked her head at Jonelle. "First, you get a kitten, which is step one to becoming a crazy cat lady. Now, you're talking about kids? Girlfriend, you need a date. When was the last time you talked to Burt?"

Jonelle groaned. Her best friend never gave up trying to get her and Burt together. "I don't worry about my social life when I'm on a case."

"You know, seems to me you like having a case to work on more and more these days."

Not wanting to start a fight, she ignored Adrienne's last comment. "The kids are three twelve-year-olds from Tamora's apartment building. Two of them, Piper and Fredricka—they call her Red Fred or Fred—live on Tamora's floor. I got the impression from Fred that her mom gives her a lot of freedom to come and go as she pleases."

"So you think this Fred knows something?"

"Maybe. These kids are bright. Not your typical 'head staring at the phone screen' types. I bet they know more than the adults in that building are willing to admit."

After Adrienne promised to call if she remembered anything else from the porn studio—known as Playcat Productions according to the flier—Jonelle headed to the office. On the way over she stopped by the store for cookies, chips and, as guilt sunk in with all the junk food, added apples, oranges, and a small bunch of bananas. When she was growing up, her mother, now a working movie extra in Hollywood, didn't care much what Jonelle consumed, so as a result she acquired a serious fast-food habit.

"Office meeting in five minutes," Rainey said as she passed Jonelle's office.

"Right." She stowed the snacks next to her desk, grabbed notes on Tamora's case, and took her place around the conference room table. Marvin sat at the head. Ben hadn't yet arrived, which was typical. Once Rainey opened the box of doughnuts, it was only a matter of seconds before the most senior agent materialized.

"Ah, there he is," Omar said, pointing at his co-worker. "We oughta commission a scientific study on how it is you can smell pastry all the way down the hall."

Ben grabbed a glazed doughnut and started to sit before going back and grabbing another.

"Diet going well I see," Jonelle said.

Ben shot her an "I don't care" look and consumed half in one bite.

Anxious to get their opinion on Lark's abduction, Jonelle signaled to her uncle she wanted to go first. He hesitated. His rule was everyone reported in order of seniority, placing Jonelle last. This time she knew her child abduction case outweighed Ben's bank fraud and Omar's cyber security breach.

"Jonnie wants to go first, if you guys don't mind," Marvin said, his eyes roaming from Ben to Omar. "She's got more information on the child kidnapping case she's working on for the public defender's office."

When Jonelle finished the recap Ben whistled softly. "Remind me how you got yourself involved in that?"

"Something I overheard piqued my curiosity, so I looked into it."

Ben shot Marvin a look, eyebrows raised.

"You guys are busy, and all Jonnie had on her plate was delivering summonses. She knows not to let this case interfere with what she does around here."

"Fine by me," Omar said. "Nine times out of ten, whoever it is pleads guilty. You tryin' to get evidence to prove the mothers innocent?"

"I'm not trying to prove guilt or innocence. Everything I find out, I give to her attorney. It's his call."

She turned to Ben, waiting for him to give his opinion so they could get on with the meeting. Instead, the senior agent remained quiet, a sly smile playing on his lips.

"What?" she asked. "Why're you looking at me like that?"

"Just thinking," he said. After swallowing the last of his doughnuts, he licked his fingers. "Of the three of us, you're the only one who wants to be what everyone thinks of as a gen-u-ine dee-tec-tive." His laughter ricocheted off the conference room walls.

She wasn't offended. In the years she'd known him, Ben supported her need to go the extra mile and, in fact, encouraged her every step of the way. Now if Omar had ribbed her . . . well, that was different. Omar hated getting his hands dirty and had a fear of guns of any kind, which pleased her far more than she cared to admit.

For a brief moment she considered discussing Piper, Fred, and Grayson's involvement but changed her mind. One bit at a time.

"So what're you thinking happened?" Ben asked.

"I'm struggling with why this child? There are other children in that building, most on lower floors. The risk to go down all those floors with a child is enormous, but someone decided the risk was worth the reward. Why?"

The senior agent leaned back in his chair. "I'm thinking you're getting the idea the mother's involved, but you don't wanna say. Have I got that right?"

Jonelle's eyes moved from Ben to her uncle and back again. "I can't prove anything like that."

"That's not what I'm saying."

Marvin cleared his throat. "Ben's got a good point. You work for the woman's attorney, but you're still obliged to keep an open mind."

She squirmed in her seat. She didn't like all the attention on her . . . not for very long anyway. In order to move the spotlight away, she asked Omar a question. "What do you know about surveillance cameras? Are they ever wrong?"

He stopped eyeballing his manicured nails. "Wrong how? They're great. They record what they see. 'Course if they're not maintained properly sometimes the time stamp is off."

She sat up. "Really? Is that common?"

"Sure. I've seen cases where they're as much as fifteen or so minutes slow."

"Plus," Ben added, "convenience stores usually have cameras only at the entrance, above the cashier. If the store's got a lot of heavy traffic in and out, your perp might blend in with the crowd."

"There's no way this lady blends in," Jonelle said.

This information wouldn't help Tamora's case, just the opposite. If she entered the store at say ten that evening, if the recording was slow, the time stamp should record several minutes before ten, not after. "You ever known them to be too fast?"

Omar shook his head, his perfectly oiled hair staying in place.

Once Jonelle finished, the rest of the team gave a ten-minute progress report, and Marvin dismissed the group with his usual request to keep him informed. He headed for his office with his usual "be safe" remark.

"Hold on a minute," Rainey said, after Ben and Omar filed out of the conference room. "I know you guys don't need to give me details about what you're up to, but what're you doing with children?"

Jonelle held up an index finger to signal she'd be back. She brought four bottles of water and three colas from the break room, grabbed the snacks and arranged everything in the middle of the conference table. "I bought some things I thought kids would like and threw in some fruit for good measure. What do you think?"

"I think I want to know a bit more about them." Rainey had raised her daughter on her own after her divorce and was now a proud grandmother of a two-year-old. The worry in the blue eyes below the white-blond bouffant hairstyle gave Jonelle pause.

"I understand your concern, but hear me out. I think they want to visit because they're curious about what a real detective's office looks like. They're savvy—the first time I met them they were headed to the IHOP by themselves. Can't swear to it, but I'm fairly confident that none of them have helicopter parents."

Rainey's head bobbed up and down before Jonelle finished. "I get all that, Jonnie. Hell, my own daughter was more mature than most her age. She didn't have a choice since I worked so much to make ends meet. How old are they?"

"Twelve."

Another frown.

"Listen. I'm not going to question them."

Rainey's eyebrows shot up.

"Well, not much," Jonelle admitted. "I'm thinking it'll be more of a conversation than anything else. Kids see and hear a lot without always revealing what they know to an adult. All I want is a true vibe of what goes on in that building. I don't know where Lark is, or who has her, but I have my suspicions."

"Lark? She the little one abducted?"

"Right. The mother has a secret life which may or may not have bearing on the case. Not only that. There are a few adults who know more than they're telling me. As soon as they find out who I am and why, their guard goes up." She paused, waiting for another reaction from Rainey. In reply, the receptionist stuck another pencil in her well-sprayed hair. Jonelle looked closely. She could already see two other implements in the frothy hairdo.

"When we're done here, I plan on driving them back to their apartment rather than having them take the bus. Depending on time, I might treat them to lunch. What do you think?"

"I think, except for your uncle, you're about the only person I trust talking to youngsters without parents present. And I also know how tenacious you are when you get hold of something, so no matter how mature they seem to you, don't forget they're only twelve." Rainey left without another word.

A few minutes later Jonelle set out napkins and cups. After admiring her handiwork, she could no longer put off calling Langford. While in the middle of punching in his number, Rainey buzzed from the front. Her guests had arrived.

"I'll come out and get them, Rainey. Thanks."

Jonelle found Piper turning her head this way and that at the large photo of Marvin Shorter, Grayson scrutinized the framed private investigator business license, and Fred had stuck her hand in the candy bowl on the desk. The redhead noticed Jonelle first and immediately withdrew her hand.

"This lady said I could have a piece."

"Of course you can. We all make sure Rainey has a never-ending supply. Help yourselves, but I do have snacks for you in the conference room."

"Can we see your office?" Piper asked.

"Sure." Jonelle led the youngsters down the hall.

"Not much to see except my license."

"Who's the guy in the picture?" Grayson asked, fingering the photo in a silver frame on Jonelle's desk.

"My late husband."

No one spoke as Jonelle led them to the conference room.

She instructed the kids to sit anywhere.

"Do you have a gun?" Grayson asked, sitting close to the chips.

"I do."

"Cool. Can I see it?"

"You cannot."

Piper giggled.

Before Grayson said anything else, Jonelle needed to clear up a few things. "Okay, guys listen up. I'm really glad you're here, and if you have any questions about a PI's life, I'll be happy to answer as many as I can. The truth is the PI business is not as exciting as you see on television." Technically, that was the truth. She didn't want to go into what she'd experienced in the past which would shoot holes in what she'd just said.

"Most of the time we do background checks and surveillance work. Work that doesn't involve car chases and shooting bad guys."

"Yeah. But you carry a gun. You said so," Grayson insisted.

"I have a gun, yes. And I keep it locked up."

"Who's the black guy in the big picture out front?" Piper asked.

Jonelle turned to her, grateful for the change in subject. The youngster's sweet-smelling perfume hung in the air. "That's Marvin Shorter. He's my uncle and owner of the business."

Piper smiled. "My mom wants her own business. She says it's gonna happen, too."

"I'm sure it will."

"You ever kill anybody?" Fred asked, reaching for the chocolate chip cookies.

Not yet, Jonelle thought. "No, and I hope I never do." No need to mention she'd shot at and wounded people in the past. "Help yourself to soda or water. I've got fruit here, too." She pushed the bowl closer to Piper who ignored it in favor of a handful of barbeque-flavored potato chips.

"I haven't been able to reach Tamora. Anybody see her around the apartment building lately?"

All eyes turned to Fred.

"Why're you guys lookin' at me?"

"You might've seen her when you, you know, walk around at night," Piper said.

Fred shrugged. "One day I thought I saw her outside the building, but she was walkin' really fast like she was in some kinda hurry."

"Was she in a hurry to get to the building or away from it?"
Tread easy, Jonelle.

"She was leavin'." Fred gulped cola.

"Anybody else see Miss Tammy around?" Jonelle remembered that's what they called Tamora.

Piper and Grayson shook their heads.

"What about seeing things that don't belong?"

Three opened mouths gaped at her.

"What I mean is have you seen any strange people hanging about?"

"Why didn't you say that in the first place?" Piper asked.

"Sorry about that. Have you?"

Piper shook her head. "Naw."

"I have," Grayson said.

All eyes turned in his direction.

"You never said," Piper replied, her tone accusing.

"You never asked," Grayson retorted.

Jonelle waited until the interaction played out.

"Anyway," Grayson continued, "my dad wanted me to take my sister's old bike out to the trash in the back. It's rusty and the frame's bent and it's too big to cram down the chute. While I was out there I saw Jelani and Randy talkin'." He paused. For a while the only sound in the office was that of teeth crunching.

"So," Jonelle prompted. "What happened? Those two never talked before?"

"Sure they have. But they wasn't the only two there. There was some other dude I never seen before. They stopped talkin' when I got closer. Jelani sees me and says, 'Lemme have that. I'll throw it away.' He, like, never offers to help anybody out, ever."

Another hesitation. More slurping. More crunching.

"Get on with it, willya?" Fred insisted around another mouthful.

Grayson, though he made a face, complied. "So after I gave him the bike, I went 'round the corner a little ways, then sneaked back. I wanted to make sure he threw it away 'cause my dad would be mad if he saw it still hangin' around. The three of 'em was still talkin'. The more they talked the louder they got. Randy kept sayin' stuff like, 'We shouldn't talk about that here,' or somethin' like that, and Jelani kept sayin', 'Chill out, dude,' over and over, like that."

"What did the other guy look like?" At this point Jonelle decided the hell with not questioning kids.

The description by Grayson sent a chill down her spine. If accurate, she had come across the man twice. Once at Tamora's workplace and again in front of the porn film studio. "Did Randy or Jelani call the other man by his name?"

Grayson shrugged.

"Did you hear them say the name Shawn?"

Another shrug.

"When did you see the three of them?"

"Yesterday," Grayson said.

"Reason we're here is because we wanted to see what a real detective's office looked like," Piper said. "And Fred said she saw Randy go into Miss Tammy's place."

"When was this?"

"Yesterday. Real late," Fred said. "I went across the street to get my mom a coupla Red Bulls 'cause my sister made a mistake and drank the last one. That's when I saw him."

Jonelle knew Tamora was at the film studio late last night. "Did you see Miss Tammy or just Randy?"

Fred's freckles merged together as the youngster concentrated. "I seen Randy at the door talkin' to somebody inside. Didn't see Miss Tammy, but who else could it've been?"

Who indeed?

CHAPTER 27

I got me a plan. Can't do it now or else I could screw it up. It's only because of the mother that we're treating the kid like glass. Somebody mentioned the kid could tell the cops because she's seen all of us. Somebody else complained that the mother's starting to crack. Beginning to ask too many questions.

My idea? Toughen the kid up a bit.

Someone pulls out a butterfly sticker and starts ripping the wings off. All but two of us laugh. I don't think it's funny. There are ways to toughen her up without ruining her favorite thing.

We could leave her by herself for a longer period of time. Instead of feeding her all the things she likes to eat, only give her vegetables, see what happens. Except. I don't like veg that much so that wouldn't work too good.

Gotta think of something, though. It ain't the first time we've done this . . . and if I have any say, it won't be the last.

CHAPTER 28

According to Fred, Randy entered Tamora's apartment. "I didn't stick around to see when he left."

"Do you know if he'd visited Miss Tammy before?"

"I dunno," Fred said. "But the only time I ever see him is late at night, anyway. I think he sleeps during the day. Or somethin'." She grinned at her two friends, who giggled at the shared joke.

"What do you think that something is?"

With her back against the chair, Fred swung her legs back and forth. "You know." She pressed two fingers to her lips and blew imaginary smoke. More giggles all around. Jonelle itched to talk to each one separately, but that was definitely out of the question. Maybe a change of scenery would trigger more information.

"How about I take you guys to lunch? Pizza? Chinese? You pick."

"Pizza!" they shouted in unison.

"Before we go, let me introduce you to Marvin Shorter. He's owned the business for about thirty years now. One of the first black-owned detective agencies in the area."

"That's cool," Grayson said. "When I graduate, I'm gonna own my own . . . business."

Intrigued, Jonelle asked, "What kind?" She sincerely hoped it wasn't a gun shop.

While proud to announce he wanted his own business, Grayson now appeared reluctant to say anything else.

"Go on," Piper said. "You started it, so you might as well tell her."

"Bakery," he said, barely above a whisper.

"He's real good at it, too," Piper added. "Baking, I mean. He calls me whenever he's just made something, and my mom gives me some money to go up to his place to see what he's got." She made a face. "He never says up front. It's always, 'Come on up and take your pick.'" She rolled her eyes.

"I don't plan stuff," Grayson said, a touch of defensiveness in his voice. "And I don't like people tellin' me what to make. I make what I feel like. Plus I charge a little extra for the sweet stuff because I don't like it as much as the savory."

"Is Miss Tammy one of your customers?" Jonelle asked.

"Naw. She always said she's watchin' her weight and she don't want Lark eatin' too many sweets. The only people on that floor that buys stuff is Piper, Fred, and Miss Maxine."

Jonelle ushered everyone back to her office. She absent-mindedly put items in her bag and checked to make sure she had her credit cards. "So, how often does Miss Maxine buy your baked goods?"

"At first, um, maybe once a month, but lately she started askin' me to let her know whenever I baked pastries with fruit, like strawberries and apple. Once she wanted me to bake peanut butter cookies, but I don't bake cookies so much, so I told her no. I don't mind her requestin' stuff 'cause she pays more than the others."

"That's nice. Let's go, guys."

With the three youngsters trailing behind, Jonelle stopped outside her uncle's office. The door stood open as usual, but there was no sign of him.

"Sorry. He must've stepped out. If you want to stop by some other time, let me know and I'll give him a heads-up." She continued on to the front.

"I'm taking these three home," she said to Rainey. "After that I have a few stops to make from there, so I'll probably call it a day instead of coming back here. Okay?"

"Fine with me. By the way," Raincy said, "when Marvin speaks at schools in the area, he sometimes passes out Frisbees with the agency's logo. You guys want one?"

"Sure."

"Cool."

"I guess so."

"There's a box over here on this side of the desk. Pick out whichever color you want."

Piper chose yellow, Grayson picked red, and after digging through the pile, Fred decided on blue.

Jonelle winked at Rainey. "Thanks a lot. Call if you need me."

She led them out of the building. Instead of turning right and heading to the open lot, she paused. A dark sedan sat illegally parked under several large trees on the median.

"What're you lookin' at?" Grayson asked.

In the time it took to divert her attention to him, the car pulled away and sped down the street. "Not sure. Did you see that car? Did it look familiar?"

He shrugged. "Looks like every other blue Nissan on the planet. Where we going?"

"Hmm. My Jeep's parked down here." Once everyone buckled themselves in, Piper spoke up.

"You know, a lot of people in the building are talking about you."

Jonelle suppressed a smile. "Good. I want everyone to know about me and what I'm doing. Makes them more likely to contact me with any information. What're they saying?"

Piper, sitting in the passenger seat next to Jonelle, turned to the two behind her in the backseat before responding.

"Mrs. Watkins told my mom to call if she sees you wanderin' around the building. Claims you're trespassing."

"Really? Then why does she keep the main doors open? Seems to me if she was all that concerned, security would be tougher than it is. Sorry. Didn't mean to raise my voice like that." Something about that woman ticked her off.

"The building ain't locked until the nighttime. When Mrs. Watkins leaves. You gotta have a key to get in after, oh, I dunno, five or six. Somethin' like that," Fred said.

"So is this key separate from the one that goes to your apartment?"

All three answered yes.

"But if you forgot for some reason," Fred added, "you could always get somebody to buzz you in."

She silently warned herself to tread carefully. "I'm guessing there's some kinda intercom, but I wonder if—and I'm not judging, mind you—I wonder if you've ever buzzed somebody in that you didn't know."

An awkward silence spread throughout the Jeep.

"Sometimes you can't hear too good," Grayson said, his voice low behind her. "I mean if you're expectin' somebody and the buzzer sounds and you say who is it and they say somethin' static-y, well, you're not gonna argue, right?"

Good point, Grayson, she thought. Out loud, Jonelle agreed. "I've done it myself in my own condo a few times, so I understand. Anyone else have a problem with me poking around that you guys know about?"

Piper squirmed in her seat. "Um. Well . . . I heard my mom say that Miss Maxine doesn't believe you're workin' to help Miss Tammy. Miss Maxine thinks you're really workin' for the cops and that you want to put Miss Tammy in jail."

Jonelle gripped the wheel tighter. "Really? And did Miss Maxine say why she thought that?"

"Somethin' about the way you ask questions. She said you was more interested in what Miss Tammy was doin' that night rather than tryin' to find out who could've taken Lark. Miss Maxine said you was almost sayin' that she had somethin' to do with it. Were you? Were you sayin' Miss Maxine is involved some kinda way?"

Keeping her eyes on the road helped her decide how to respond. "I was hired by Miss Tammy's lawyer to find out as much as I can about the night Lark disappeared. The main problem right away was . . . how much time Miss Tammy said she was gone when Lark vanished. So, to help Miss Tammy prove that she's right, and the police got it wrong somehow, is to ask as many people I can to corroborate, um, that is verify, that everything Miss Tammy says is true."

"I know what that word means," Piper sniffed.

"Sorry. Don't mean to talk down to you guys."

"Hey," Grayson said. "You got a gun in here somewhere?"

Fred groaned. "You and guns. I think you're gonna be a gangbanger one of these days. I know. Why don't you make a bread-shaped pistol?"

"Why don't you shut up? I'm not gonna be no criminal. Already told you I'm gonna own my own bakery. I wonder if the gun's someplace in here is all."

Jonelle steered them back to the main issue. "What else are people saying?"

"I heard one of the ladies say she was in the laundry room and saw you and Jelani and that he got upset about somethin'," Fred said. "She also said that Miss Maxine was goin' around tellin' people not to talk to you no more."

"She say why?" Jonelle's face burned.

"Naw. Only that if you came around askin' more questions that they was to let her know, so's she could make sure Miss Tammy heard about it."

Jonelle pursed her lips together to keep from blurting out what she thought of Miss Maxine. She guessed it was time for another visit to—quoting Randy—"that old busy body down the hall."

With Grayson on her right and the other two across from her in the booth, Jonelle ordered one medium cheese and one medium meat lover's pizza. She added a tossed salad to alleviate feelings of guilt. Everyone agreed on lemonade, and while waiting for the pizza to arrive, Jonelle's need to learn more outweighed any former reservations about asking more questions.

"I'm curious about Mrs. Watkins. For some reason I got the impression she stayed in her office most of the time. Does she ever make personal visits to the units?"

Piper, the vegetarian in the group, hence the cheese pizza, answered first. "Not that I ever saw. One time my mom wanted me to tell Mrs. Watkins we needed a new showerhead. When I went downstairs, Miss Maxine and her were talkin' and watchin' this small television."

"Do you remember what they talked about?"

Piper shrugged. "Whatever goofy soap opera thing that was on."

Jonelle addressed her next question to Fred. "Do you remember seeing Mrs. Watkins go into Tamora's apartment?"

"Only time I seen her go inside was when Lark had a birthday party, and Mrs. Watkins brought her a gift."

Damn. Jonelle tried something else.

"When you guys take care of the pets, do you ever see anything odd?"

"Do you mean do we see anybody acting suspicious around the building?" Grayson asked. He plucked a pepperoni from a slice of pizza and chewed.

"Yes."

"My dad says everybody's a little weird."

"Well, I think it's *weird* that all these people are so worried about Miss Tammy that I think they're forgetting about Lark," Piper said. "That's why we put up fliers. Somebody's gotta do something to find her. I mean, where is she? How come nobody's organizing a search party or something?" Anger in the youngster's voice came through.

"That's a good question. What do you think the answer is?"

The plastic cushions in the booth squeaked when Piper leaned back. She picked at the cheese on her pizza. Jonelle waited.

Piper looked at her friends who stared back, slowly chewing.

"I think," Piper said, "what I mean is, we've talked about this, so it's not just me."

"I understand," Jonelle said. The waitress came with the check, and Jonelle asked for containers for the uneaten pizza.

"We think Miss Maxine knows something and so does Miss Tammy. I don't mean they know who took Lark or anything," Piper said, frowning. "Heck, now I don't know what I mean."

Jonelle thought she knew and had been considering the same thing herself. What she came up with was the only way a mother would seem so nonchalant about her child's abduction is that she knew what had happened. She wouldn't say this to the kids. She felt she'd gained their trust and didn't want to jeopardize that, so she kept that idea to herself.

She paid the bill, gave the cheese pizza leftovers to Piper, and said, "Grayson, you mind sharing the other leftovers with Fred?"

"She can have the whole thing. I don't like used pizza," he said.

The way he said it sent off warning bells. As Jonelle followed the trio out of the restaurant, she took in Fred's skinny arms and legs poking out from under shorts that were frayed at the hem. What she'd thought was adolescent gawkiness she now wondered if it could be something else.

"Tell me something. Every time I've been in your building Miss Maxine is always there. Does she ever go out?"

"For the past couple months, every Saturday at nine in the morning," Piper said. "My mom says you could set your calendar and watch by what she does."

"Where does she go?"

Grayson shrugged. "Mrs. Watkins picks her up. We figure they go play bingo or something."

Once inside the Jeep, and after everyone had buckled up, Jonelle again broached the subject of Lorraine Watkins. "I understand Mrs. Watkins lives somewhere else and that if there's an emergency you call another number. Is that right?"

"Yeah," Grayson said. "But most of the time after she locks up, she goes over to the shopping center." He snickered.

The girls giggled.

"How do you guys know that?"

More giggles.

"Okay, everybody. What's so funny? So she goes shopping when she leaves work. I do that sometimes myself."

"I don't think you're shopping for what she's shopping for," Piper managed between fits of laughter.

"Okaaay. Fill me in, please."

"Here's the deal," Piper said. "Me and my mom went to the discount shoe place, and we saw her talkin' to this guy. My mom said she oughta be ashamed flirtin' with a guy could be her son."

Jonelle had to make sure she heard right. "You positive it wasn't Jelani she was with?"

"Him?" Fred snorted. "No way."

"Nope. Not Jelani. We was close, and when she saw us, she ducked inside the auto parts store."

Jonelle glanced at Piper, silly smile still plastered on the girl's face. "Can you describe what he looked like?"

"Black guy. About your complexion. Not ugly, not cute either."

"Do you remember what he was wearing?"

"Normal clothes." Piper shook her head. "He looked regular. You know?"

Jonelle suppressed a sigh. She glanced in the rearview mirror at the occupants in the backseat. "Is it possible that it's the same guy Grayson saw with Randy and Jelani?"

"We maybe could pick him out of a lineup or something, if you got one," Grayson said.

The kid definitely watched too much television. "It's too early for that, but I'll give it some thought," Jonelle said.

"We think she hangs out there 'cause I seen her, too," Fred said. "My sister took me to get shoes a little while ago and, whaddya know, there she was. But we seen her talkin' to a black guy *and* a white guy."

More fits of laughter.

"Say," Grayson said, once he caught his breath. "You want us to keep an eye on her when she goes to the mall?"

"Absolutely not. Seriously, guys, please don't interfere. We, um, don't want to tip the bad guys off, now do we?" Jonelle's heart sank. She hadn't intended for the kids to get so involved. Now that they were caught up in the case, she had to find some way to diffuse the situation.

"Tell you what. Since I can move around more quickly, I'll handle everything away from the apartment. What would be a huge help is if you watch—and I mean watch only—what happens around your building."

She pulled the Jeep in front of the apartment building. The three youngsters hopped out and stood outside the driver's side window. Jonelle reached into her bag. She always kept a supply of small notebooks to jot down impressions on a case. Reaching inside she found three unused pads but no extra pens or pencils. As she looked up, she noticed a figure staring at the group from a distance. She couldn't tell if the person was male or female. Whoever it was saw her staring and turned and hurried away.

"Here," she said, handing a notebook to each.

"What're these for?" Piper asked.

"For taking notes on what you see that you think might help Miss Tammy."

Piper didn't look too sure about that, but Grayson caught on.

"I get it. Like when the detective wants to remember stuff, he writes it down for later, right?"

Jonelle agreed.

"Cool. So we're kinda workin' the case, too. I got lots of pencils at home if you guys need one," he said.

"You've gotta promise that *all* you'll do is take notes. Promise?"

Two heads nodded. The scowl on Piper's face indicated she wasn't sold on the idea.

"What's the matter, Piper?"

"I'm not sure my mom'll like it if I hafta go to court or somethin'."

"Oh, no. No way this'll ever go that far. Don't think of yourselves as anything other than reporters. If—and that's an 'if in all caps—you see something out of the ordinary and can't get in touch with me, write it down and I'll look into it. Okay?"

Piper still hesitated.

"Listen. No pressure. In fact, now that I think about it, having you write stuff down might not be a good idea. I'm really sorry, so forget I suggested it. I sometimes get carried away and don't always think things through the way I should. So,"—she held out her hand—"if you want to give me the notepads, I'll stick them back in my bag."

Grayson shoved the pad deep in his pants pocket. "I wanna keep mine."

"Me too," Fred replied.

"I dunno," Piper said. "If somebody doesn't like what I'm writin', then I hafta give them the notes. My mom says—"

"Oh give it a rest, willya," Fred shouted.

Piper's eyes flashed. Before an argument ensued, Jonelle jumped in.

"Tell you what. You guys are a team, so if one member doesn't want to do something, that's okay. No worries. The fact that I've learned so much from you guys from the little time I've known you has been a tremendous help."

"Can't we still report on stuff, though?" Grayson said with a tinge of sadness.

"Of course. And you can call anytime." She smiled and held out her hand for Piper's notebook. Instead of placing the pad in the palm of Jonelle's hand, she tucked it inside her purse.

All three waved and entered the lobby's glass doors. Jonelle resisted the urge to park and seek out the apartment manager and decided instead to check out the local strip mall first.

Before she set off, she turned to the spot where someone stood watching the group. She drove through the lot, parked near the street, and observed the main entrance. After ten minutes, when no one went inside, she aimed the Jeep for the street.

She checked her mirrors before pulling out and yawned. Dealing with tweens exhausted her. Another quick check in the mirrors revealed a dark blue sedan behind her. The same sedan she'd seen twice before.

CHAPTER 29

A plastic sheet covered the license plate, preventing her from reading the tag of the sedan still one car behind. Jonelle pulled into the open lot of the strip mall and parked close to the front of the Little Caesars. The vehicle on her tail slid into a space one row behind and several cars down. The person behind the wheel needed to work on his tailing skills. Unless, of course, he wanted his presence known.

She removed her weapon from the lockbox, fastened the holstered pistol around her waist, and pulled out her shirt to hide the gun from view. Satisfied, she left the Jeep and headed over to the parked sedan, using the full lot to cover her movements. Several shoppers milled about the lot, a few staring open-mouthed at the black woman weaving in and out of the parked cars. Someone honked at her to get out of the way.

She waved a "hold your horses" and, with eyes still glued to the sedan, closed the distance. Even with the tinted back windows, she made out the silhouettes of two people. Jonelle stopped. The figures had their heads turned to each other. Hands waving through the air from both indicated some sort of disagreement. Jonelle ducked behind an olive green Land Rover.

She figured that if anyone in the vehicle carried a weapon, most likely he sat on the passenger's side, so she scooted over to the driver's open window. Angry words floated out of the car.

"Now what? We jus' sittin' here. What you wann do, man? I ain't got all day."

"Me neither," Jonelle said, popping up, hand resting on her weapon. "Help you boys?" She swallowed a gasp as the driver turned at the sound of her voice. Randy stared back, hazel eyes wide in disbelief.

"Well, hello there," she said. "For some reason I didn't think you got up this early." She bent down and recognized the passenger. Shawn's face perfectly matched Randy's expression.

"Didn't know you guys were friends. We need to talk. Wanna do it here or maybe go inside somewhere for a chat?"

Randy faced forward, jaw clenched. "Ain't no place to sit around here."

Jonelle didn't know if either man carried a weapon, but she'd use hers if necessary. She pulled the back door handle. Locked. "Open it," she demanded.

"What?"

"Open the damn door. I'm hot, and I'm tired and I'm not playing games." She patted the side of her waist for emphasis.

Randy's eyes grew large. He disengaged the lock.

"Thanks." She slid in behind him.

"How you doin', Shawn? Seen Tamora lately?"

Shawn faced the dirty windshield.

"Don't want to talk? Well, that's okay . . . for now. I don't mind starting the conversation. Here's the deal, guys. I don't like being followed. Pisses me off, to tell the truth. So, which one of you wants to explain the reason why this is the third time?"

"Don't know what you talkin' about, lady," Randy said.

"I think you do, but that's not why I'm here."

"Wasn't me you think you saw, but, hey, I like drivin' around. Lookin' at the view." Randy turned his head toward Shawn who ignored him.

"And I'm the best view you got? Really, guys, I'm flattered. I know Shawn here likes other things to look at, right? Such as helping very attractive former co-workers in their new acting jobs.

Though, I think in that particular case, those people aren't called actresses. They're called models. Am I right?"

That got him to turn around. He glared at Jonelle. "What the hell you talkin' about?"

She removed the flier about Playcat's latest production and waved the advertisement in his face. "This. This is what I'm talking about."

He made a grab for the ad, but she pulled away. "Not so fast. Listen, ordinarily I wouldn't give a damn what someone does in his or her free time. But Tamora's involved and so I'm involved. Whatever she does, whomever she talks to, and wherever she goes may impact what happened to her child. And since I'm sure everybody connected to her knows that, I get real suspicious when the spotlight turns on me. Understand?"

Randy mumbled something under his breath.

She leaned forward. "What was that? Speak up, Randy."

"I said, that porn crap got nothin' to do with me."

"Don't care one way or the other. Someone saw you outside Tamora's apartment when she wasn't there, talking to someone inside. Who was it?"

"I didn't do nothin' to that kid," he said.

"That's not what I asked."

His hands tightened around the steering wheel. An angry silence hung in the car.

"What did you need inside her apartment?"

"Don't say another word, man," Shawn cautioned.

"Look, I can't let her sit here and accuse me of kidnapping," Randy yelled.

"Calm down," Jonelle said. His outburst froze shoppers heading for their vehicles. She didn't want to deal with some guy going off. She smiled and called out through the open window, "No problem, folks. Everything's all right." Jonelle lowered her voice. "I'm not accusing you of anything, yet. Right now I'm only interested in what happened to Lark. Whatever else goes on in her place is between the two of you." And Langford's since the situation involved Tamora, but she didn't tell him that.

"Weed, okay? And if I'm lucky, I can score some snow."

"Shut up, fool." Shawn aimed a fist at Randy's face.

"Wouldn't do anything rash if I were you," she said, slapping the leather holster for emphasis. "All we're having here is a nice conversation, so relax. Go on, Randy."

He moved as far away from Shawn as he could. "She's got stuff stashed in her place and said I could go inside and grab some. We got a real easy deal. All I gotta do is leave the money in the fridge under the milk."

"If she's not home, how'd you get in?"

"Ah, I get where you're goin' with this." He turned halfway around and grinned lopsidedly at Jonelle. "Yeah. You're right. Ole busybody Maxine would let me in."

That wasn't where she was going.

"You dumb sonofabitch," Shawn said. "Stupid junkie don't know how to keep his mouth shut," he grumbled. "This is on you, man. I'm outta here." He made to reach for the door handle, but Jonelle's voice stopped him.

"We're not done. I don't care about drugs or porn. But, if you leave this car without answering my questions, I'm taking everything I know to the cops. I've got a pretty good idea of events leading up to and including how someone got in and grabbed Lark. But then, what? I know you wander around at night, right Randy? All that going up and down halls, in and out of the building. How much do you know about that night?"

Both men clamped their mouths shut.

"Let's go back to Miss Maxine. Was she the one in Tamora's apartment you were talking to?"

Randy stayed quiet.

"I heard Maxine hangs out around this mall with Mrs. Watkins. Hate to lean on an old lady, but a woman's gotta do what a woman's gotta do. Wonder what the cops'll say when they find out Maxine lets people in Tamora's apartment. And that Watkins probably knows all about it. They might put two and two together and get five." She made to leave the car.

"Hold it, willya?" Shawn swiveled in his seat. "Leave her alone."

Something about his face, especially around the nose, the eyes. "Oh, hello? What's your relationship to Lorraine Watkins?"

He turned back around so fast it was a wonder he didn't get whiplash.

"Let me guess," she said, warming up to the idea. "You probably told Watkins Tamora ditched her day job. You were already involved in Playcat, so you offered to help. You suggested a way Tamora's, um, attributes could earn her some real cash. Be a better deal than sitting on your butt all day and night earning minimum wage. For half the work, she could make at least twice the amount of money."

Randy spoke up. "What're you guys talkin' about?" He flicked a thumb toward the backseat. "She's sayin' Watkins and you are related? What is she, your ma? Damn, dude. You could've told me. That explains a lot."

Shawn grunted and stared straight ahead.

Jonelle leaned her forearms on the front seat. "Seems a lot of people are keeping you in the dark about things, Randy. I'm guessing the reason is because they don't trust you."

"Don't listen to her, man. She's fishin' around. She don't know nothin'," Shawn said.

"I know you haven't denied anything I said," Jonelle shot back. "This is how I think it works. Tamora met Shawn at her day job. I suppose she got the night job on her own. She gets fired from both jobs but keeps to the same routine for the benefit of the neighbors. Next, Shawn here turned her on to the studio. I think she's so popular that she's not only filming at night but also during the day."

Jonelle wracked her brain. "Wonder what else she's doing. You got any ideas on that, Shawn?"

"Whoa," Randy said. "She gets naked for money, huh? Cool. You think I can get in on that action?"

Jonelle wanted to smack the idiot upside the head. "I haven't figured out the connection with Maxine or Lorraine Watkins . . . yet. I've got a detective friend who could check if either woman has ever been arrested. Hey, Shawn. You wanna save me some time?"

He grunted.

"I'll take that as a no. What about you, Randy? What else are you doing inside Tamora's apartment besides trolling for drugs?"

"Told you I ain't touched that kid."

She didn't think he snatched Lark. His drug use probably fried several brain cells, and swiping the child required some finesse. She leaned in close to his ear. "What did you see the night Lark disappeared? Don't insult my intelligence, Randy. You saw something. Otherwise your friend, here, wouldn't have anything to do with you. Am I right?"

Shawn turned in his seat and glared at her. "Don't try and pin that kidnapping on me, either. I didn't take the kid."

"Stop trying to screw with us," Randy said. "You got the wrong idea, lady. Why don't you check out Mrs. Watkins?"

"Shut up, fool," Shawn hissed. "I'm tellin' you she's fishin'. She don't know nothin'."

"I ain't going down for somethin' I didn't do. You want answers, talk to her," Randy said. "Or Maxine."

"Thanks for the suggestions. Assuming for one minute you really didn't take Lark, or know who did, what did you see that night?"

His fingers picked at the lesions on his face. A few times he glanced over at Shawn who resumed pretending Randy didn't exist. A trail of sweat flowed from Randy's short, dark hair, down to his chin. He stopped gouging his face long enough to wipe the moisture away.

Jonelle scooted to the center of the backseat to get a better look at him. "Not leaving until you tell me what happened that night."

A tense silence hung in the car for several seconds. Finally, Randy spoke up in a voice so low, Jonelle demanded he speak louder. "I said, the first time I walked up to her door, I changed my mind 'cause Tamora gets mad if I come back too many times. So, I went to the stairwell and sat inside for a minute, thinkin' about what to do." He let out an exasperated sigh. "So, after a while I figured I didn't care if she got pissed. Tamora never stayed mad for very long."

He paused.

"What time was this?"

He shrugged. "Don't know."

"Go on."

"I left the stairwell, stopped at her door, and almost knocked but went on down to my own place at the other end of the hall. It was gettin' kinda late, and she hates it when people disturb her daughter sleepin'. But I still needed my . . . "

He hesitated so long that Jonelle wanted to scream. "So," she prompted, "you went back again. Was the door open or closed?"

"It wasn't open all the way. Only cracked. All I did was peek inside. I didn't go all the way in. Honest!"

Her heart raced. "What did you see, Randy?"

His fingers continued attacking his pale skin. "Somebody dressed in black was holding something. I couldn't see too good because their back was to me."

"Man or woman?" she asked.

"What?"

"The person you saw, was it a man or woman?"

He glanced at Shawn out of the corner of his eye. "I . . . I'm not sure. Man, I think. I ran back to my room."

"What were you afraid of?" Jonelle wanted to scream. Instead she marveled at the fact these idiots didn't drop breadcrumbs so that anyone could follow what they were doing.

"I didn't say nothin' about bein' scared."

"So why did you run back to your place? Did you have some idea of who the person was in Tamora's apartment?"

Randy sniffed several times and kept his mouth shut. Both men refused to answer any more questions. She resisted the urge to nudge Randy with her pistol, realizing that would probably freak both men out and push the situation to a dangerous place.

She slid out of the backseat. "I'm not done, so you might want to consider being more upfront next time. You should know that when I get hold of something, I don't let go."

Neither man responded.

Jonelle zigzagged back to her Jeep, taking advantage of the almost-filled lot to conceal her movements. While the men didn't know where she'd parked, from her vantage point behind the wheel of her Jeep, she kept an eye on their car.

She reached into her console and removed a pair of mini binoculars and trained them on the car's occupants. "Dumb and dumber are probably arguing about what to do next," she mumbled to herself. "Good." Instead of leaving, she decided to wait and follow them out. See how they liked someone shadowing their bumper. A quick check of her emails revealed nothing pressing, so she settled back against the car seat and let her mind wander.

Everything Tamora did, she did for herself. While she tried not to judge, she found the young woman seriously lacking in common sense. Slowly, she began to consider the possibility Tamora had something to do with her daughter's disappearance. But why? Jonelle needed to do more than sit in a hot car waiting for . . . what?

A little excitement, that's what. Something to happen so that she could get on with finding Lark. There it was. No longer did

Jonelle care if Tamora did or did not have an alibi for the night Lark disappeared.

She shook her head. Gotta concentrate. There was one other option for why the two men hadn't moved—they were waiting for someone.

CHAPTER 30

*D*on't like that I've been told to shove off. After all I've gone through. Shuffling back and forth from one place to the next. Did I complain? Well, not much. Not as much as that stupid ass Jelani. And for what? Nobody was supposed to get hurt. Especially not the little ones. They want me to give up my turn with my Butterfly Princess but I'm worried. Butterfly Princess. That's how I've come to think of her.

Had a close call in the building. My lookout gave me the all clear to grab some stuff from storage. Nobody was supposed to be down there. Nearly crapped on myself when I seen them two ladies. Don't think they recognized Lark, though. Had her disguised pretty good. She loved dressing up different, with wigs and stuff. To her, playing pretend is a game. Only now the game needs to get rough.

People are starting to panic because that detective is getting close. Wasn't for her there'd be no problem. We'd take the pics and that would be that. And we wouldn't put 'em on social media, either. Too many eyes. We're talkin' private parties, here.

A few preview snaps of Lark to see if anybody's interested in kids that young. The contact said they're not dirty—they're art. Art my ass. I seen enough smut to know what's what.

They want art? Hell, I'll show 'em what art's all about. The more I look at my Butterfly Princess the more she wants to be with me and me only. I can tell. She looks at me different from before. And, hey, I'm seein' a side of her I didn't before.

We all been lettin' that detective run around like she owns the place. She's scarin' people into doing things they shouldn't, causing everybody to make mistakes. Not me. She don't scare me none.

Time for somebody to put her in her place. Once I do that then the little Butterfly Princess will be safe. Safe with me, not with her whore of a mom.

CHAPTER 31

For several more minutes she sat sweating and staring at every car that passed by while at the same time keeping one eye on the still stationary sedan. She wiped her face with a tissue, checked again for messages, and fumed. The hell with this. She inserted her key into the ignition and decided those two would have to wait until later. Before she put the Jeep in gear, the slow movement of a silver SUV caught her attention.

Tamora's face stared straight ahead in the passenger seat. Unable to see who sat behind the wheel, Jonelle tracked the vehicle to a spot farther down on her right. Sure enough, the sedan with Randy and Shawn followed. Jonelle slid down in her seat. They knew her car, but she counted on them wanting to relay what happened to their contact as fast as possible.

It was one thing to surprise two people, but four? Jonelle's phone chimed. The display read Thelonius Burton. She groaned. "Hi, Burt. I'm kinda busy now, so—"

"This isn't a social call," Burt said. "I wanted to let you know that we got a tip from Baltimore's western district PD which may have some bearing on the disappearance of that little girl in your case."

She sat up. "You found her?"

"That's not what I mean. Vice says they're watching someone involved in drugs, and possibly child pornography. Apparently activity in this area increased recently, and they're running down several leads."

Jonelle's stomach lurched. If she told Burt about Tamora's staring in porn films, he'd want the police to take over her case. She didn't want that to happen. This was hers. She fought for the opportunity and worked too hard to get this far. Yet . . .

"You still there?"

"Yeah. I uh . . . oh hell. I know something about the mother that might link to the suspect and his activities." Jonelle wiped more sweat from her brow. She craned her neck to where she'd last seen the two vehicles but couldn't find either one.

"You better come in to the precinct. Now, rather than later," Burt said. "And I didn't say the suspect was male."

The edge in his voice warned the invite wasn't open to debate.

She swore under her breath.

"I'll ignore what I thought I heard. See you in half an hour." Burt disconnected without waiting for her response.

Jonelle started her Jeep and headed in the direction she last saw the two vehicles. Burt could cool his heals for a few extra minutes. She needed to confirm the driver of the SUV was, indeed, Lorraine Watkins. She scanned the rows and drove up and down the last two sections. Nothing.

After a few minutes she gave up on trying to find the SUV and exited the mall's main entrance when something Burt said came back. He'd hinted the person Baltimore Vice was interested in could be female.

The drive to the Howard County police department took a little over thirty minutes. She signed in, got a vistor's badge and headed upstairs. Standing beside Burt's desk she said, "So, haven't seen you in a while. How're things going?" Jonelle pointed to his tie. "I like that one. Can't go wrong with the Roadrunner."

With one hand Burt wordlessly indicated for her to take a seat. She obliged by holding her tongue and sitting in the guest chair opposite his desk.

"I'll cut to the chase," Burt said.

"Please do," Jonelle responded. She didn't know what his problem was, but this all-business attitude coming from him wasn't something she was used to. "Listen, if you're upset because I didn't tell you about Tamora's acting in porn films before, it's because I found that out not too long ago."

Burt tapped a manilla folder. "While waiting for you to come in, I got a copy of the Baltimore Vice operation. I glanced through the report and found something interesting. Seems there's some new talent offering her services. The description doesn't fit you, but it does match a friend of yours." He slid the folder in front of her. "Why don't you review this and tell me if the person sounds like someone you know."

Uh-oh.

With some trepidation, Jonelle read the words on a summary of surveillance at a place identified as Playcat Productions. The document listed dates and times of all individuals going in and out of the establishment. Her heart raced, sure her own name would appear. She double checked the dates and almost fell to the floor. Vice's surveillance included the night Adrienne entered the location.

"You okay?" Burt asked.

"Sure," she croaked. She cleared her throat. "I could use a drink of water."

She waited until he left to read the rest. Behind a list of vehicles recorded near that place, as well as their tag numbers, were photographs of people exiting each one, walking across the street and going up to the door.

Sweat popped out on her forehead. She wiped her hands on her pants to keep from smudging the pages. There stood Adrienne, fuzzy but recognizable, entering the building.

Several photos later showed a light-colored SUV parked at the curb. A familiar-looking female leaned out of the driver's side window, talking to Tamora.

"I'll be damn."

She flipped through several more pictures. A few were of a woman carrying a tote full of supplies. "Who's that?"

"Cleaning woman. She's legit. Comes in once a week in the mornings. Vice doesn't see any need to get her involved and doesn't want her changing her routine." Burt placed the water bottle on the desk and sat in his chair.

She slid the folder back across without looking at the rest of the contents.

"If no one's called Adrienne yet, they will soon. Now, I don't know her as well as you do, but she doesn't seem the type to deal with this kind of business. Also,"—Burt slid the folder back—"you should study the rest of these. Adrienne wasn't the only to have her picture taken."

Jonelle found the photo of herself. "Ohmigod. How. . . ?"

Burt ignored the question. "You've been ID'd, and the fact your PI license is clean and up to date is a plus in your favor. They know you didn't go inside, and when you went around the back where the garbage bins are, they assumed you weren't there for an audition. Not so in Adrienne's case." He paused.

Jonelle gulped water. It was one thing for her to get called in by the cops. That was part of the job. Adrienne was a different matter. Her best friend had an important position in the University of Maryland's Admissions Office, and any hint of scandal could jeopardize her career.

"I know this looks bad. Adrienne was only there because I pressured her to see if she could get inside and find out more about what goes on in that place in order to check on Tamora. Obviously, she'd have a better chance of getting inside than me, plus she thought it would be a hoot."

"Hoot, huh? You see me laughing?"

An imaginary hand reached inside Jonelle's chest and squeezed. For a moment she had trouble breathing.

He squinted at her. "Your claustrophobia acting up?"

"Burt, this is all my fault," she gasped. "You've got to do everything you can to get her out of this."

"What about you?"

That did it. "If you're accusing me of something, go ahead and do it and stop treating me like a kid."

Burt pursed his lips, grabbed the folder, placed it under his arm, and stood.

"Wait," Jonelle said, eyes wide. "I'm sorry. I'm being selfish here. I really don't want Adrienne involved. I'll do whatever you want so long as her name isn't included." She nodded at the folder.

Her phone rang. The frown on Burt's face warned her against answering, so she turned the cellphone off.

For several seconds the only words spoken were those of the other detectives in the unit.

"Burt?"

"Yeah. I'm thinkin'."

Burt had loosened his tie as he leaned back in his chair and studied the ceiling. Never one to sit still while waiting, she picked up a pen covered in a rubberized version of Dory the fish from "*Finding Dory.*" She turned the object around and around until Burt spoke.

"Okay," he said, sitting upright. "You need to back off that place. Vice knows what's going on, and they're more interested in the drugs. For now. But the slightest hint of kids anywhere near that place and all bets are off. I don't think I need to tell you that just because you don't see cops, doesn't mean they aren't there."

Jonelle worked for the lawyer for one of the porn stars and could always claim she had a right to scope out the place. Unfortunately she'd drawn not only Adrienne but also Luther into her plan.

"Okay. I hear you. I'll find some other way to pin Tamora down."

"Hope so. What else you got?"

She swallowed hard. "I've talked to three youngsters who live in the building where Lark disappeared."

"About this? What the hell're you doing?"

"No, not about this and there's no need to shout. It's related to the case, but not the, um, drugs or adult film angle."

"Kids are tricky," he said, his voice an octave lower. "How old are we talking about here?"

"Twelve."

"You interviewing them with or without their parents?"

"I'm not interviewing them, per se. They wanted to talk to me, and I said yes. It was more of a social thing rather than a Q and A session. They didn't mention wanting to bring their parents, and I didn't insist."

"'Social,' huh? You sure about that?"

She ignored the sarcasm. "Well? Am I in trouble here?"

He rubbed his chin. "You should be okay. You know, of course, that whatever they tell you can't be used in any legal sense."

"All I want is to know what everyone's gossiping about or who they've seen hanging around that apartment. If I'm lucky I'll find out something new, but I won't press. I promise."

"Fine. But to cover all your bases, why not run what you're doing by the attorney first?"

Without comment Burt reached inside his desk and pulled out a pad of paper. He selected the same "Dory" pen from the holder on his desk and slid both to her. "Write down everything you found out about that place and everything you know about Tamora Phelps and her connection to adult films. I also want the names of everyone involved."

Jonelle picked up the pen without comment.

"When you're done here, I'll contact vice and explain your actions, so don't leave anything out."

Burt treating her like this made her face burn. "Last I heard naked lady pictures weren't against the law," she said.

He leaned across the desk, inches from her face. "An adult taking her clothes off isn't the only issue. We're talking drugs and underage kids. And last *I* heard, those are definitely against the law. They tracked Adrienne out of that place and noted she didn't seem too steady on her feet."

Crap. She'd forgotten that Adrienne, in order to fit in, had smoked pot. If Adrienne had seen kids in there, she would've said something. "Listen, all she had was a little weed, nothing heavy." At least Jonelle hoped not. "She didn't bring any drugs with her, and she damn sure doesn't know anything about kiddie porn. She'd have told me, and we'd have come straight over here."

The only reason Jonelle didn't fill an entire sheet of paper with one oversized crude word was knowing that if she did, she'd get her best friend in serious trouble. She sighed deeply and began addressing everything in the vice report, filling in the events from the time Adrienne left the car until she returned.

After reading over what she'd written, she scribbled the names Lorraine Watkins and Miss Maxine . . . and added Randy, Shawn Mowerby, and Jelani Hill. Even though she didn't know some of the last names, she provided the location where each lived. A few words of her suspicions about the two women without going into a lot of detail might warrant a visit from the cops. In turn, that could spook them enough for either or both to make a mistake. A mistake that she could use to her advantage.

CHAPTER 32

Jonelle didn't like the tension that slid between her and Burt almost without effort. When she finished writing, it became clear after ten minutes of waiting that he wasn't going to return anytime soon. So, Jonelle dashed off a short note expressing regret again and signing it with an "I'm sorry" and smiley face. Her phone chimed as she left the division and entered the hall.

"Sorry to bother you, hon," Rainey said. "But one of those kids called. Think she said her name was Piper. I wouldn't have called you except she sounded excited. Said she'd tried to call but your phone went to voicemail. She didn't want to tell me anything except that it was an emergency." Rainey recited a phone number.

Instead of continuing down the hall and toward the lobby, Jonelle found a ladies room and ducked inside. She punched in the number, and after only two rings a young voice answered.

"Piper? It's Jonelle Sweet. I understand you're trying to reach me. I got hung up here at the police station but I'm heading to your building now. Should take about fifteen, twenty minutes. Where can I find you?"

"Police? You arrested or something?"

In spite of the pain pounding in her head, Jonelle smiled. "No. Not yet, anyway."

"Oh." Disappointment came through the line. "So. I'm home. Grayson and Fred are on their way. And my mom's here. When I told her what we heard, she said she needs to talk to you."

"Heard what?"

"We were outside out back, foolin' around on the swings, and we heard a couple ladies sayin' that they heard somebody say they'd seen Lark."

"On my way." Jonelle hurried out of the precinct. She called Adrienne and left a voicemail stating it was urgent she see her concerning Tamora and the porn studio.

The drive over to Piper's apartment gave Jonelle time to fume about the mess she'd gotten her best friend into. "No more," Jonelle murmured as she parked close to the building's entrance, though she'd made the same comment several times before.

A flash of light and a reflection of an SUV glinted in the glass doors. Jonelle turned and faced the profile of Lorraine Watkins pulling the silver vehicle into an assigned spot near the front. The apartment manager exited the vehicle, followed by Miss Maxine who, upon looking in her direction, stared open-mouthed at Jonelle.

"Hello, ladies," Jonelle said brightly. "Nice to see you both again."

Watkins frowned. "Don't know if Tamora's in or not. We just came from, uh, shopping."

Jonelle held the glass doors open and stepped aside. "Not here to see Tamora. I got a call from someone who says they have information about Lark."

Maxine looked from Watkins to Jonelle. Her hand settled near her throat. "You sayin' they found Lark?"

"You don't seem very happy, Miss Maxine. Something wrong?" Jonelle asked.

"She's got to get upstairs, right Maxine?" Watkins said.

Miss Maxine hesitated as if confused as to whose question she should answer first.

"I'll talk to you later," Watkins said in a loud, firm voice.

Miss Maxine scurried off, stabbed the elevator's up button several times before finally entering and staring at the floor. After the doors closed, Jonelle followed Watkins into the manager's office.

"Can't talk to you now, I'm busy." Watkins sat and shuffled through papers covering the surface of the desk.

"I saw you guys at the strip mall up the street," Jonelle said.

Watkins hesitated slightly before continuing to rearrange papers on the desk.

"This was after I had a little conversation with Randy and a friend of his named Shawn."

The apartment manager's movements slowed.

"But I guess you already know that since you all got together, right?"

Watkins looked up. "I don't know what you're playing at, but you are getting on my nerves. My business is my business and—"

"Not if it involves an abducted child," Jonelle said.

"Don't try pinning that on me. I had nothing to do with whoever snatched Lark."

Jonelle pulled the visitor's chair closer to the desk and sat.

"The problem with this whole thing is why Lark. There are a lot of children in this building, all ages, sizes, colors. Someone went all the way up to the seventh floor, up to the door, walked in without Miss Maxine's knowledge—or so she claims—entered, and grabbed the child. Why did he or she pick Lark?"

"How the hell should I know?"

"And why didn't Lark scream?"

"Same answer. You better leave before I call the cops. You're trespassing and—"

"I just came from the cops where we discussed Tamora's acting gig as a porn star. Along with drug use and possible involvement with kiddie porn. You know anything about all that?"

"I . . . I don't believe you."

Jonelle indicated the manager's desk phone. "Go ahead and call the cops. Ask to speak to homicide detective Thelonius Burton."

Watkins' cellphone chirped on her desk, making the woman jump. She stabbed a finger on the screen, silencing the ring. "I want you to leave."

Jonelle stood. "Vice has the studio under surveillance. Did you know that? They have several photos and asked me to ID anyone I knew. Funny thing. One of the pics showed a heavyset black woman dressed in a knit dress leaning out of a car Tamora had exited. The two were laughing. When I looked more closely, I could swear that person looked like you. Thing is, vice didn't need me to identify the woman because they already know her name."

Deep worry lines cut into Watkins' face.

"I'm going upstairs to talk to some people. You're welcome to join us if you'd like."

The apartment manager turned and stared out the window. Her phone chimed again. She made no attempt to answer.

Jonelle leaned over the desk, and read the screen. The Baltimore police department's name and number showed. She pointed an index finger. "Better answer that."

Still smiling, Jonelle took the elevator up several floors and approached the door to seven fifteen. Her arm was still raised when the door flew open. "What took you so long, Miss?" Piper held Jonelle's gaze with one hand placed on her hip.

"Watch your manners, young lady." Mrs. Enruth came up and stood behind her daughter.

"Sorry." Though the word sounded sincere, the expression on her face indicated Piper wasn't pleased.

"They're getting a little anxious," Mrs. Enruth said, ushering Jonelle into the neat apartment. Seated around the dining room table were Grayson and Fred munching on plates of sloppy joe's and chips. "Take a seat. Fix you anything?."

"I'm having a cheese and tomato sandwich," Piper added. "Want one?"

"No thanks, I'm fine." She marveled that the youngsters could still eat after all that pizza a few hours ago.

"Something to drink then? Coffee? Tea? Something cold?"

Though anxious to find out what the kids knew, she waited until Piper's mom had placed a cup of coffee in front of her. "Aren't you having anything?"

"She's already had two," Piper said.

Mrs. Enruth pulled out a chair. "Snitch."

Jonelle smiled at the easy relationship between the two. "What've you guys got for me?" She sipped the steaming hot coffee.

Grayson looked at Piper's mother, who nodded slightly.

"We were out back on the swings 'cause we finished walking the dogs and didn't have anything else to do," he said.

"She doesn't wanna hear that part. Jeesh," Fred said.

"You go and tell it, then!"

"Knock it off you two," Mrs. Enruth scolded. "Go ahead, Grayson."

He made a face at Fred before he continued. "There was these two ladies from my floor, and one of 'em was sayin' she thought she saw Lark in the basement."

"What?" Jonelle didn't believe what she was hearing. "You sure they were talking about Lark?"

All three nodded.

"What else?"

"They were arguing. One said no way, and the other one said it was true 'cause she seen this guy before, washing little kid clothes. And she said he didn't look like the type to go around washing anybody's clothes. Stuff like that."

Jonelle's head was spinning. If true, that meant Lark was someplace close by. "Do you know who these women are?"

"I've seen 'em before, but I don't know any names."

Jonelle raised her eyebrows at Piper's mother.

"Grayson described them but I can't figure out who they are."

No one had used the cards she'd left on that floor.

"Did they mention the name of the person with Lark? If it was her, that is," Jonelle said.

All three shook their heads.

"Could it have been Randy?"

Fred snorted. "If it was they woulda said. Everybody here knows Randy."

"Did they mention if they'd seen this person before?" She directed the question to Grayson.

"Don't remember. Anyways, after they said that we went into the basement. We figured we could poke around a little. Save you some time."

"You never told me that," Mrs. Enruth said, giving Piper a stern look.

"I was gonna . . . but I kinda forgot," Piper said sheepishly.

"Did you guys find anything?" Jonelle ignored the frown on Mrs. Enruth's face.

"We checked the laundry room, but nobody was in there," Fred said.

"That's because too many people go in and out of there all the time," Piper added. "So we figured it had to be a room that locked. I went upstairs and got the storage room key."

Mrs. Enruth muttered something under her breath.

"There's dirt and dust everywhere in that place. No way could anybody hide in there. But we looked anyway," Fred said.

"All we saw was junk," Grayson added.

Jonelle turned to Piper's mother. "I was down in the basement the other day. Does anyone know if Jelani ever locks the maintenance room?"

They all shrugged.

"I was also in the trash room. That wasn't locked, either."

"Trash room? What for?" Grayson asked.

"So that's why you smelled so bad that day." Piper giggled.

"Guilty as charged. I left pretty quick, so I didn't do any exploring. I'm assuming there's a room that provides the power. Anything else?"

"You can't hide a child down there and nobody notice," Mrs. Enruth said.

If what Grayson said was true, somebody did notice something, Jonelle thought. While Lark might not be hidden down there now, she might have passed through at some point.

Jonelle couldn't figure out why anyone would risk the child being seen. Unless they wanted it that way. "Think I'll go back down and have another look," she said.

"Can we come, too?" Piper asked.

Her mother responded with a resounding no, giving Jonelle no chance to answer.

"Your mom's right. It'll be easier and safer if I go poking around there myself."

"Are you carrying your gun?" Grayson asked, huge smile on his tomato-and meat-covered lips.

"Let's just say I can take care of myself."

"Why don't you ask Mrs. Watkins to help?" Piper suggested.

Jonelle shot Mrs. Enruth a look. "She's probably busy."

"Bet she's not," Fred said. A smug look crossed the freckled face.

"Why do you think that?" These kids were full of secrets.

"'Cause I been seein' her a lotta different places lately." Fred shoved more chips in her mouth. She took her time sipping soda. To Jonelle it looked as though Red Fred enjoyed being in the spotlight. Instinctively Jonelle knew not to rush her, so she waited.

A loud burp was followed by "'scuse me" and a giggle.

As Jonelle shifted her attention to Piper, Fred spoke up.

"When Lark went missin' we told Mrs. Watkins we wanted to put up posters all around. At first she said no, she didn't want the place messed up. Then she changed her mind. Said Jelani would do it, but he didn't so we did. One night after that I left to go to the store—"

Jonelle lifted an eyebrow at Mrs. Enruth.

Piper's mom gave a slight nod.

—"and I seen her tearin' the posters down. Why'd she do that? Anyway, next day we put 'em back up again."

Another swallow of soda.

"Other times when I. . . when it's too late to visit these guys,"—she pointed a thumb at her friends—"sometimes I sit in the stairwell on the top floor. Mostly on account of it's cool and quiet in there. This one time wasn't quiet. I heard voices. Yellin' real loud somewhere down below. I heard Mrs. Watkins' voice and the other one coulda been Randy. Then I heard this other voice, and I coulda sworn it was Miss Tammy."

Finally. "What were they saying?" Jonelle asked.

Fred scrunched up her face in concentration. "Don't remember all of it."

"Prob'ly 'cause you was smokin' a joint, right?" Grayson erupted in laughter.

Piper chimed in with, "See, told you to watch yourself." She wagged a finger at Fred who stuck out her tongue.

"Oh, shut up," Fred yelled.

"Later," Mrs. Enruth told Jonelle in answer to a question she hadn't asked.

"Go on, Fred. Ignore them," Mrs. Enruth said.

"I heard about some kinda plan. They said people kept changin' the plan. And Miss Tammy said she knew Lark's daddy was gonna make a stink, and the cops were gonna arrest her again and her stupid lawyer wasn't gonna stop them. And Mrs. Watkins kept tellin' her to calm down, it's all gonna work out. Like that."

CHAPTER 33

*T*he kid's getting anxious and so am I. This thing is screwed up.
Everybody's been fartin' around like we got all the time in the
world. Hell, I can do better on my own. She likes me best anyway.

Been looking at different possibilities. Way back when we agreed
on this I had an idea but got voted down as usual. What if Butterfly
Princess and me take a little trip? After all, there's plenty places
besides around here that'd pay good money for a few private pictures.
As long as I do the picture taking it shouldn't be a problem. She likes
games. I'll make sure to treat it like a game.

Since that PI's keeping everybody busy, it'll be a while before
anyone knows we're gone. I'm getting tingly all over thinking about
it. But first, I gotta get her away from where she is now. Tried
hinting about the possibility of me and someone else going out on our
own. Easier to split the money in half than what them fools are
thinking of doing.

He said he'd think about it. He's getting tired too, but I suspect
he's not used to being around little kids. Suggested that the way things
are going, he better not think too long.

CHAPTER 34

Instead of taking the elevator, she used the back stairs, eyes glued on the metal steps, searching for signs of people who'd recently used the area. And trying not to think about the lack of windows. A rank smell assaulted her nose. Discarded cigarette packs, candy and gum wrappers, all showed signs of having been there a while.

On the bottom floor Jonelle ignored the laundry and maintenance rooms. She stopped in front of the door marked "Storage" and tried the handle. Locked. She inserted the key obtained from Piper's mom. The door opened easily into a dark room. Jonelle found the switch and flicked on the lights.

Rows and rows of wire mesh storage cages covered most of the area. Each cage had a number and a lock. Because of the mesh, most of the contents were clearly visible. A few enterprising souls covered the contents of their cages with blankets and tarps to protect—and conceal?—what lay inside. She couldn't imagine a child living in one of these, at least not for very long. On a temporary basis? Maybe—but only for a few hours. Like in an emergency.

From where she stood in the front, she couldn't tell what the back cages stored, so she headed for the ones farthest from the door. Instead of covering specific items, one compartment was lined top to bottom in a brown tarp and secured with a padlock. Jonelle removed a tool from the lock pick set in her purse, and within seconds the lock snapped open. "Easy-peasy." She pulled aside the tarp.

Two small, somewhat battered, roller totes and several cardboard boxes filled the space. "Why would anyone bother to hide this junk?" She secured the lock and closely examined the other bins.

Most of the cages used padlocks. Several more inspections of covered units yielded the same result. Of the few that dangled combination locks in front, the contents were displayed with items so benign the owners must've felt confident no one wanted the articles. She made one more circuit of the room and turned to go when something caught her eye. A butterfly cutout lay on the floor of the next to last unit way in the back.

Jonelle picked it up. Very little dust. The unit above held several boxes. Even though it contained a padlock, she'd originally ignored it since she could easily make out what was inside.

Several small hooks hung from the top most edge. Perfect to attach a tarp or other cover. Her pulse quickened. She picked the lock and opened the unit. Her hand reached for the first box.

Noise from outside stopped her.

Too late to run and turn off the lights, she hid in a darkened corner, willing whoever it was to keep going. They stopped. Someone jiggled the knob.

"Did you bring the key?" Demanded a female voice.

"You said you had it," answered a male.

"Shit. Don't feel like going all the way back upstairs to get it." Another wiggle of the knob and the footsteps faded away.

She needed to get out soon as the familiar tightness in her chest started to spread. A quick search of all the boxes revealed nothing but towels, sheets, old dishes and utensils, and books. Nothing to indicate the containers once held a child.

She put the paper butterfly in her purse, turned off the light, opened the entrance door a crack, and listened. Whoever was there earlier hadn't returned. She slipped out of the room.

No point in searching the trash room again. The recent sighting of Lark, if accurate, proved the child was still alive.

Time to confront Watkins.

The door to the manager's office was closed. In all likelihood Watkins had stuck to her routine of leaving the building at five, but Jonelle knocked anyway. No response. She tried the knob. Locked.

"She's gone," said a man's voice behind her. "You gotta call that number if you need something."

"Thanks." Jonelle smiled and made to copy the number until he exited the building.

With no one else around, she quickly picked the lock. Instead of turning on the light she used the sunlight seeping through the blinds to search the room.

She tried the desk drawers, which opened easily. Too easily. She doubted the woman would keep anything incriminating in her office, but looked anyway. Under an appointments calendar in the middle drawer she found two pieces of information. Evelyn Clifton's name and address was scribbled on one slip of paper.

She scowled at the other name with a 717 area code.

Jonelle punched in the Pennsylvania number. After several rings a female voice answered.

"I'd like to speak to Lorraine Watkins, please." Jonelle held her breath.

"She's not here. Try Maryland."

"I already did. No answer."

"Well, then. You wanna leave a message?"

"Yes, uh. Tell her it's about Tamora . . . and Lark," Jonelle said.

The silence on the other end stretched for several seconds. "Hello? You still there?"

"Who is this?"

"A friend."

Labored breathing followed by silence.

Whoever it was hung up.

Scribbled on the other slip of paper was a street address with a question mark but no city, followed by "Rental" and another question mark. What did they rent? Car? Apartment? Jonelle shoved the papers inside her bag.

A quick search of the metal cabinets behind the desk uncovered information on each tenant. The files were in alphabetical order, and since she hadn't thought to ask for Randy's last name, they weren't of any use. She slipped her hand all the way to the back of each set of folders. Behind the middle drawer of the last cabinet, her hand closed around a slim, square object. She pulled and out came an Ipad. "Well, well, well."

The desk phone rang.

Jonelle's hand flew to her chest. "Jesus, Mary, and Joseph."

She peered at the caller ID display. The call came from the same 717 number with the name Mary Burroughs.

Jonelle waited for the phone's answering service to click on. Instead of leaving a message, the caller hung up. She made a note of the name, tucked the computer under her shirt, and after opening the door a crack to make sure no one lurked close by, left the office.

Unable to wait until she got home, Jonelle sat in her Jeep and turned on the Ipad. The computer was password protected. On the third try she typed, "Playcat" and it worked. She poked around for several minutes until she found a file of photos. She clicked the icon.

In a sub file marked "test" were several shots of Tamora in various poses, both dressed and without clothes. Jonelle hurried through those. What adults did on their own time wasn't any of her business. Several other photos were of the same style as Tamora's but were of different women and a few men.

Jonelle sighed. Looking at naked people pictures made her want to take a long, hot bath. She continued scrolling through the photos but didn't come up with anything else.

She opened the email file, unsure of what she was looking for.

On the second page several items were marked FYI. She opened one from the previous week which read, "The customer wants to be sure that none of this gets traced back to him. NO SOCIAL MEDIA." Watkins had given her assurances.

Jonelle scrolled up, looking for more emails from this particular account. There were several. One included two words—"package received."

What package? And what did this have to do with Lark?

A sick feeling in her gut warned that someone—Watkins?— might want to take pictures of the child to sell. Since the file name was also the name of the studio, Playcat was probably used as a place to take the photos. While that made sense, Watkins couldn't risk anyone seeing kids going in and out of a crappy warehouse.

The idea forming in her mind was ripe for Adrienne's assistance, but she'd already gotten her friend in trouble. Who else?

Luther.

While he might dispute it, Jonelle considered him a friend. He never went into any detail about how he ended up living on the street, and she didn't care. The man was sharp as a tack, and she valued his insights. Slipping the Ipad in her shirt once more, she left the Jeep and, standing with her back next to a trash can, dumped the thing inside, not caring if Jelani found it or not.

She made a side trip to the grocery store and bought deli meats, cheese, bread, fruit, and a few bags of his favorite chocolate chip cookies. Even though he preferred something stronger to drink, she selected a few large bottles of fruit and vegetable juice. When he saw the drinks he'd make a face, but she also knew that whatever she brought he'd share with the others.

She parked her Jeep at the curb next to his building. A few of his gang were already easing though the gaping hole in the chain link fence on their way to settling in for the night. They smiled, waved, and yelled "Hiya, lady!"

"Back so soon?"

"Whatcha got?"

"Sandwich fixin's, fruit, and juice," she said.

A few groans at the mention of juice.

"Luther around?"

"Should be," answered a lady of undeterminate age. Jonelle had asked her name before, but she'd glowered and walked away. Too soon.

She struggled through the fence with the bags. No one offered to help, and she didn't ask. Primary on their agenda was grabbing their favorite spot. The LED camping lights illuminated the cavernous space.

"You need me to go back to that dirty movie place?"

Jonelle pivoted toward the sound of his voice.

Luther limped in her direction. "I'm gonna start callin' you Mama Jonelle if you don't stop buyin' food all the time." He held out his hands for the bags.

Although he'd never told her his age, she pegged him at somewhere over sixty, but not yet seventy.

"By the way, you know the cops is watchin' that place, right?"

She followed him over to the southeast corner where he opened the bags, took out one pack of deli turkey, a few hard rolls, apples, and a couple oranges and the cookies. He left the remaining items in the bags and called out, "Ladies first. And if I see somebody that ain't a woman, I'm gonna knock you upside the head. Got it?"

He indicated for Jonelle to sit on one of two plastic milk crates. He took the other.

"So. Whatcha want this time?"

Had it come to this? "Sorry if the only time you see me is when I want something, but—"

"They's all kinda relationships in this ole world. This is ours. It's what I call our business relationship. 'Sides, every time you come 'round you got bags of stuff." He patted his stomach. "Think I gained ten pounds since firs' time we met."

She took a deep breath. "The cops know I was at the studio, and they have a picture of my friend. They also have a photo of the manager of the apartment from where Lark was abducted."

Luther whistled. "You think they got the child stashed somewhere in that place? Don't her mama do the nasty in them films?"

"Yeah. Tamora's one of their main performers. They produce adult videos, and I suspect this group takes and probably distributes photos of little kids."

"With no clothes on?"

Jonelle nodded.

"Damn. Them kinda people don't need to be breathin' the same air as you and me. Whaddya want done?"

"I'm gonna need to get inside that studio again, but the cops already warned me off, and if I'm on any more surveillance images, they could pull my PI license."

Luther pulled out Lark's photo from his pant's pocket. "Plenty of naked people places around here. Don't have to be that particular one. Mostly the cops look the other way, or get themselves free DVDs, if you know what I mean."

"Vice thinks they're also dealing drugs."

"They know about them kiddie pictures?"

Jonelle didn't think so. Burt seemed genuinely surprised that one of the performers was the mother of the missing child. "Don't think so. I've got to figure out a way to get proof without telling them how I found out."

A chuckle rumbled from deep within Luther's chest. "You done somethin' illegal? Why do I get the feelin' that one 'a these days I'm gonna have to bail *you* out?"

He had her there.

"Why you wanna go back, anyway?"

"To find evidence that there's more going on inside that place besides doing drugs or filming adult videos. I think Tamora may have gotten herself in some kind of terrible mess that involves Lark. I've got a sick feeling that this may only be the beginning of something much worse."

He rubbed the stubble on his face. "You know, I bet Riley could help. The cops around here ain't seen her. Wouldn't recognize her, anyway, 'specially the way she looks now."

Jonelle waved her hands in a dismissive gesture before Luther finished.

"No. I can't get anyone else involved. I might not know exactly what I'm looking for inside that place, but I'll know when I see it. Besides, she'll only complicate things if she gets caught. So, thanks, but no thanks."

His next comment set her back.

"Why you think that just 'cause she lives here she don't know 'bout things? Truth is Riley was a cop before she hooked up with us."

"Cop? What happened?"

"Fell into drugs, stole some stuff from the police, and they kicked her out. Didn't give her no jail time on account of she paid them back and was damn good at the job before things got rough. Later, she hung out with a lotta crazy men, which led to sellin' herself to get by. She's stayed clean as long as she's been here 'cause we don't allow no hard core druggies."

Jonelle lowered her voice to a whisper. "If she's getting herself together, why's she still here? No offense."

He snorted. "She likes the company. You wanna see if she can help or not?"

In spite of herself, the idea intrigued her. "Sure. I'd like to meet her."

The same woman who'd answered Jonelle earlier, walked beside Luther up to where she sat perched on the milk crate.

"Luther says you're lookin' for somebody to help with some kinda porno film actress," Riley said, her eyes flitting from Luther to Jonelle.

Now that the idea of getting into the studio was taking shape, she was having second thoughts. "They're probably still surveilling that place, so I've gotta think of some other way to get the information I want. Thanks anyway, Riley."

"Listen, if it weren't for the fact Luther says there might be kids involved, I'd tell you to screw off."

Jonelle gasped at the woman's abrupt attitude.

Luther laughed.

Riley turned to go.

"Hold on a minute," Jonelle said. "I'm not rejecting the offer of help for any reason other than I don't want to get you in trouble. How would you explain why you're in there if you got caught?"

Riley glanced at Luther, who nodded slightly.

"Them places need cleaners, don't they? And I'm guessin' they use individuals rather than a regular cleaning service. So, you get me some rags and some cleaning supplies, and we'll see what I can do."

"As a matter of fact they have a regular person. I've seen photos of her."

"She look anything like me?"

"Nope. But maybe if you wear some kinda scarf on your head. Might work."

"Or you can tell them whatshername is sick and I'm her replacement."

The kernel of an idea popped in her head. "Or, how about this? The date and time stamp was on the photo. There's really only one way in and out of that street. We'll park at the head of the street, about a half hour before the cleaning lady's scheduled to start. I'll approach her and say . . . something like you're gonna help out temporarily. To get the place ready for a special shoot or something."

Riley wrinkled her nose but kept her mouth shut.

They tossed around several more ideas, but none were any better than the first.

"Let's try this. You and I will sit at the end of the block in my Jeep. I'll pick you up here at eight tomorrow morning and—"

"—Make it eight thirty."

"Um. Okay. Eight thirty. We head out to the studio and wait until ten or so. If nobody shows, I'll see if I can figure some other way to get you inside. We might have to go back another day, but I'd hate to waste much time."

"Lady, I know how to get inside. What I wanna be sure of is what you want me to do once I'm in there."

Jonelle bit her tongue. Riley's abrasiveness grated on her nerves. "I'm looking for photos of children, especially this one." Jonelle took the flier from Luther and gave it to Riley.

The woman studied it closely and returned it to Luther.

"Also, I think someone is hiding the child somewhere, and if you see signs of people living there—"

"—Didn't you notice that before?"

Jonelle's tongue was in danger of turning bloody. "I haven't been inside," she said through gritted teeth. "My focus at first was the mother. Now I'm looking at the apartment manager, along with two or three other people. At this point I need something to hold the manager's feet to the fire. If I can find proof she's involved, she might tip her hand and lead me to Lark. Right now I don't want the cops to raid the place and scare everybody off."

At roughly the same height and weight, one black, the other white, the two women sized up each other. Luther hadn't said a word. His head twisted from one to the other, a crooked grin on his face.

"Well," he said, slapping his hands together. "Much as I like watchin' this program the two of you got goin', I'm gettin' hungry."

Without another word, Riley turned her back on Jonelle and left.

"What's with her?" She'd come across people like that and thought she knew the answer.

"Nothin'. She's different is all—same as the rest of us. Once you take the time to learn who she is, ain't no big deal."

Jonelle didn't have a lot of time. She stared in the direction where Riley had gone. "I don't know, Luther. What if I get here and she's changed her mind?"

"Then I guess you'll have to think of somethin' else."

CHAPTER 35

J onelle arrived at the warehouse a minute before the agreed upon time. Before she had a chance to turn off the Jeep's engine, Riley slid through the opening in the chain link fence, and climbed into the passenger seat without comment . . . or invitation.

Not one for chit-chat herself in the mornings, Jonelle nodded a greeting to Riley who returned the gesture. All the way over to the studio, Jonelle thought of starting a conversation, but judging from the woman's expression, changed her mind. Let her make the first move, she thought, and immediately felt guilty for her juvenile attitude. After all, Riley was doing her a favor.

"What're you starin' into space for?" Riley asked, pulling Jonelle back into the here and now.

"Thinking about something I have to do later. Here's the street. I'm gonna pull behind that large dumpster." The dashboard clock read a little after nine.

"Here's a burner phone I got. If things get hairy, gimme a call. I already programmed the number." She got out and went around the back of the Jeep.

"Hey. Where you goin'?"

"Gotta find some way to get the cleaning lady to stop here." Jonelle removed a bucket of cleaning supplies from the back and placed it on the ground. Next, she withdrew two orange cones. "These should slow her enough for me to run up and talk to her about how you're here to help."

"Got a better idea. You give her some cash to stay out all together, and I'll get inside and do my own thing."

Jonelle sighed. The urge to tell off this irritating woman was so strong it made her teeth hurt. Instead of letting loose, she carried a cone in each hand and stomped to the front of the Jeep. A few steps before rounding the trash container to set up her mini roadblock, a silver SUV roared from the opposite direction and flew down the street.

"Who the hell's that?"

Jonelle jumped. She hadn't heard Riley walk up.

"Unless someone else drives the same car, that's the apartment manager, Lorraine Watkins."

"So, what do we do now, Sherlock?"

Jonelle turned and faced Riley. "You know what? Not gonna be any 'we.' I'm taking your sorry ass back to the warehouse. I'll figure out something else on my own." She stomped back to the car.

Riley didn't move from her position near the Jeep's front bumper.

She flung the cones in the back.

Riley stood by the road, staring into the distance.

Now what? Although she'd rather leave the woman standing there, she didn't want to upset Luther. After counting slowly to twenty, she went and stood next to her.

"The driver went inside. Alone, from what I can see," Riley said, pushing dirty blond hair from her forehead. "Look, uh, Jonelle is it? I ain't good at bein' nice. You want help findin' that little girl, I'm in. But don't expect sweetness an' light 'cause that ain't me. Got it?"

"Fine. Now let me tell you a little about me. I can take a lot of abuse as long as it's not disrespectful. And I like being in charge. Oh, I'll listen to suggestions. But don't for one minute think I'll give up control, 'cause that ain't *me*. Got it?"

A sideways peek at the slight upturned corner of Riley's mouth and a quick glance at the woman's beady blue eyes told Jonelle the two understood each other. "Okay. Let's start over. For some reason Watkins seems in a hurry. No idea what's so important."

"You think maybe the kid's in there and she got spooked by you nosing around and came back to move her somewheres else?"

"Could be. If the kid's in there, that's a whole new can of worms."

When Adrienne went inside, she'd focused on the office area. Not the storage areas, studios, nor any possible open spaces in the back. Playcat used as a hiding place? Maybe.

A loud muffler signaled the arrival of a green sedan. The loud rumbling was accompanied by exhaust and the caustic smell of burning oil. The sedan slowed to a stop before rounding the corner where Jonelle and Riley stood.

Jonelle's "helper" strutted over to the driver's side window.

"Hey. Didn't you get the message?" Riley demanded.

Dammit. There she goes again, Jonelle thought.

She elbowed Riley away and held the wide, doe eyes of a brown-skinned woman sitting behind the steering wheel. Two rosaries, one black and one white, dangled from the rear view mirror.

"Sorry about that." Jonelle's eyes demanded Riley keep her mouth shut. "We're not here to keep you from doing your job. Only . . . well, the guys inside have a big production planned and need an extra special clean-up job. And, so here we are. No worries, though. It's only for today."

Riley snickered.

In a firm voice Jonelle said to Riley, "Why don't you go get your cleaning stuff? And bring me my purse . . . please."

With smirk still planted on her narrow face, Riley gave a mock salute and headed to Jonelle's Jeep.

Jonelle turned back to the woman. "Sorry about the confusion," she said. "Guess nobody told you we're here to help out. So, how about this? I'll pay you for your inconvenience if you'll let my friend go with you to the studio in your car 'cause, uh, I've gotta take my Jeep to another appointment."

"So how she get back home? Once I'm done I gotta go to my next place. No way I got time to take her to . . . wherever."

"Don't worry about it, I'll pick her up. So, how long does it take for you to do that whole place by yourself?"

The woman shrugged. "Couple hours. Only gotta clean office and studios."

"See, that's why we're here. To clean the rest of it."

Another shrug. "Whatever."

Riley returned with the bucket of cleaning supplies and Jonelle's bag. She set the bucket down next to the car.

Jonelle dug inside, pulled out a twenty, and handed the money to the woman who stuffed the bill in her pocket without comment.

"Now what?" Riley raised her eyebrows at Jonelle.

"Be right back." She gave the woman her best conciliatory smile and motioned Riley away from the sedan. The thought of sending someone she now considered two bottles short of a six-pack into an unknown situation filled Jonelle with a sense of unease. This was wrong, yet the only way to get inside the studio without alarm bells going off was to send someone that Watkins—and vice—didn't know.

"Are we gonna do this or what?" Riley crossed her arms in front of her ample chest.

"Maybe using you isn't such a good idea. I'll think of something else." She indicated for Riley to hand her the cleaning supplies.

"Oh no you don't. I've been lookin' forward to this since last night. Listen. If I didn't wanna be here you'd be over there standin' next to that wreck of a car by yourself. But here I am, so let's get this party started."

After a slight hesitation, Jonelle plastered a smile on her face, ambled back to the car, and indicated for Riley to get in the passenger seat. She passed the cleaning materials through the window to Riley.

"Here's what we'll do, ladies." She hurried on, not wanting Riley to say anything else. She addressed the cleaning lady. "If you don't mind, please give . . . Susie—"

"Susie? I look like a Susie?"

"—a quick review of what you do and she can clean the rest of the area."

Normally Jonelle would ask the name of whomever she was dealing with, but in this case, the less she knew the better. If the cops questioned her about the cleaner, she could honestly say she didn't know the name.

"Aye, aye, captain," Riley said.

Ignoring Riley's drone was getting easier, so Jonelle addressed the cleaning woman. "I think there might be a light-skinned black lady inside who may question why there's somebody with you, so you can tell her she's your assistant for today, okay?"

"I know the lady you mean. I seen her before. She don't look at me, so I don't gotta say nothin'."

"How many other people, besides the, um, actors are inside this time of day?"

"Depends. If they're filmin', two guys. One guy on camera, the other guy tellin' the naked people what to do."

Riley giggled. "This could be a perk. How many naked people we talkin' about here?"

"Two. Sometimes three. I don't look too much." She crossed herself.

"C'mon. Let's go and get 'er done," Riley said, between fits of laughter.

The green sedan coughed and sputtered down the street. Jonelle's eyes followed as the car parked next to the curb, behind the silver SUV.

CHAPTER 36

*W*hat's with the damn crying all of a sudden? Fed her all her favorites. She left most of the food on the paper plate and she's still upset.

Got a headache last night. Haven't had one this bad in a long time. Left my pills behind since I had to leave in a hurry. Tried reasoning with her at first. She acted like all of a sudden I was speakin' some kinda foreign language. Every time I told her to shut up she cried louder. Could be going out on my own wasn't such a good idea. Except . . .

Maybe I can use all this crying. Took some pictures. Whoever invented this digital stuff had the right idea. Don't need to worry about going into the drugstore to buy film—or get anything developed and call attention to myself.

Told her I was gonna send everything to her mama to show her what a good little girl she was. She got quiet for a little while after that. But she started up again.

To keep everything on the up and up, I send a text saying everything's fine and that I'm still followin' the plan to keep movin' around.

I know everybody's pissed off they can't find me. Correction: Can't find us. Ignored all the texts demanding my location. Told them it's safer this way.

Maybe I should get one of them burner phone thingys.

What a hoot. Feels like I've been liberated. If they only knew my plans.

Decided from now on she's gonna have to beg for anything butterfly related. That includes games, puzzles, toys.

If she starts whining I know of a way to stop her and not spoil the merchandise.

CHAPTER 37

That detective lady oughta have a tougher spine if she's gonna make it in the business, Riley thought. Her cleaning companion hadn't said a word since they drove off, but that didn't surprise her. Most people gave Riley a wide berth. Probably had something to do with the do-it-yourself whack job of a haircut and the fact that she smelled as though regular baths were a thing of the past—which they were.

And that she talked to herself on a regular basis. Luther had tried getting her to stop by saying if she didn't folks might think she was crazy. Fact was that's exactly what she wanted. People tended to leave a person alone that way.

Both women left the sedan at the same time. Riley pulled out a cigarette, but before lighting it the cleaning woman said, "No. No smoke."

"Fine." She put the unlit cigarette back in her pocket. "Let's rock an' roll."

Without another word, the cleaning woman knocked on a door painted a high gloss black. A small peephole was centered high in the middle. No number and no sign afforded the place the desired anonymity.

"Hiya," Riley said to the skinny white guy who opened the door.

Instead of acknowledging her greeting, he looked at the cleaning woman.

"She help out today," the woman said.

"Yeah. She's showin' me the ropes so I can fill in . . . in case she gets sick or somethin'. You okay with that?"

The cleaning woman scowled. Riley's expression warned her to keep quiet.

Before he could answer, a voice from the back shouted, "Who is it?"

"Cleaning lady, er, ladies," he replied, stepping aside to let the two enter. "Since there's two of you, this shouldn't take long, right? We've got an extra shoot to do."

"No problemo," Riley said brightly.

The other woman snorted her reply.

Once he disappeared around the back, the cleaning woman motioned for Riley to follow.

"Hold on a sec." Riley reached out and, with thumb and forefinger, rubbed a few of the robes which hung on a long clothes rack in the narrow hallway to the right of the small entranceway. Most were made of cotton, but there were also a fair amount made of a glossy satin material. Some of the robes were long, some short, and all of different colors.

"We don't do laundry," the cleaning woman said.

A vending machine with an "out of order" sign sat against the wall next to the robes.

The woman led Riley back in the direction the man had disappeared. She entered a large, windowless room. Five armless chairs sat against one wall. The cleaning woman took out a dust cloth and motioned for Riley to do the same.

"Dust everything but don't bother equipment," she said.

Riley had no intention of touching the cameras, and she couldn't reach the overhead lights. She pointed to a wooden table with two metal folding chairs.

"Do I polish that table?" Riley asked.

"No. Only wipe off. We gotta scrub floor. Get water from large sink around here."

She followed the woman into another large room. This one contained a slightly antiseptic smell, like a doctor's office. Riley pressed up and down on the soft, malleable floor with her trainers. The squishy floor grossed her out a little. She wondered if the reason the floor was spongy was because if passions took hold and somebody fell, they wouldn't hurt themselves. She giggled at the thought of bodies bouncing on the floor.

With water bucket filled, Riley grabbed a large sponge, squirted some liquid cleaning solvent on top, and waited for a clue as to what to do next. The cleaning woman began scrubbing around cabinets, tables, and chairs.

Riley followed suit.

Once every available surface was wiped off, the cleaning lady prepared to leave the room.

"Hold on. What do you do with all those bottles, tubes, and stuff piled up on that cabinet over there?"

"Nothin'. Don't touch. I'll get in trouble."

Fine. Maybe I won't touch, but there's so many I wonder if they'd miss a few, she thought. Riley peered at the labels. "Eww. No way do I want any of that stuff." Multiple tubes of lubricants and jellies sat alongside boxes of baby wipes.

"C'mon," the cleaner said. "Only make sure floor cleaned off in here. In next room don't touch the cage. Only dust off."

Cage?

"Make sure leather stuff wiped down real good. Use this." She handed Riley a large spray bottle of saddle soap.

"Um. What kinda leather stuff we talkin' about here? Saddles?" Where the hell would they keep horses, then she figured these people probably rode something else.

"You'll see. Follow me." Around the corner a small door opened onto an even larger room. Various leather collars and whips, plus different lengths of chains hung on hooks covering one entire wall. Above that hung a metal cage suspended from the ceiling and held in place by a system of pulleys. She whistled softly. On the surface of a square table several screwdrivers and pliers were arranged by size.

"What do I do with that stuff?" Riley asked.

"Wipe off leather with soap. Then use this stuff." She handed Riley a bottle of Huberd's leather conditioner. "Don't touch chains."

"No need to worry about that."

"Leather most important. Next important are the two beds in next room. They change linen and take to laundry. You don't do that. Only wipe down bed frame real good and mop floor extra good. If anything broken, they'll let you know how to replace. Got it?"

Riley got it all right. During the little tour she didn't see signs of anything other than a few guys fiddling with the lights and cameras.

Except for that room with the cage suspended from the ceiling and the leather and whips and chains. She noticed another door near the back but hadn't said anything. Time for another look.

"Okay. How about I go back and clean off that leather stuff hanging from those hooks? Some of it looked grungy to me."

"Only do that twice a month. Not time yet. Next week."

"Well, I'm here now. So . . ."

The cleaner had already begun mopping the floor around the bedroom. She waved Riley away in a "do whatever you want" motion.

Riley grabbed the bottles of saddle soap, conditioner and a cloth and hurried next door. She looked both ways and, seeing no one, headed for the door in the back.

She turned the knob. Locked.

In the large pocket of her cotton smock her hand closed around the Swiss Army knife—her most prized possession. The best thing she ever stole. She selected the metal file and small screwdriver. Within a few seconds the flimsy lock gave way, and she found herself staring into a darkened room. Her hand found the light switch.

A weak, overhead bulb illuminated tables, chairs. Wooden bed frames leaned haphazardly against two of the four walls, alongside several mattresses not even she would lie on. Large cardboard boxes of trash bags, condoms, lubricants, and paper towels were stacked on the floor. Along the wall opposite the door wooden pallets, stacked one on top of the other, almost reached the ceiling.

Except. Riley squinted. The wall didn't lie flush against the ceiling. A thin sliver of light filled the break. She pushed against the wall and it gave a little under her fingers. "Huh," she murmured, "wonder what's back there?"

Riley probed the entire partition but couldn't find a way inside. She kicked it with her foot when she couldn't get behind the false wall and almost kicked it again until she remembered why she was there. Mumbling to herself, Riley wiped the knob on both sides of the door she'd entered and moved on to the next closed door.

Disappointed to discover what amounted to a regular break-room complete with table, chairs, and microwave—plus the smell of rancid, burnt popcorn—Riley concluded that detective was even more clueless to what was going on in that place than she originally thought. She turned to leave when raised voices caught her attention.

Instead of heading toward the main studio, Riley headed in the direction of the noise. She followed a dark, narrow hallway down to an open door on the left.

"Look. Like I said before we don't do that kinda thing. I could do serious jail time, so no way. Go somewhere else," said a male voice.

A female voice responded. "And what I'm saying is we need more space. All I want is use of the studio. Hell, you don't even need to be here. A few props, some lights. I've got my own photographer."

Riley was tempted to peek around the corner but held back.

"I don't want you touchin' my equipment."

"I'm not gonna use your precious equipment. We're not doing video, only stills. I've already explained that. You don't wanna get involved, fine. This is a business deal. Your cut for use of the studio is thirty percent. How about it?"

A pause stretched for so long Riley wondered if the two used a different exit to move to another room. She inched closer, intent on peeking inside when the man said, "That don't sound like enough to me. You're gonna need props so you gotta pay extra for those." Riley pulled back.

The tone in the woman's voice shifted. More confident now, less pleading. "I know that. And you need to pay more for Tamora. I know she's one of your most popular stars, so we're gonna need to renegotiate her contract. Make sure me and her aren't getting screwed." The woman laughed.

"Hey. Whatya doin'?" The cleaner stood behind Riley. "We don't go in there if there's people."

The voices inside stopped.

Riley pushed the woman aside and ran down the hall and into the main studio. She didn't care if the cleaning lady followed or not. She snatched a sponge from the cleaning bucket, dabbed some soap on it, and scrubbed the slatted headboard on the bed positioned in the middle of the floor.

"I already done that," the cleaning woman said. Through narrowed eyes she added, "I told you no going inside office. Why you there and not cleaning the back?"

"I cleaned back there already. Didn't I tell you I was quick? If not, my bad. You can call me Speedy Gonzalez if you want."

"You don't look like a Gonzalez to me. I almost got in trouble when they see me there. Had to explain what I was doin'. Told them about you helpin' an' they wanna meet you. Now."

Shit. Riley forced herself to put on what she considered her best subservient look. Someone who didn't know her would assume she was having a bad case of indigestion. She trudged down the hall, head down, shuffling her feet. She knocked on the door frame.

"You wanted to see me?"

The large black woman—Mrs. Watkins, according to the PI's description—stood next to a dilapidated metal desk, the surface overrun with paper and photos. What few bare surfaces showed through, were covered with brown stains.

A skinny white man—the same one who let her in—sat in a wooden chair, picking at some scabs on his face.

In her previous life, Riley was trained to observe people. Their mannerisms and nonverbal ticks often revealed more than their words. Although years had passed since she'd last worn a uniform and seen the other side of a police station, her mind had cleared sufficiently since she'd hooked up with Luther and rid her system of the hillbilly heroin that threatened to destroy her. What she saw before her was a guy who didn't give a damn about anything except how to keep the money coming in so that the drugs could keep flowing.

The black lady was something else altogether. Gotta stay alert around that one.

"Who are you?" Watkins demanded.

"I'm helping the regular cleaning lady. In case she gets sick or goes on vacation or something."

"That's not what I asked. What's your name? Where do you come from?"

Riley snorted. "I come from the streets, lady. Before that, my mama's womb. Even folks like me need money to live. Can't always depend on handouts, especially when most people try like hell to pretend I don't exist."

"Don't sound to me like we can trust you to show up when needed, then." The man glanced over at Watkins to see if she agreed.

Watkins ignored him. Laser focused on Riley, she leaned in and studied the woman so closely that had she not been a good cop in the past, Riley would've betrayed her nervousness. As it was, she matched Watkins' stare.

"Homeless, huh?" Watkins walked a tight circle around Riley. "You sure do look like it. Only problem is, you seem a helluva lot more interested in what's going on in here than doing your job. You wanna explain that?"

"Look, lady, keep your drawers on. I heard voices, okay. I only wanted to ask if you knew how much I'm gonna get paid since, uh, nobody told me that part."

"So why'd you run off?"

"Got scared when I got yelled at. Didn't wanna get her in no trouble, either."

The guy who'd been following the exchange with half-closed eyes, addressed Watkins. "We done here? She seems okay to me and since you seem to forget, lemme me remind you. I run this place. She wanna clean it, I got no problem."

Watkins indicated the door. "Go on and finish what you gotta do."

Riley was almost tempted to make a snarky remark until she saw the sneer on Watkins' face. Her head pounded out a mantra—keep it cool, keep it cool. Don't blow it.

Heading back the way she came, she nearly missed a corridor only big enough for one person to slip through. A quick turn of the head proved no one was looking. She slipped through.

Black walls and floor gave her the impression of being in a tunnel. One bare lightbulb hung in the middle and only illuminated a few feet on either side. The darkness didn't bother her. Fact was the less light the better. Comfort came at night.

Much to Luther's chagrin, Riley preferred to wander around after the rest of the community was tucked in for the evening. There were fewer mind creatures at night. Fewer creepy-crawlies traveling up and down her arms. Fewer people who stared when she screamed.

And now, for the first time in a long time, she had a purpose. Riley chuckled. If she was Jonelle she'd have kicked her own ass to the curb for all the attitude. Now she understood why Luther let that detective lady into their lair.

Riley stopped on the far side of the light. A dead end.

Or not. A flaw on the right side of the wall high up in the corner caught her attention. She placed her hand against the surface and followed a narrow seam up, over, and down. Another false wall.

Riley smiled and grasped the Swiss Army knife. Many times when money got low she thought about pawning it and had even walked into several establishments—and immediately backed out again. That decision had saved her life on several occasions.

She pulled out the small blade, inserted it in the crack, and pulled. Nothing happened. There must be some way inside, otherwise why not seal the whole thing? Several tries using the large blade, bottle opener, and scissors yielded the same result.

Sweat poured down Riley's face as she inserted the nail file. A voice called out. She yanked the tool from the wall and the seam gave way, allowing enough space for her to insert the tips of her fingers and pull. A space as wide as her shoulders opened.

The voice grew louder.

Riley slipped into darkness.

CHAPTER 38

Thirty minutes after Riley and the cleaning woman entered the studio, Jonelle received a call from Adrienne. Damn.

"Don't be mad. I didn't know about the surveillance. Burt's gonna help me straighten everything out. We're gonna make sure you don't get in trouble at work. Promise."

"And hello to you, too," Adrienne said.

Jonelle relaxed a little. Her friend's voice held its usual sarcasm. If Adrienne were truly pissed, she would've said a lot more than hello.

"I promise never, ever, to get you involved in anything like this again."

A slight pause. "I don't remember you twisting my arm. If I said I wasn't nervous about a phone call from a cop not named Burt, I'd be lying. You could've given me a heads-up, though."

Jonelle flinched. So much was happening so fast. "You're right. I totally forgot when the kids called and said someone thought they'd seen Lark and—"

"They found her?"

"Not yet. I'll fill you in on everything when I see you. But, um, I've gotta hang near the studio because I've got Riley in there poking around. To see if that place can serve as a hideout. Plus, I saw Watkins drive up. She's inside, so I'm hoping Riley can get a bead on what Watkins is up to."

"Who the hell is Riley? Girlfriend, you got some serious explainin' to do."

"I will. But I can't leave now. I've gotta stick around and find out what Riley discovered and then drive her back to . . . well, I don't know really. Wherever she wants to go."

"Been a busy little do-bee, haven't you?"

"I gotta keep my eyes on the prize, as it were. Time's something this kid doesn't have." Jonelle sat in the driver's seat of her Jeep and, with her arm across the steering wheel, put her head in her hand.

"You still there?" Adrienne asked.

"Yeah."

"How much longer you gonna stay at that studio?"

"Until Riley comes back or the shit hits the fan," Jonelle said.

"You parked out front or somewhere else?"

"Down the block. Right before you turn onto that side street. Why?"

"We need to talk. In person. I can be there in, what, twenty minutes I think."

Jonelle was shaking her head before Adrienne finished. "Oh no. No way. You are so out of this, it's not funny. Stay away. I'm serious."

"Yeah. Me too. See you in twenty."

Jonelle paced back and forth. She squinted at the watch on her arm, aware that the practice of wearing one was obsolete these days given that everyone carried a cellphone, yet she couldn't give it up. Almost an hour had elapsed since Riley entered the studio. If Riley wasn't out in another half hour, or if Watkins' car hadn't left, she'd find another way inside.

A familiar gray sedan approached and parked behind the Jeep. Adrienne emerged from behind the wheel and met Jonelle on the corner. "You walking back and forth like that might give some dude the idea you're looking for work," Adrienne said.

"At least there's no competition," Jonelle shot back. "Believe I asked you not to come."

"Since when do I pay much attention to your demands?"

"Since I got your face splashed in photos that are in police possession," Jonelle said. In a softer voice she added. "You've no idea how crappy I feel about that. Whatever I need to do or say to . . . whomever, I'll do and say it to get you out of this mess."

"Not in a mess. Your Burt did a helluva lot to prove my innocence, so when I talked to some detective with Baltimore vice, all I had to do was reiterate how everything was your fault." Adrienne giggled.

Jonelle tried to hide the relief in her voice. "'Your' Burt? What the hell's that mean?"

"It means you owe him more than a mere thank-you, if you catch my drift."

"You're right. I'll take him to dinner, or something."

"Pretty sure the guy would prefer the 'something.'"

Jonelle waved the comment away. "Can't deal with that now." She headed to the corner where she could see the front of the studio.

Adrienne matched her stride. "How can you see anything from here?"

Jonelle wiped sweat from her brow. "I can tell if someone goes in or out. That's all I'm concerned about right now. If Riley doesn't come out in another half hour, I've got to figure out a way inside without becoming the next feature event on *ID Investigation Discovery* TV. Speaking of which, I've been thinking about how they managed to set up the cameras."

"What do you mean?"

"Playcat probably has their own surveillance, so I'm guessin' the cops must've set up theirs nearby, probably next door. Problem for them is they don't have anything past the entrance because there were no shots of you beyond the outer door."

"True. Wondered about that. But what if they didn't show you everything?"

"Burt would've said something."

Adrienne lifted an eyebrow. "Interesting. So. They don't care about the naked stuff. They wanna know who's going in and out because it might tell them about the drugs."

"Right," Jonelle agreed. "Plus, they know about Watkins. While their focus is drugs, I don't think that's the reason she's in there now."

Adrienne stopped short. "Sounds like it's getting crowded in there."

"And it might get even more so," Jonelle said. "Fire department requires all commercial buildings have two exits, so there's another way inside there."

"Probably in the back," Adrienne said.

"I went around there when you went inside the other night. Luther going through the trash distracted me from searching around, plus it was hard to see. Gotta find out what's back there. You stay here," Jonelle said.

For once Adrienne didn't insist on accompanying Jonelle. That whole surveillance thing with her face splashed everywhere must have scared her best friend more than she was willing to admit.

Somewhere in the distance, the sound of a CSX train rumbled. Before searching the back, Jonelle studied the front of the building. While she hadn't seen anyone else go in or out of any of the other doors, the long concrete building contained several windows on the main level covered with mesh, and long narrow windows above. All indications pointed to the fact that the structure housed businesses other than Playcat.

Parked at the curb on the end closest to the entrance of the dead end street was a white delivery van, rear doors facing her. She couldn't tell if there was writing on the side or not.

"What're you gonna do when you get around the back?" Adrienne asked.

"Not sure. You got your phone?"

Adrienne nodded.

"If I get into trouble, I'm gonna call nine-one-one first. You'll be my second call." After pausing to glance once more at the front, she left Adrienne and started to cross the street.

"Just so you call somebody. Hey!"

Jonelle stopped.

"Let's synchronize the time. If you're not back in an hour, I'm callin' . . . somebody. Even if it's only Burt." Adrienne's brow furrowed.

Jonelle took advantage of her friend's anxiety. "Stick around and keep watch on the vehicles. If anybody gets too close, pull out your pepper spray and call for help."

"You sure you don't want me coming with you?"

"I think you'd be more help here." Jonelle patted the holstered gun secured around the waistband of her cotton capri pants and covered with the tunic top she wore.

"Makes me nervous when you take that gun," Adrienne said.

"It'll make me more nervous if I don't," Jonelle replied.

Jonelle inspected the front once more and hurried to the back. While she hadn't seen any movement in front, that didn't mean the occupants weren't there.

The belabored rumble of another CSX train thundered in the distance. Her rubber-soled shoes crunched along as she skirted broken bottles and crushed cans. Up ahead, next to a large trash container stood a blue recycling bin. She grabbed a handful of the cans and dumped them inside.

"Help you, Miss?" The deep voice startled her. She turned and faced a black man holding a large plastic garbage bag.

"Didn't see any sense in these lying on the ground when there's a perfectly good recycling bin sitting right there."

"You do that a lot, do you? Go around picking up other people's trash?"

"Only when necessary." He didn't smile at the remark, so she'd best get on with it. "Actually, I'm a PI and a client of mine, works in, um, well, she's an actress. I'm helping her out on a case that involves the film studio a few doors down."

He inclined his head. "So how come you're back here?"

"Research." Even though technically she was on his turf, his questions were getting on her nerves.

After a few more seconds studying her without comment, he broke into a grin, threw his head back, and laughed. He strolled over to the green trash bin and flung his bag inside, throwing up rotten smells of wasted food and used up debris.

"Don't mean to trespass," she said, attempting to gain control of the situation, "but I couldn't figure out any other way to get to the back of this place. What do you know about that adult film studio—Playcat, I think it's called?"

"Not much. Guy who owns it's named Jasper. Only conversation we had is an agreement that we keep the gang bangers from hangin' out. You let 'em loiter, and they're like leeches. They grab hold, suck you dry. As long as those folks keep their business inside, I don't bother them. They do their thing and I do mine. So far it's working out."

"What is it you do?"

"I own a barbershop slash beauty supply house. We cater to most of the shops around the city by providing most of what they need, from equipment to shampoo, creams, lotions, whatever. Except stuff for manicures and pedicures. Don't get into that."

Sweat rolled down her face. "Mind if we stand over there under the shade?"

"This gonna be a long conversation?"

Instead of answering, Jonelle walked to the overhang between his store and the one next to it with boarded up windows.

She waited for him to catch up. "All I'm interested in is what you know about the studio. Especially the guy who runs it and whether or not you've noticed a silver SUV coming and going."

"You wanna know a helluva lot."

"I'm a PI. It's what I do."

Jonelle's phone chimed with a text from Rainey insisting she call the office. She turned off the phone without responding. She thought about asking the guy his name then decided against it. Best keep the whole thing loose and informal. "So what about the guy and the car? Anything?"

"Don't know Jasper's last name. Only speaks when you speak first. Keeps to himself, though he does spread fliers around when he's got a new, uh, film coming out."

"What do you know about one of his most popular actresses? Her name's Tamora."

"Actress?" He snorted with derision. "You call what they do acting? Besides, Jasper did say once they're referred to as models. As if that makes it all right."

He stared off in the distance as if trying to put together the name with a face. "Think I know who you mean. Pretty, got bazoomkas out to here. Skinny waist. She don't speak, either, but I caught her smiling at me a couple times. Don't want the kinda grief her kind would cause, and, besides, my wife would kill me . . . and her, too."

Her kind? Jonelle studied him a little more closely. While he didn't give up a lot, she got the impression he didn't miss much, either. "She has a little girl, and the little girl has been abducted. I'm trying to find out everything I can about what could've happened."

He whistled softly. "She got somethin' to do with that?"

"I don't know. Hope not. The only way I'll be satisfied is if I exhaust all possibilities. Where do you suppose the back of the studio is?"

"Down here. Easier if I show you. C'mon."

Jonelle followed the broad-shouldered back about three-fourths of the way down. Considering that half of the spaces were boarded up, she was surprised the area was relatively clean. "Who else has a business here?"

He turned his head slightly. "There's also Cho who sells dry cleaner supplies, and Monty's got a wholesale button company."

"Buttons?"

"Yep. They gotta come from somewhere."

He stopped and pointed to a recessed door. "That's the place. Don't think you're gonna get inside without a key, though, 'cause like my place, and everybody else's, the back's always locked. The front's on a security system, and you gotta be buzzed in. Or have a key. But I suppose you already know that."

He turned to go.

"Wait a sec. What about the car?"

"Oh yeah. Been seein' that a lot more lately. Snooty bitch . . . uh, sorry. She ain't too friendly which is okay by me."

"Is she always by herself?"

"Seen her sometimes with an average-looking dude and a raggedy-looking light-skinned guy. They don't speak, neither."

For some reason, Jonelle didn't want him to leave, but there was nothing else, except . . .

"Before you go. I'm curious about something. Do you own or rent your space?"

He cocked his head, a slight smile playing on his face. "Rent. And because we're, according to the state, reclaiming the area for commerce, the city gives us a huge tax break. As long as Playcat keeps their nose clean and don't get into anything too hinky, everything's okay. We all look after each other. If you're interested in learning more, you know how to find me." With that, he gave a mock salute and left her standing there.

She needed to find a way to get inside without anyone seeing. Her eyes wandered all around the structure. A small security camera was aimed high above the door.

"Damn." Did it belong to Playcat or the cops? Was it real or for show? Too late to worry about that now. She hoped the thing was fake and only used as a deterrent or at least no one was staring at a monitor with her face splashed across the screen.

She patted the phone clipped to her pocket, slightly guilty she'd turned it off. She turned it back on and checked the screen. Messages from Rainey and the kids would have to wait. She skirted the door and stood next to the first mesh window. Even as tall as she was and standing on tip-toe, she couldn't reach the window. Someone had placed several plastic buckets next to the trash bin. She walked over and picked the largest one that could hold her weight.

That done, she stood on top and, shielding her eyes, tried to look inside. Nothing but black. They'd painted the windows, which made sense considering the business. Angry at wasting so much time, Jonelle considered leaving the bucket where it was. Instead, she hauled her makeshift stand over to the other window and got the same result except for a round spot which looked as though someone had scratched off the paint.

Jonelle squinted through the hole.

A pair of eyes stared back.

CHAPTER 39

*G*ot me one of them throw-away phones. Had to take her in the store with me to get it. A few nosey busy-bodies commented about how cute she was, but most didn't pay us any attention. Bought her a bag of chips. She wanted a butterfly coloring book but they didn't have any so she chose a brown-and-white stuffed puppy.

She's been quiet for a while, but it's hard to go in and out when I need to check mail. Everybody's so busy chasing their tails, going here and there. I'm done with that. Been thinking about hiding somewhere that nobody'd think to look for us. Problem is how to sneak in without anybody seeing?

Need a good lie. Or maybe not. The mother ain't too bright. Sometimes I think the contact's feeding her drugs in order to keep her quiet and agreeable. I hinted my suspicions in my text yesterday. Only response was to keep my ideas to myself.

One person sent me a personal text agreeing with what I said. Big surprise.

Claims he knows some stuff nobody else knows. Alls I do is wave a couple bills in front of the guy's nose and he tells me what I wanna know about the drugs. He don't care what happens to who, when.

That PI hasn't been around in a while. Wonder what that's about?

CHAPTER 40

D ark eyes stared back at Riley. She ducked. One hand flew to her mouth to squelch the scream threatening to explode from within. Was the vision real or . . . ? Once she caught her breath, she rose slowly and brought her eyes back to the hole. The other eyes were gone—if they were there in the first place.

Riley took out her knife and, going as fast as her shaking fingers allowed, chipped away at more of the paint to get a better look. She didn't plan on sticking around for someone to complain about what she'd done. All she saw was bright sunshine, blue sky, dark green trash bin. She scraped away more paint and . . . brown hands gripped the mesh on the window.

Fascinated, Riley's eyes first took in the dark hair, dark forehead, brown eyes, and a face she recognized. She groaned.

The detective mimed opening the window. Riley shook her head. She'd already tried that. Next, Jonelle pointed to the right and mouthed the words "door" and "open."

Riley shrugged. "What door?" she mouthed. She'd stopped at the seam in the wall.

More frantic pointing.

Riley hurried back the way she came and slipped inside the narrow hall. Though she couldn't hear any voices, somebody must be looking for her by now. She hurried to the end of the short corridor and faced another wall. She tapped gently. A hollow sound echoed.

Unable to see clearly, she gently pushed against the wood. The wall gave way slightly. Riley dug her fingers inside and shoved. The wall slid a few feet to the left. "I'll be damned," she said under her breath.

A windowless door stood on the other side with a sliver of light creeping through a crack at the bottom. Her hand touched a cold, steel bar. If she pushed the bar and opened the door would an alarm sound?

"Already screwed, anyway," she mumbled, leaning her weight against the steel. The force caused Riley to stumble out into a brightness that nearly blinded her. Jonelle grabbed her before Riley fell to the ground.

Riley braced for the sound of an alarm that never came.

"Don't let the door close," Jonelle yelled, letting go of Riley and lunging for the edge of the door. Too late. "Dammit!" Jonelle turned. All she saw were trash bins. No sign of Riley.

"What the hell?" She couldn't worry about that dipsy woman now. Instead of returning the way she came, Jonelle ran in the opposite direction. The distance to that end of the building was closer, and she wanted to go around the side and observe the front.

Riley was on her own, and good riddance, though she worried what the woman would say if caught.

"Hey," a voice hissed.

Startled, Jonelle couldn't tell where it came from.

"You deaf or somethin'? Over here."

A face she came to dislike peered from around a trash bin a few feet away.

Jonelle shook with anger. Riley was supposed to follow her lead, not take it upon herself to go her own way. On top of everything else, she'd let the door close instead of giving Jonelle room to get inside. Sick and tired of being thwarted every which way, the only thing stopping her from hurling every obscenity she could at the woman was the fact that someone might hear. She gestured for Riley to come close.

Riley shook her head.

Jonelle felt for the gun. For a brief moment she wondered who'd miss the woman if . . . ashamed of those thoughts, she breathed in and out deeply. No time for emotion. She had to think.

A quick glance at the studio confirmed no alarm sounded. No one came to check out the noise she made, so Jonelle relaxed a little. While curious what—if anything—Riley discovered inside, Jonelle couldn't question the woman until she'd slowed her pulse and calmed down.

Ignoring the homeless woman huddled next to the trash container, Jonelle crept to edge of the building and around the side and peered around the corner. The silver SUV was still parked out front. She pulled out her phone and called Adrienne.

"What's going on?"

"Did you see anyone come out?" Jonelle asked.

"All I've seen were a couple vans pulling up front and then leaving. I didn't know this place had other occupants."

"Me neither. At first. Ran into a guy that sells barbershop and beauty supplies. He says in addition to his business and the studio there are two other occupants. He's seen Watkins before but no child."

A few moments of silence, then, "You sure the child is still alive?"

"Yes." She refused to believe otherwise. "What makes me sick is that I think Tamora knows where Lark is, but for some reason, even though she could go to jail, she's keeping quiet. Lark is somewhere safe—I feel it in my bones—which is why Tamora's kept her mouth shut."

Jonelle had thought long and hard. "If the child's not in the apartment building somewhere, the only other place is with Watkins."

"You sure? Doesn't Tamora have a sister? It'd be easy to hide the kid with the others that go in and out of there, considering she runs a daycare."

A door opened. "Hold on. You seein' what I'm seein'?" Jonelle asked.

"Yep."

The cleaning woman stood in front of the entrance. Hands on hips, head swiveling back and forth.

"Shit," Jonelle said.

"What?"

The cleaning woman got inside her car. The engine roared to life, and she made a U-turn.

"Look. The woman in that car's gonna drive up, and she'll either stop and ask about Riley, or she'll take one look at you, see it's not me, and leave. If she stops, put her on the phone."

"That thing needs a new muffler."

While she waited for Adrienne to come back on the line, Jonelle returned to the rear of the building. No sign of Riley. She breathed a sigh of relief. Good riddance.

"Jonelle?"

"Yeah?"

"She slowed down. When I walked up to her, she sped off. Sorry."

"Don't worry about it. I'm on my way. Keep an eye on that SUV. If it moves before I get there, call me." Jonelle decided to stay at the back of the building. She kept close to the trash containers, using each one as a cover in case the building had a silent alarm and Watkins, or anyone else, came looking out the back. At this point she didn't care if the barbershop guy spied her and thought she was weird or not. Plus there was no sign of Riley anywhere.

Jonelle sprinted to the spot where Adrienne stood between the Jeep and her own vehicle.

"Where's the other one?" Adrienne asked, as Jonelle came and stood beside her.

"No idea. She went inside posing as another cleaning woman, next thing I know she's staring at me out a back window. She let the damn door slam before I could slip inside. And she split before she could tell me what she found out. Damn Luther for suggesting her in the first place."

"What'd he do that for?"

"Thought she could help. She was a cop before the drugs took hold and she lost everything."

Adrienne made sympathetic noises. "What's next?"

"You go back to your place. I'll give you a call later."

"Where're you going?"

"Home. I've gotta think all this through. Plus, I feel bad about neglecting Gracie."

Adrienne slid inside her Saab. "Since you've already become a certified cat person, why not get the little one a friend?"

Jonelle's mouth gaped open. "Are you kidding me? You'd come visit knowing there were *two* cats?"

"As long as you get one as cute as her, I have no complaints." She waved and took off before Jonelle could respond.

One more look at the stationary SUV in front of Playcat and Jonelle made a decision. The supply guy mentioned seeing Watkins with men resembling Randy and Shawn. If she couldn't lean on Watkins, she'd pay both another visit.

She jumped at a tap on her shoulder.

"You need some work on your detecting skills."

Jonelle turned and faced a smirking Riley.

Before she could rip the woman a new one, the sound of a racing motor forced her to swallow the words bubbling up to a boil. Tires squealed as the silver SUV careened down the street, passed Jonelle, and headed in the opposite direction. Not only was Watkins in the driver's seat, but Jonelle glimpsed someone in the passenger seat. Someone with long hair.

"Hurry," Riley said. "Maybe you can catch her. But you ain't leavin' me standin' here. I'm coming, too."

"Hop in."

Instead of following Watkins, Jonelle drove her Jeep to the front of the studio.

"What the hell're you doin'?"

"Shut up. Something's wrong."

Jonelle eased up to the door and got out. The entrance door wasn't completely closed. "Jasper? You in there? Anybody?"

No answer.

Vaguely aware that a camera somewhere watched her enter, and with Riley hovering close behind, Jonelle followed the short hallway around to the left. There, in front of her, racks of robes were strewn about; some trampled on.

Jonelle continued into the main studio. "Jasper?"

No reply.

Jonelle pulled the gun from her waistband.

A low whistle sounded behind her.

She ignored Riley and stepped into the studio, skirting a few overturned chairs.

"Office is back that way," Riley said, attempting to go past Jonelle, who quickly stepped in her path.

"What's your problem?" Riley asked.

"Be quiet," Jonelle said.

A sense of unease gripped her. Too quiet. For the amount of time Watkins lingered inside Playcat, there should've been others around. Where were they?

Jonelle moved on. The prop room's door stood open.

The smell of sweat, leather, and bodily fluids assaulted her nostrils. Her chest tightened when she registered the lack of windows in the cramped space.

"No place anybody can hide here," Riley said. "I already checked."

With a firm grip on her weapon, Jonelle walked over to the long closet on the back wall. She slid each door to the side and went through all the clothes. Nothing. "Gotta check the office," she said.

"Finally realized I'm standin' here, huh?"

Jonelle pressed her lips together and wondered how long it'd take for someone to find the body if she crammed Riley inside that closet.

Papers lay scattered everywhere inside the office, including the floor. The desk drawers and file cabinets stood open and in disarray. Yet no sign of anyone.

A small safe stood next to the wall. She pulled the handle but it didn't open.

"Show me where you were when I saw you at the window," Jonelle said.

"So I ain't the invisible woman after all," Riley huffed. Without another word, she turned on her heel and headed down the narrow corridor.

"This here's a hidden room." Riley placed her hand on the panel and frowned.

"What . . . ?"

"Shh! I hear something," Riley whispered.

Jonelle motioned for Riley to move over.

She put her ear to the wall. Voices. Or, more precisely, one voice. She couldn't make out any words. Jonelle didn't bother motioning for Riley to stand aside. The dipshit woman would've ignored her anyway. The closeness of the hallway aggravated her claustrophobia and made the decision easier. She placed her hand against the panel and pushed.

Nothing happened.

Riley elbowed Jonelle aside, pulled out her knife, and inserted the blade in the seam and pulled.

Although her back was turned, Jonelle imagined a snide look on the woman's face. Focus, Jonelle, she told herself.

The wall gave way and the two squeezed inside.

Jasper lay on his side facing them, a rag in his mouth and duct tape binding his legs and arms behind his back. His eyes, wide with fear, relaxed somewhat as Jonelle leaned over him.

She returned the gun to her holster. "Hold on," she said, yanking the rag out of his mouth.

He gagged in protest.

"Oh shut up," Riley said. She didn't bother to help as Jonelle struggled to remove the tape from the man's arms and legs.

"Ignore her," Jonelle said, helping him sit up. "If we're lucky, she'll go away."

Jasper rubbed his head. "Crazy woman knocked me over the head with that." He motioned to a two by four on the floor nearby. "What the hell she do that for?"

"And how the hell would we know that, Sparky?" Riley asked, hands on hips.

"You. Be quiet. Not gonna repeat myself again. Stand over there," Jonelle said, "and keep your mouth shut. You've almost used up the allotment of patience I've given you."

After a few beats, Riley slumped over to the exit.

Jonelle returned her attention to the film maker, still massaging the back of his head.

"Before I call the cops, tell me what happened."

"Nope. No cops." He peered at her. "I don't know you. How'd you get in here?"

"My name's Jonelle Sweet. I'm a PI working for Tamora's lawyer. I know she works here, and, well, I need to find out what might've happened to her daughter. This is as good a place as any to search."

"Yeah, well. She turned on me quick. And after all I've done for her, making her a star and all. That's freakin' gratitude for you. Now I've gotta find me another model." Pale eyes looked Jonelle up and down.

She ignored his obvious assessment. "Turned on you how? Tamora did this?"

He struggled to his feet and staggered past her. "Naw. Not her. That other one. Her so-called manager. Gotta get back to the office."

"Somebody ransacked the place," Jonelle warned.

"Figures. Bet Watkins did that. Worst day of my life was when I met that woman." Jasper stumbled out of the room. Jonelle followed and Riley brought up the rear.

"Oh, shit," Jasper yelled.

Jonelle entered the office.

He paced through the small space, touching everything as if not believing what his eyes told him. He turned toward the safe. "Thank, God they didn't take anything," he said.

Jonelle frowned, wondering why he didn't check inside to make sure. "I don't think she was after money. There's something in this studio that means a lot to Watkins . . . and Tamora. You got any idea what that could be?"

Jasper sat in the creaky office chair and with elbows on the desk, put his head in his hands.

Jonelle waited, grateful that the only sound from Riley was her raspy breathing.

He shook himself and absentmindedly fingered several of the papers on his desk. While she waited for the director to come to grips with what happened, she picked up a handful of the pages, read a few words that meant nothing to her, and began stacking them in a neat pile.

"Hey, get a grip you two," Riley demanded snapping her fingers loudly for emphasis. "Grow a pair already, Mister. And as for you—"

The look on Jonelle's face stopped Riley from continuing. "I'm taking her home and then I'm coming back here," Jonelle said to Jasper.

"What if I don't wanna go back yet," Riley said, crossing her arms in front of her chest.

"Not asking for your opinion." she swallowed the words, *you freakin' fool.* Jonelle had never thought about anyone like that before.

"Woo-hoo. The black de-tec-tive is growin' a spine."

"She with you?" Jasper asked, his eyes covering first Jonelle, then Riley.

Riley walked over to the desk, picked up several sheets of paper, and began stuffing them into the pockets of a skirt that hadn't seen detergent in a long time.

"Hey, cut that out. What the hell's she doing? Stop it already." Jasper reached over and grabbed for Riley's hand.

She brandished the Swiss knife at him.

He backed off.

"Either put that away or give it to me." Jonelle pulled out her gun.

Riley studied Jonelle before slowly putting the knife back in her other pocket.

"You pull that stunt again and everybody's gonna know you as one-legged Riley." Jonelle motioned for Riley to hand over the papers.

After a slight hesitation, Riley lobbed them in Jonelle's direction, a lopsided smile plastered on her face as the sheets floated to the ground.

"Go ahead and shoot her," Jasper said. "I won't tell a soul."

"Tempting though that is, I don't wanna risk losing my license." She retrieved the papers and handed them to Jasper, who smoothed them out. "Tell you what. Since there's surveillance around, you okay with letting the cops know that all I was interested in was Tamora? Not drugs, not—"

"Whoa. Surveillance? Drugs? I don't know what you're talking about."

Riley piped up. "Cops come lookin', they might find somethin', but it ain't gonna be weed." She patted the skirt pocket that held the knife. "She's mainly talkin' about them times that little girl coulda been hidin' out in that back room."

CHAPTER 41

Although cool air spread through the office, sweat broke out on Jasper's brow. "I . . . I don't know what the hell you're talking about. There're no kids anywhere in or around my studio. Don't go there, no how, no way. I told Watkins we don't touch kids. Never have, never will. This is a legitimate business dealing with adults only." His eyes pleaded for Jonelle to understand.

"I think you better tell me all you know about Lorraine Watkins."

He let out a frustrated sigh. "She found out about my business through a mutual contact."

"Shawn?"

After a slight hesitation, Jasper nodded.

"What's your connection with him?"

"Came by one day. Said he was looking for part-time work, so I offered him work here."

"You've gotta know where this place is to find it. You tellin' me he showed up one day out of the blue?" Jonelle believed that story as much as she believed a rabbit could deliver chocolate eggs. Since Shawn wasn't her immediate worry, she motioned for him to continue.

"After that, Watkins came over, introduced me to Tamora, and after a quick interview, I decided Tam had everything for success in this business—the looks, the attitude. No problems for about a year. Tamora proved so popular I actually started seeing monthly profits.

"Next thing. Watkins starts coming around more and more wanting me to let her use the studio to take pictures. Stills only, she said, and that she'd pay. Claimed it was all gonna be innocent. Said famous people in the past took so-called art pictures and that's all she wanted to do. Art." He grunted. "Yeah, right."

"What'd you tell her?"

"Told her no. Don't want no part of that. Figured I was probably on the cops' radar,"—he glanced at Riley—"on account of they're prejudiced against someone like me trying to make an honest living. All I'm doing is giving the people what they want."

"Save it, Sparky," Riley yelled. A sideways look from Jonelle stopped her from saying more.

"Go on," Jonelle said.

"Cops get wind of kids hanging around here, they'd be swarmin' around this place faster than a bunch of flies landing on a pile of shit."

"If she was okay with the 'no kids' rule, why'd she tie you up? Doesn't look like she robbed you, so what message was she sending?"

He shrugged.

"C'mon Jasper. You've gotta start giving me something I can use. Think about an innocent little girl caught up in all this. If you have any information as to where Lark might be, I've gotta know. There might not be much time left."

Several seconds passed. No one spoke while Jasper looked as if he was struggling with how much to reveal.

"Figured tyin' me up was a warning. She said much worse would happen if I didn't cooperate. Claimed she'd start spreading rumors about what was going on in the studio. Said the cops would investigate and close me down until they figured out the truth. The back room where you found me is the space she wants to use to take the stills. I can't afford to lose this business," he whined. "I got bills like everybody else. Hell. Now you're telling me the cops are watchin', anyway."

Poor guy looked as if he was about to cry. Yet something was off about his performance. "We've got a problem here, Jasper. See, you're not being totally honest with me. Part of me accepts the fact that tying you up was a warning, but I don't believe it was an empty threat of what she might do if you didn't let her use the studio. She's got something on you.

"What I think is you *did* let her shoot pictures here. Or somebody else who works here did. Or maybe you helped her hide the child—or children—at least temporarily, and you wanted to squeeze her for more money. Am I getting close?"

He licked his lips. "Nope. No way did I do any of that." The words tumbled out a little too quickly.

"Why is the room hidden with false walls and the windows blackened?"

The expression on his face hardened. He pressed his lips in a tight line.

"That area is pretty big and empty except for a few pallets, so obviously you're not using it for storage. You tellin' me you're paying rent on space you're not using?"

"Don't want nosey people looking in," he grumbled.

"What would they see if they did take a peek?"

He folded his arms and leaned back in the chair which screeched in protest.

For a brief moment Jonelle wanted Riley to open her big mouth, tick the man off so he'd yell something she could use. For once, the woman stayed quiet.

"So tell me, what actually happened? 'Cause I'm starting to wonder if you staged this whole thing." The close quarters bothered her, so she paced around the cluttered office. "You guys probably got nervous when you saw Riley hanging around." Jonelle ignored Riley next to the door.

"Yeah. And I tied myself up. Try again."

"I agree it's possible Watkins tied you up. And I bet the cops would get an anonymous tip—from a female— on where to find you. Looking around at this mess and not finding the drugs they knew you had, they might believe your story that you'd been robbed." She looked sideways at Riley. "I doubt all you had in here was a little weed. The cops wouldn't bother with that. Did Watkins agree to remove the drugs in exchange for use of the studio? Was it the cleaning lady?"

Riley clapped her hands as if approving Jonelle's deductions.

"All you're doing is speculating. You can't prove any of this," he sneered.

"Don't need to, Jasper, 'cause I don't give a rat's ass about you, nudie films, or drugs. All I care about is finding that child."

Riley backed out the door.

"Where're you going?" Jonelle asked.

"Gotta pee. Be right back."

Jonelle picked up a few papers from the desk. Most contained the words "Production Schedule" written across the top. Below were lists of names followed by the word "Model" and notes about the kinds of scenes set for videoing. Based on the titles, they were all various takes on that old "Debbie Does Dallas" theme.

Jasper remained seated, watery eyes following her every move.

The man's relaxed posture meant she wouldn't find evidence of anything involving underage kids, yet she continued studying the sheets until she found something interesting. At the top of a yellow piece of paper was the word "Staff." Her eyes went down the list. Most of the names were male, and in addition to Shawn, one other name stuck out—Jelani Hill. Next to his name the words "part-time."

She tapped the sheet. "Jelani works for Watkins at the apartment complex where Lark was abducted. Coincidence?"

"As the saying goes, 'it's hard to find good help nowadays.' Same thing applies in this business. I use a lot of people on a part-time basis." Jasper sat up in the chair.

"Says here he's a part-time photographer. Does he take stills or shoot video?"

"Whatever's needed." He stood. "I'm getting tired of all these questions. You ain't a cop, so I want you outta here."

Jonelle patted the small of her back where her weapon rested against her skin. "Not done yet." She knew she was close to finding the connection between Lark's disappearance and this studio but unable to wrap her head around the missing link.

Her eyes settled on the safe. "Noticed you didn't open that when you walked in here. Seems like you'd check to make sure nothing was taken. What do you keep in there?"

"None of your damn business."

"So something important, then. Video, stills, SD cards. Stuff that probably means more than money. If the cops examined the contents, what would they find?"

"Probably find out this loser here is doin' kiddie porn," Riley said, entering the room once more.

"Told you I don't—"

"Yeah, yeah," Riley interrupted. "Save it, Sparky. Lookee here what I found." In one hand she held a pale green child's blanket and in the other a sheet of butterfly stickers.

Jasper looked as if he were about to upchuck his last meal.

"Where'd you find those?" Jonelle asked. She held out her hands for the items and relaxed when Riley released them without comment.

The homeless woman cocked her head in Jasper's direction. "Same place we found him. First time I went back there, I smelled something. Familiar, you know? Couldn't place my finger on it. Went over to one of those windows and started scrapin' off that black paint so I could see better. Anyways, I didn't get a chance to really search that place before you stuck your big head on the other side of the window and nearly scared the crap outta me."

"Why'd you let the door close, then? I wanted to see what was back there." Jonelle bit her tongue. The loony woman got to her every time she opened her mouth.

Riley's hands waved dismissively. "Anyways, I went back there 'cause of that smell. It hit me all of a sudden. That's what they feed you mostly in them shelters. Been eatin' a whole lot better since I been with Luther. He treats us good. Gets us all to share and—"

"I agree Luther's great," Jonelle said. "What'd you smell?"

"Cheese."

"Cheese?"

"Yep. Mac and cheese. So I looked around. I'm thinkin' they stuffed Sparky in there to throw us off from taking too close a look. I found that blanket and stickers behind another false wall."

"Show me." Jonelle made to move past Riley.

"What about him?"

"The cops already know about him." And us, she figured. "Let's go."

Jonelle hurried back down the tight hallway. She allowed Riley to lead her to the spot where she found the blanket.

"Back here," Riley said.

A solid wall appeared behind the spot where Jasper was bound. On closer inspection, the wall didn't go up to the ceiling. There was a narrow space that wasn't obvious unless a person looked for it.

Riley marched to a spot where the back partition met at right angles to another wall. "Watch this." She pushed against the edge, and the wall opened about a foot.

Jonelle shoved, slipped inside the wider opening, and stepped into a room with a long counter but no furniture.

Except. On the floor were several scuff marks. She sniffed. Now that Riley mentioned it, she, too, smelled cheese.

"It'd be real easy to move stuff around from one place to another. This entire studio is full of furniture and moveable walls.

All they'd have to do is rearrange it when they needed this space. And it's hidden. You can sneak anybody inside. Kids can come and go out the back way at night. The few other businesses are nine to five establishments. No one would see anything. Plus, the surveillance photos I saw were taken from the front only."

"What's next?" Riley asked. Gone was the woman's crappy attitude. All business now.

"Where'd you find the blanket and stickers?"

"On the floor over there." Riley pointed to the far edge of the room, next to another wall. "Guess they must've been in a hurry and left this stuff behind."

Jonelle felt around the walls, but unlike the one that allowed her access, this wall was solid. "In a hurry because . . ." Jonelle frowned. Where the hell was Tamora?

CHAPTER 42

*G*etting sick and tired of dragging the little brat from place to
place. Gotta find someplace no one would think to look. Need
to lay low until I figure somethin' out. Tried sending emails to a few
customers, pretending I was the contact and asking for new customers.
Not one person came back with any information. Seems they want the
merchandise for themselves.

So, what if I manage to find some new subjects? What if I check
out what else is out there? Got me some money saved. Got me some
names. Got me some relatives in the Carolinas that might be willing
to help out. Don't think it'll take much to convince them of what I
want to do.

After all, the money's good and nobody's gonna get hurt.

CHAPTER 43

J onelle knew Watkins didn't go to the apartment building on weekends. After almost dragging out a protesting Riley in front of Luther's warehouse, she drove around the corner, parked, took a deep breath and turned on her phone. Several text and voice messages were from Rainey—most marked urgent. She frowned. Working weekends was rare. Did she miss something? Initially the voice messages were firm and then got downright angry.

"If you don't call Marvin now to explain why you're not here, I won't be able to protect you from his anger," one message from Rainey said. Jonelle checked the time. Over an hour ago.

Jonelle punched in the agency's number. The phone was picked up so fast she didn't even hear it ring.

"Where the hell're you? As long as you work for this agency, you're supposed to make yourself available. You know that, Jonelle. That's one of your uncle's strictest rules."

She'd never heard Rainey so angry. Jonelle didn't respond. She wanted her heart to stop pounding in her chest first. She waited for more verbal onslaught from the receptionist. When nothing else was forthcoming, she risked explaining.

"I'm sorry," Jonelle said, somewhat surprised she didn't feel as contrite as she should. "But I was in a dicey situation that called for split-second timing. There wasn't time to get everything all nice and neat. Besides, I forgot we were working this weekend."

"Not asking for 'neat.' A little consideration and respect for your status around here is the point."

Jonelle clenched and unclenched her hand several times. The silence lengthened. "Is there an emergency?"

"You were supposed to serve two people who have court dates coming up next week. You promised this case of yours wouldn't interfere with your work around here. The least you can do is make an attempt," Rainey said. She lowered her voice and added, "I'll leave them for you on my desk. They better not be there when Marvin comes in Monday."

She murmured she'd take care of everything and sat looking out the window of her Jeep. Why was Rainey so upset about a few lousy summonses? Because Marvin liked control. Well, so did she. The rest of the messages were from Adrienne and a couple were from Piper. Jonelle contacted Piper first.

"Hey, Miss. We were wondering if you found Lark yet."

Jonelle groaned inwardly. "Still looking, but you guys can do me a huge favor. If Mrs. Watkins returns to the apartment, call me immediately, okay?"

"What d'ya mean? She doesn't work weekends."

"I think I've seen her car around, so if she turns up, let me know. Thanks." Jonelle disconnected before Piper asked any more questions. Too many people wanted too many things all at once. She felt as if she was a lump of taffy being pulled in all different directions.

Instead of driving to the office, she headed home. Letting herself into her condo, she went in search of Gracie and found the kitten curled up on her kitty bed. She leaned over and kissed the feline on the top of her head. Gracie opened one eye, yawned, stretched, and snuggled back into her original position.

Next, she called Adrienne with an update on Playcat Productions.

"So, you've got a new sidekick, huh? Excuse me for saying this, but she didn't look like she could find a doughnut in a bakery, much less be of any help in finding that little girl."

"Truth is she's a pain in the ass, but she showed me something I don't think I would've found on my own. She threw a fit when I took her back to Luther's. Kept insisting *I* needed *her* help. Fat chance. Honestly, if I never see her again, it wouldn't hurt my feelings one bit." She let out a frustrated sigh. "Forgot about going to the office and picking up a few summonses, and Rainey and Marvin are pissed. After the day I've had I needed a kitty fix."

"What's the fur ball doing now?"

Jonelle smiled. She wasn't fooled. The little "fur ball" had attached herself to Adrienne's heart whether her best friend wanted to admit it or not. "She's sleeping. As usual. Even though Marvin's complaining about my absence, I can't let Watkins' trail get cold. When I have time to catch my breath, I want to run something by you. I'm looking at all my, um, professional possibilities."

"Sounds interesting. Wanna give me a hint?"

"Not yet." Jonelle disconnected feeling a little better. She punched in Burt's number.

"I was about to call you," Burt said, picking up on the second ring. "I assume Adrienne's already given you the lowdown on her interview. Am I right?"

Now that she heard his voice, she wasn't sure what to say next. So she plowed on through. "Yeah. She wanted me to make sure I thanked you—these are her words—properly for all you've done."

His deep chuckle came through the line. A slight tug pulled at Jonelle's heart. Burt was such a good guy. Why couldn't she—

"What's up?"

She bit her lip. "You won't like this, but I have to give you a heads-up. My face might appear on more surveillance photos.

Along with a scruffy-looking white woman whose name I'd rather not give you."

The silence stretched on to an uncomfortable level. "Guess I should be thankful for the alert," Burt said. "Truth is we've already seen your face—and that other woman's—today. I already warned everybody you weren't gonna let this drop, so nobody was surprised. Though I've gotta tell you I'm starting to wonder about the company you're keeping these days."

Jonelle relaxed. "She's a friend of Luther's—"

"Figures."

"—and since she used to be an ex-cop, I didn't see the harm in her snooping around."

"Did you say ex-cop?"

"Yeah. Don't know the story on that, yet. Anyway, she found a child's blanket and butterfly stickers in a hidden room near the back of the studio. If those people are dealing in anything worse than weed, you better check the safe in the office."

The only sound that came through the phone was Burt's breathing.

She took his silence as permission to continue. "I think these people might be dealing in kiddie porn. The beginning stages, at least." She stopped, waiting for Burt's reaction. When none came, she asked, "You still there?"

"Yeah."

"We, that is the other woman and I, discovered Jasper—the owner slash producer—tied up in a hidden room. He claimed Lorraine Watkins knocked him out and tied him up. But that doesn't make sense. If he wanted to untie himself, he could have. His wrists were wrapped in duct tape in front of his body, not behind, leaving his hands free. I watched Watkins leave, but I haven't seen Tamora."

Jonelle debated whether or not to tell him more of her suspicions, but his silence unnerved her somewhat. "I saw a list of employees, and Jelani Hill's name was on it as part-time. Jasper, the owner, says Jelani works as a part-time videographer. Are you gonna say anything, or would you rather I keep rambling on?"

"Where are you now?"

Finally.

"Home. But I have to swing by the office first."

"Where're you going from there?"

"Not sure. Watkins isn't going back to the apartment building anytime soon. If she goes back at all. She's spooked. I'm gonna fax Langford Tamora's movie poster to let him know his client is not as innocent as she claims."

Papers rustled in the distance.

"He already knows," Burt said. "He called to tell us he suspects Tamora Phelps may be involved in her child's abduction. He wants permission to try and contact her first so he can bring her in voluntarily. Guess he plans on using you for that."

Damn. In spite of everything, she still didn't want to believe the young mother was involved. "What tipped him to Tamora's involvement?"

"You, actually. When you reported about her losing her jobs and appearing in adult movies, he tried to reach her. For the past several days, with no results. He'd also like to hear from you ASAP."

Jonelle felt bad she hadn't been providing as many updates on the case as she should. Things were heating up, and she didn't want to take the time to report in. "I'll give him a call as soon as I hang up from you."

"Would it be too much to ask you to let me know if you find Tamora first?"

The sarcasm wasn't lost on her. She chose to ignore it. "I'll call. Heck, I'll even bring her in if you want. Save you guys some time."

"Don't be shitty," Burt said, his voice tight.

"Sorry. My rubberband of a life is stretched in different directions, but all I care about now is finding Lark. Oh, um, by the way . . . Now, I don't mean to tell the police how to conduct their investigation—"

Burt groaned.

"—but I think it'd be better if you watched Jelani Hill and Shawn Mowerby, instead of Playcat. Think I may have spoiled that studio for you. Not that I meant to, of course."

"And what makes you think we're not watching them?"

"Are you?"

"Instead of telling me what you think I should do, I suggest you check in with the attorney. You're still working for him, right? 'Cause if not, well, you know the drill."

She sure did. They'd warn her to stay away from the investigation. Therefore, she couldn't afford to get fired from Langford's team. That was her only excuse for being on the case in the first place.

As soon as she disconnected from Burt, she drove by the office.

The reception desk was vacant.

Voices from the back proved Ben and Omar were working. Ashamed she felt only a smidgen of guilt, she snatched the summonses and left. Next, she called Langford's office and left a message telling him everything she'd found out at Playcat Productions and the involvement of Watkins, Jelani, Shawn, and Randy. She omitted mentioning how the kids and Riley helped her and the fact Piper, Grayson and Fred were keeping an eye out for Lark. She advised him she hadn't found Tamora but would keep searching.

Instead of going to the apartment building, she hustled over to Tamora's sister's house. Evelyn Clifton had to know the whereabouts of her baby sister. Plus, what better place to hide a small child than among several other small children.

She drove by the daycare, noting the lack of activity outside as well as the lack of available parking spots near the front of the home. Just as well. Unlike her first visit, Jonelle didn't want to announce this one.

She turned down the next street over and searched for a parking spot. Finding none, she steered the Jeep back to Evelyn Clifton's street. She braked hard when a familiar SUV skidded down the narrow road in front of her and pulled up to a stop. A tall figure sprinted out of the passenger side.

From where she sat in her vehicle, Jonelle couldn't make out who it was but was fairly certain the person was male. And alone.

Was Tamora somewhere inside?

A car honked from behind. She put her arm out the window and waved the person on.

The SUV sat there, double parked near the entrance.

"C'mon," Jonelle urged. "I need to know if my hunch is right and Tamora's inside."

Her phone buzzed with a text message.

"Hey, Miss," the text stated. "Smthng's hpng. Hurry." Piper had added three exclamation points.

"Wl b thr soon," Jonelle replied.

"K."

The silver SUV continued idling.

Jonelle moved her Jeep as close to the curb as possible while keeping an eye on Clifton's house.

Her phone buzzed again. Before she could check the screen, the person with the same body type as Shawn returned with a duffle bag and slipped inside. The SUV sped off.

Instead of following, Jonelle double parked in front of the daycare, set her emergency flashers, and got out. She walked up to the door and knocked.

The door flew open. "Now what? Oh, uh, thought you were someone else." The lines in Clifton's brow deepened.

"I'd like to speak to Tamora," Jonelle said.

"She ain't here." Clifton made to close the door.

Jonelle slipped her foot between door and frame, glad she'd thought to change into her cross trainers. "What about Lark? She around here someplace?" She swiveled her head in an attempt to see beyond the woman's body but couldn't.

Clifton blinked several times and glanced behind her shoulder. She quickly turned back to Jonelle. "Don't know what you're talking about. If you don't get off my porch, I'm gonna call the cops."

"Go ahead. See, I talked to a detective friend of mine a little while ago, and they'll probably be paying you a visit any time now. Before I leave, who was that just now? Shawn? Didn't get a very good look."

"Get off my damn porch. Right now," she said through clenched teeth. She slammed the door.

Jonelle took her time settling inside her Jeep. She checked her phone. Another text from Piper: "U cm now Miss. Miss Maxine nds u."

Maxine? Jonelle had dismissed the elderly woman when she'd concentrated on Watkins. She responded with "coming" and aimed toward the apartment building.

A scant half hour later, Jonelle targeted Watkins' spot near the front of the apartment building. Instead of an empty slot, the silver SUV sat in its usual assigned space. In order to make sure it was the same vehicle, Jonelle slipped out of her Jeep and placed her hand on the SUV's hood. Not only was it still warm, but the faint ticking sound still emanated from the engine. The "Reserved Maintenance" spot was vacant. Jonelle slid in and parked. The heft of the weapon against her lower back reassured her somewhat.

"Hey, Miss." Piper opened the glass doors.

"Where've you been? I thought detectives were supposed to look around the scene of the crime," Fred said, her voice rising.

"Knock it off," Grayson added. "She's here now. We got news for you."

The door to the manager's office was closed.

"How long have you guys been waiting in the lobby?"

"Since I texted you," Piper said.

She pointed to the closed door. "You guys see any signs of Mrs. Watkins?"

All three shook their heads.

She walked over and tried the door knob. Locked.

"You gonna break in?" Grayson asked.

"You want us to turn our backs so we don't see anything? In case the police question us?" Fred added.

Jonelle sighed inwardly. What she wanted was for the trio to leave her alone to do her job, but she had nobody to blame but herself. "You said something about Maxine. Is she in her apartment?"

"She's with my mom. That's why we're waiting for you. So's you could come right up and not go anywhere else." Piper motioned for Jonelle to follow her to the elevators.

Where the hell was Watkins?

Jonelle itched to get inside the manager's office. She wanted to search the place for evidence of Watkins' relationship with all three suspects as well as each one's involvement with Playcat Productions.

Piper ran out of the elevator and knocked once on her door. It opened as Jonelle and the other two walked up.

"I was about ready to call the cops," Mrs. Enruth said. "Maxine's in a state, and I don't know how to calm her. Says she's scared and doesn't want to go to jail." She stepped aside for Jonelle to enter but blocked the two kids. "Oh, no. Time for you guys to go on home."

"Shoot," Grayson said. He opened his mouth to object but abruptly shut it when Piper's mother made a warning noise. He shoved his hands in his pockets and left without further comment.

That left Fred. "If Piper can stay and listen, why can't I? Not like anybody cares if I go home or not."

"Go on home, Fred," Mrs. Enruth said in a soft voice. "Your mom may need you. As for Piper, she's going to her room and close the door. Right?"

The scowl on Piper's face indicated she didn't want to do anything of the sort, but after giving Fred a long look, turned and headed down the hall to her room.

A slight tinge of worry pulled at Jonelle about Fred. Of the three youngsters, Fred seemed the most vulnerable. However, Jonelle had no doubt that if Mrs. Enruth believed Fred was in any kind of distress, she'd take action. What she had to discuss with Maxine wasn't fit for a twelve-year-old's ears. "See you later, Fred."

Fred muttered something Jonelle didn't make out and stomped down the hall.

"Where's Maxine?" Jonelle asked after Piper's mother had closed the door.

"Kitchen. She's here, Maxine."

The elderly woman entered the living room. Gone were signs of the prickly attitude from that first encounter. In its place stood a frail old woman who looked as if she hadn't been taking care of herself lately.

Jonelle wanted to ask Mrs. Enruth to leave but couldn't direct the woman's actions in her own home, so she sat on a chair while Maxine took her place next to Mrs. Enruth on the couch.

"Where's Lark?" Jonelle asked.

"Right now? I don't know."

"Let's start from the beginning. Don't leave anything out 'cause I've had it up to here with being jerked around by you and just about everybody else. You're in this mess with Watkins and maybe even Tamora."

She ignored the small gasp from Mrs. Enruth.

"So let's start there. Do you know who took Lark?"

Maxine picked at the hem of her cotton dress. "I think so. I mean, I know who was supposed to, but that's not how it worked out."

Mrs. Enruth inhaled sharply.

"What the hell does that mean?" Jonelle asked.

Maxine's face crumpled as if she were about to cry. "It wasn't supposed to get this serious. When Tamora left that night, I was supposed to call Lorraine so she could get inside. I called but for some reason, she didn't answer. I kept peeking at the door. The stupid girl was only supposed to be gone for a few minutes. Five minutes tops, she said."

Maxine sniffed and dabbed at her eyes with the sleeve of her dress. Mrs. Enruth handed her a tissue.

"Go on." Jonelle pulled at her handcuff and pistol necklace.

"I kept an eye out, but Tamora didn't come back. And Lorraine still wasn't answering, so I got nervous. Since the door was um, open a little, I was afraid somebody else would get inside, somebody who might hurt Lark."

"Didn't you think that what you were doing to that child was also hurtful?"

Maxine started crying.

Shit. No way was she going to comfort the woman. "What happened next?"

"The only person I could think to call was Randy. He went inside and got Lark. Everything would've worked out fine if Vaughn hadn't called the police."

Jonelle wanted to strangle the old lady. She fought to keep her voice calm. "So, Lark's been with Randy this whole time?"

"No. Not the whole time. He grabbed her and took her to his place. We snuck her out the back way until . . . somebody else could come get her. We had to keep moving her because you kept snooping around the place." Maxine glared at Jonelle through wet eyes.

"Where is she now?"

The woman started wailing. "I don't know. I honest to God don't know. Nobody does. It's all messed up."

"I saw Watkins' SUV, but her office door is locked. Do you know where she is?"

Maxine wadded up the tissues she'd already used and dumped the lot on the coffee table. Piper's mom slid the entire box over to her. "Her car is outside?" Maxine looked frantic. "She said she was going to her mom's place to figure out what to do next." She grabbed Mrs. Enruth's hand. "What am I gonna do?"

"What about Jelani and Randy? And Shawn?"

"Jelani said he'd had enough," the elderly woman sniffed. "Said things were going off the rails. He got scared. Shawn said everything was up to his mother now."

"His mother? Watkins is his mother?"

Maxine nodded. "Don't know about Randy."

"I'll be right back," Jonelle said. "You stay here."

"I want this over with," Maxine cried.

Jonelle rushed to Randy's apartment. She knocked several times and got no response.

"He ain't home," said a woman opening the door of the apartment across from his.

"How long's he been gone?" Jonelle asked.

The woman shrugged. "The last time I seen him was two, three days ago."

"Was he alone?"

"Every time I've seen him he's been alone," she said, closing her door before Jonelle could ask any more questions.

Jonelle returned to Piper's apartment. She entered and paced around the small living room. No matter what Maxine said, Watkins's vehicle was here, so where was she? "Besides Jelani and Randy, who else in this building was involved?"

"Nobody. I don't know of nobody else. But Lorraine didn't tell me everything. When things started getting . . . difficult, I told her I didn't want to know no more."

Jonelle walked up to Maxine and stared down at her. "You telling me the truth?"

The elderly woman flinched and slowly nodded.

"Why do this? Why Lark? Why now?"

Maxine sipped from a bottle of water. "We figured nobody'd make too much of a stink about a missing little black girl, especially if the mother didn't make too much noise and laid low. But the cops got involved and then you showed up." She sniffed and glanced at Mrs. Enruth as if seeking her assistance. Piper's mom kept her mouth firmly shut.

Maxine sighed dramatically. "Lorraine said as long as Lark stayed hidden for a week or two, things would cool down and everything would work out okay. Jelani could take the pictures of her and Tamora together and nobody'd be the wiser. Tamora agreed to everything so what's the harm?"

"Where was the last place you saw Lark?"

Maxine clutched her neck. "That . . . studio," she said, each word seeming to struggle out of her mouth.

Piper's mom stood. "Ohmigod. Are you saying they took that poor child to where they shoot those adult films? What the hell's wrong with you, woman?"

Jonelle no longer had to worry about restraining herself from pummeling Maxine. Piper's mom was ready to do that herself.

A loud pounding stopped Jonelle from continuing.

Mrs. Enruth rushed over to open the door.

"Hey, Miss Jonelle. You best get downstairs 'cause I just seen Miss Watkins leave the building." The words left Fred's mouth in a rush.

"Dammit." Jonelle turned back to Maxine. "Where's she going?"

"Prob'ly her mother's house."

"Where's that?"

"Pennsylvania. Just across the line off of I-83 in York."

"Address?"

Maxine looked as if she was weighing whether or not to tell Jonelle the truth.

"Don't even try lying," Jonelle snapped.

"Calm down, Miss Sweet," Piper's mother urged. "Both of us getting mad isn't gonna help anybody. Besides, I know where Lorraine's mother lives. She gave me her number and address—in case she had an emergency I'd know who to contact."

Jonelle resumed pacing, aware Fred hadn't moved from the doorway. With all the problems she had with this case, the last thing she needed was to get a minor in danger.

"Thanks for the information, Fred. You go on down to your apartment now."

Fred squinted at Jonelle. "Aren't you gonna go after her?"

"She's had a head start, so no need for me to rush. C'mon, let me take you home." Jonelle turned to escort Fred down the hall. The youngster didn't move.

"No."

"Pardon?"

"I'm not going home. My mom don't know if I'm around or not. What you're doing is a lot more interesting."

Before Jonelle could demand the child go home, Piper's mother called out. "You can stay here with Piper for a while."

"I don't want to," she said, crossing her arms in front of her chest.

That did it.

"Go. Stay. Whatever. Listen, I don't have children for a very specific reason. I've got work to do, and I'm going to do it. Without you."

Fred's mouth popped open but no words came out. Jonelle moved past her and hurried down the stairs. After trying the knob on Watkins' office door once more, Jonelle rushed outside to her Jeep. Sure enough, the silver SUV was gone.

Angry at herself for not staking out the woman's vehicle, Jonelle headed for the highway that would take her into Pennsylvania.

CHAPTER 44

The navigation system in the Jeep announced she'd arrived at the address for Watkins' mom. She pulled in front of a gray-shingled house on a quiet corner in a neighborhood of single-family homes and parked under a regular street light, not one of those sodium orangey things. She gazed back at the dwelling and wondered what everyone behind those gray walls knew of everything that had transpired.

She didn't see the familiar silver SUV and, for one awful moment, considered the possibility the manager hadn't come here in the first place.

Dogs barked in the distance. While lights were on in all the nearby homes, few cars rolled down the street, and there was no foot traffic. Jonelle drove around the corner and stopped. At the back of the house, under a carport, sat the vehicle she was looking for. She parked next to the driveway. As if the occupants knew she was there, a light came on and the back door opened. She made out two figures; one stooped and the other slightly taller and rounder.

Afraid to move, fearing Watkins might recognize her Jeep, Jonelle strained to hear what the figures were saying. Based on the arms flailing about, the shaking of fingers and heads, it looked as if the two were engaged in a heated argument. Sure enough, voices grew to a level where she made out the words, "never," "can't believe," "crazy," and "help."

Tired of waiting to see what happened next, Jonelle slipped out of her seat. Neither woman noticed. Good. While the front of the property was open, the back was enclosed by a chain link fence. Not good. A large evergreen bush hugged that side of the house. Jonelle scurried over and used the bush for cover. From this vantage point she listened to more of what they said.

"I want you to leave, right now," said the voice of the person Jonelle didn't know.

Watkins responded with, "I told you it's temporary. No one's gonna get you involved. Hell, there's no way anyone would know. 'Less you tell them."

"I'm too old for this. You know better. I didn't raise you to turn out like this. No. You got to go. And take that woman with you."

Jonelle held her breath. What woman? Tamora? The words *"what about Lark?"* thundered in her brain so forcefully it was as if she'd said them out loud.

"I can't do this out here," Watkins pleaded. "The whole neighborhood can hear."

"Then leave. The sooner you get out the better."

Shuffling noises followed. Jonelle risked peeking around the corner.

"Open the damn gate," an angry-sounding Watkins demanded.

She pulled back.

Something clanked, followed by the squeal of a rusty gate opening. Footsteps followed.

She chanced another look. Tamora stood next to the opening.

Jonelle willed her not to look next to the house.

While she couldn't see her expression, Tamora's shoulders sagged, head bowed.

The SUV pulled out, and Tamora closed the gate and opened the passenger's side door.

Jonelle sprang into action. "Stop," she yelled, ran around to the driver's side, and grabbed the handle. "Get out," she demanded.

Watkins' eyes bulged in surprise.

Instead of hopping into the SUV, Tamora stepped back.

"I said, get out. Now."

Whether it was the anger in Jonelle's voice or the lack of her passenger, Watkins slid down her window.

"What do you want?" she hissed.

Jonelle threw her head back and laughed. "Are you kidding me? 'What do I want'? How about I yell the reason for one and all to hear on this street? I bet your mother, or whoever it was you were talking to before, wouldn't be too happy about that."

Tamora backed up.

"Don't move," Jonelle demanded.

The young woman obeyed, eyes wide with fear.

"Where's Lark?" Jonelle asked, over the hood of the vehicle.

Tamora turned and glanced at the house.

Jonelle pulled out her weapon. "Get out," she ordered Watkins, who only hesitated for a fraction of a second before complying. Jonelle reached inside the vehicle and removed the keys. Without saying a word to either woman, she marched up to the house through the open back gate and pounded on the back door.

The door flew open. "Who're you?" Sharp eyes appraised Jonelle.

"Are you Lorraine Watkins' mother?"

In response, hands knotted with arthritis grabbed both arms.

Jonelle pulled out her investigator's license. "I'm working with a Maryland lawyer looking for Lark Phelps. All I care about is finding the little girl. What the police do to you and your daughter is not my concern. Is Lark here?"

A quick head shake.

"Do you know where she is?"

"She's—" The woman's mouth gaped open.

Pain erupted from the back of Jonelle's head as bright flashes of light exploded behind her eyes. She fell to the ground before total darkness consumed her.

Her head hurt. Worse, when she moved her arms they scraped against something hard and rough. She tried moving her legs. They worked but also rubbed against the coarse surface. She opened her eyes. A fuzzy bright light shot more pain into her head. She tried to sit up, but dizziness took over so she lay back down again, breathing heavily.

A voice floating from somewhere in the distance called out. Rough hands shook her shoulder. "Miss, are you woke? Miss?"

Jonelle groaned. She wanted to go back to sleep to ease the pounding in her brain.

"Miss, see if you can drink this."

Something sharp was placed under her nose. Her hand swatted the smell away. She opened her eyes and blinked rapidly.

"Can you sit up? I can't bend down much, so you need to sit and drink a little of this whiskey I got. Might help."

Jonelle worked herself back up to a sitting position. "Please turn that light off for a minute," she managed.

The darkness helped the pain somewhat. She turned her head slowly toward the voice. Watkins' mother held out a tumbler filled with what looked like small amount of brown liquid. She managed to grab the glass with both hands and sipped, wincing as the fire spread down her throat.

"Can you stand?"

"In a sec." She sipped more liquor. This time the burning didn't seem so intense.

The world began to take shape again. The hardness she sat on was the back porch, a soft blanket curled around her legs. She moved it aside, handed the cup to the woman and slowly rose to her feet.

"Careful. Don't want you falling down. Again."

"Me neither." She managed to stand, though her knees were wobbly. Jonelle patted her waist. "My gun. Where's my gun?"

"Down there. Next to the steps. I ain't touched it, so if you want it you better pick it up yourself 'cause I don't want nothin' to do with those things."

"Fair enough." Once steady, she bent down to retrieve the weapon but almost fell over from dizziness. "Guess I need another minute." She breathed in and out several times, leaned over, and retrieved the weapon. With the gun secured in her waistband, she grasped the back door knob and followed the woman into the kitchen.

"Sorry I had to leave you out there, but I live alone, and you're too big for me to drag in the house by myself."

Jonelle supported herself on the kitchen counters and made her way over to a small table where she sat heavily, the pain in her head diminishing.

"Think you can manage some aspirin?"

"Yes. Thanks."

Jonelle took a few of the pills, waved away the whiskey, and instead accepted the offer of water to wash down the pills. "What'd your daughter hit me with?" A lump formed on the back of her head, but as far as she could tell, she wasn't bleeding.

"I'm guessing she used a piece of firewood I always keep back here. I'm so sorry. I raised her better than that. Don't know what happened to her when she left home. She used to be such a good girl."

"Where's Tamora?"

"She left with Lorraine."

"And Lark?"

The woman glanced away. "I'm not sure. They wanted to bring the child here, but I told them no. I don't want to get involved in whatever mess they cooked up."

"Where were Tamora and Lorraine going when they left?"

"Back to Maryland somewhere."

"Why . . . I'm sorry, what's your name?"

"Mary Burroughs."

"Why were they here in the first place?"

Mrs. Burroughs sighed and placed her arthritic hands in her light green polyester pants pockets. "I'm too old for this nonsense. Last time a child stayed at my place—"

"Was it Lark?" Jonelle asked.

"No, some other child. Teenager really. It took me a helluva time to force them out. First it was, we only need a place for a week, then it was two weeks. Only when I demanded that I meet the child's family did they finally go someplace else."

"Where's this 'someplace else'?"

She got up and poured herself a couple fingers of the whiskey. "I don't know because I don't wanna know," she said.

"Give me some idea. If they didn't confide in you, you must've overheard them talking about things. Tell me everything you saw and heard."

She swirled the brown liquid in the glass. "Lorraine went on and on about pictures. They didn't want video, only pictures. Still pictures, she said. And they already had a photographer that wouldn't cost them because it was one of the young men from that apartment building she managed."

Jonelle had sketched out that much so far. "Whose this 'they'? Any names besides Lorraine and Tamora? Any other locations?"

Another large swallow of whiskey followed by a grimace. "My grandson Shawn's name was mentioned, but he never stopped by. And before you say anything, I already know he finds women to act in them perv videos. I also heard of Jelani and Randy. Them two take the pictures. I was okay with that 'cause I thought all them was adults, and to each his own as long as nobody gets hurt." Her eyes lost their focus. "I heard a rumor that turned my stomach. Don't care if it was true or not, I wanted that filth out of my house and away from me as fast as possible."

Jonelle understood. "But what about Lark?"

The elderly woman gazed wistfully around the small kitchen. "As God is my witness, no little child ever stayed here."

"They wanted her to, though, right?"

"Yes."

"If she wasn't here, do you have any idea where they kept her?"

After a slight hesitation, a quick nod.

Jonelle sat back, arms folded across her chest, and waited for the woman to continue.

"I don't know all the places. I made Lorraine tell me most of it because I'm not one of those stupid people you see on TV that got evil stuff going on right under their noses." She examined the liquid in her glass as if wanting more but afraid of what might happen if she filled the glass again.

"They kept moving her around. Tamora said they made a game out of it, so's the child wouldn't get scared. Some game, huh? Tamora claimed they wasn't doing nothin' wrong 'cause most of the pictures would be of her and Lark. Mother and daughter. Like that. And they had a private list of clients so nothing would go on the Internet. Or . . . whatever.

"When she explained it to me, it didn't sound so bad. At first. But then I got to thinking about what she meant when she said 'most.' Why didn't she say 'all' instead?"

Tears formed in the elderly woman's eyes. In spite of what she'd heard, Jonelle reached over and patted the gnarled hand. "I'm not blaming you for this . . . mess."

Mrs. Burroughs shuddered. "You do what you can," she said, addressing the ceiling. "You raise your kids the best you know how. Teach them to be God-fearin' people and what happens? They end up doing the devil's work."

"It's not your fault." Even to her own ears the words rang hollow.

"Maybe not all, but part. Lorraine was twelve when her daddy was killed in a hit-and-run accident. She was sittin' right next to him in the front seat. It was a miracle she wasn't killed, too. She used to be such a sweet girl before that happened. But now . . . I don't know anymore."

The pain in her head subsided to a dull ache, so Jonelle stood and paced from one end of the kitchen to the other. Odd they hadn't taken her pistol. "Does Lorraine carry a weapon?"

"No. She wouldn't dare. Not since she saw a friend of hers shot when she was in high school. She's been scared of the things ever since." She frowned at Jonelle. "Only reason I let you in here with that thing is 'cause you're hurt."

Jonelle stopped pacing. "Where are they going from here?"

"I don't know. I wanted her out and didn't much care to find out." The elderly woman placed a hand under her chin and looked off in the distance. Jonelle briefly thought of her own mother on the other side of the country, trying to find herself as late middle age fast approached. Her mother had no qualms about leaving Jonelle on her own. Some parents not only carried their burdens, but those of their children as well, for their entire lives.

"You must have some idea. Think. Where's the last place they talked about?"

CHAPTER 45

I'm not sending any more texts. Somebody might trace them back to where I am, throwaway phone or not. It's hard to keep writing stuff down, but if I don't I'm afraid I'll forget where I've hidden the information about the bank accounts. And if anything happens, it's not gonna fall on my head. It was the . . . contact's idea to open three of them, at different banks. Everybody voted on me being the logical one to apply; who'd suspect somebody who looks like me, of doing anything wrong? Once the money starts rolling in, I'm supposed to start depositing the cash. They trust me that much. Idiots. What I've got in mind is worth all the grief I've taken these past several days.

Got me an idea the other day when we was in the store. Woman comes in with three kids, all looking like they was under five. The oldest—a boy—was quiet like Lark. I started getting ideas. Be easy to pose the two of them together. They wouldn't do anything—I'm not a pervert.

Something to think about.

CHAPTER 46

Mrs. Burroughs clasped her hands. "They said something about leaving the parking lot. Too many people around or something. I never asked what parking lot . . . or where. Or what they meant." Mrs. Burroughs confirmed Jonelle'd been unconscious for less than ten minutes. Add that to the time she'd spent in the kitchen, and that meant Watkins had about a half hour lead. Lead to where, she wasn't sure. Parking lot? Were they keeping the child in a car or van? While Watkins didn't confide everything to her mother, the woman had sharp ears, which is why, though exhausted, Jonelle needed to get back to Maryland.

She thanked the woman for her help and once inside the Jeep, plugged in the directions from York south to Baltimore. The best route was interstate 83. She'd contact Burt when she got the chance and suggest they issue a BOLO—be on the lookout—to find Shawn, Randy, and Jelani.

On the highway, she relaxed a little until fast approaching headlights in her rearview mirror forced her out of the center lane and over to the right. The car moved with her, practically sitting on her bumper. She hated that and tapped her brakes in an effort to get the idiot off her tail. If she moved any more to the right, she'd end up on the shoulder.

She touched the brakes again. The tactic didn't work, so she strained to get a look at the nutcase behind the wheel.

Two people sat in the front of a familiar-looking sedan. She groaned. Were Randy and Shawn so stupid as to follow her again? She eased off the gas to see if he'd go around.

He didn't. When she sped up, so did the car. She slowed, he slowed. Only mildly concerned, Jonelle decided as long as they were cruising along like this, no problems. Several miles later and with the driver not making any move other than to stay so close that no one could drop in behind her, she remained calm.

"Whatever floats your boat, Randy," she said out loud. Her gun was loaded and within reach, and she'd use it if she had to.

She turned the radio up to help take her mind off of the past hour and soon got lost in the soft jazz sounds of a mellow saxophone coming through her speakers. Up ahead the highway information sign indicated she had about an hour and change to get to Baltimore, and she perked up. The sedan still hovered near her bumper. If he left the interstate when she did, well . . . she'd see what happened.

What happened was not what she expected. A jolt from behind startled her. "What the hell!"

Another bump, this one harder. The Jeep rocked dangerously. She gripped the steering wheel with both hands. While she loved her Jeep, it wasn't the safest vehicle around, even with the roll bars. She fumbled for her pistol and placed it close to her hip. At first she considered pulling into a gas station, but then what? Not knowing what these fools had in mind encouraged her to keep driving.

One thing she knew for sure: it wasn't Lorraine Watkins. Another bump and she went from apprehensive to pissed. More concerned about the damage they were doing to her vehicle than at their efforts to intimidate her, she set a course for Tamora's apartment building. The music that filled her Jeep, at first comforting, now annoyed her. She needed her wits about her, so she turned off the radio.

An exit sign for Shrewsbury appeared. In two miles she had to make a decision—either get off the highway to address the situation or keep going. One mile gone and above the treetops on her right a blue-and-white sign of a Hampton Inn beckoned. She steered for the hotel. She'd have a better chance of defending herself and calling for help there rather than risk getting killed on the highway.

She waited until the last second to pull onto the off ramp for W. Forrest Avenue, the Jeep rocking dangerously and her tires squealing in protest. Had she lost the tail? Headlights appeared again. He'd managed to stay with her.

The road she found herself on was relatively deserted. The assholes behind her had stopped their aggressive driving but stayed close. She raced down the two-lane road, and followed the signs to the hotel. The hotel entrance rose up ahead on the right. She pulled in, parked in front under the lights, and put the gun in her bag.

The sedan followed, but instead of coming close, stayed in the shadows and continued on to the far end of the parking lot as though the occupants needed time to figure out what to do next. And avoid the security cameras.

Through the hotel's glass doors a dark-haired woman dressed in green stood behind the registration desk talking on the phone. No one else was around. Jonelle shut off her Jeep, exited and locked the doors. If they made any attempt at attacking her car further, she'd shoot first and ask questions later.

Keeping an eye on the vehicle idling in the shadows, she went to examine the Jeep's back end. The bumper as well as the spare tire carrier had several dents and scrapes, none deep but still obvious. "Sonofabitch," she screamed into the night. Enraged, she withdrew her gun and with the weapon at her side, stormed over to the sedan.

Her anger reached the boiling point. She stopped at the edge of the building where a maintenance man, eyes bulging at the tall black woman brandishing a gun, dropped a push broom and ran to the front, hands covering his head as if anticipating an imminent attack.

She stopped and took several deep breaths. She put the gun in her bag and picked up the broom. The implement had seen better days. She unscrewed it from the base. Made of wood instead of cheap plastic, she lifted the handle up and down. Perfect.

The idling car didn't move.

"Excuse me, Miss," said a female voice behind her. "Is there a problem?"

While tapping the broom handle on the ground, Jonelle kept her voice as calm as possible. "No problem. Sorry for scaring your employee, but me and my boyfriend over there"—she indicated the sedan—"are having a slight disagreement. I'll be finished doing what I need to do in a few, so no need to call the cops."

Seconds passed as the young woman appeared unsure of what to do next. "Well. Um. I think I need to go call my supervisor."

Jonelle had to hurry. While the brief exchange tamped down her anger somewhat, the urge to exact revenge still bubbled within. Alone again with dumb and dumber, she raised the handle above her head, moving it in a circular motion. There was only one thing she wanted to do, and if anyone tried to stop her, well . . .

She marched up to the car and smashed the broom handle on the hood. The loud *thunk* echoed in the darkness. "You're so brave. C'mon, get out of the car." She whacked the car again and again, ignoring the muffled shouts of protest from the men inside.

Still rotating the broom handle like some deranged baton twirler, she walked in a wide arc toward the back and walloped the trunk. Over and over she bashed, her hand aching with each pounding while enjoying every moment. In the back of her mind she knew what she was doing was not only dangerous but wrong. And probably on video. Yet once she started she couldn't stop.

Finally, the two inside stepped out.

"Are you out of your fuckin' mind," Shawn screamed. He jabbed a finger at Randy. "Told you we shoulda brought a gun."

"I ain't going down for shootin' nobody," Randy yelled. "That wasn't part of the deal, especially now that—"

"Shut up fool."

Fascinated by the drama unfolding in front of her yet unsure of what the two numbnuts had in store she again took out her weapon. She pointed the gun first at Shawn then at Randy. "The three of us are starting to know each other very well. So I don't need to remind you I'm not afraid to use this. If I have to."

"Yeah. Well the joke's on you," Randy said, backing away from Jonelle. "Nobody knows where the kid's at now."

"Asshole," Shawn yelled at Randy.

"Uh. That's if we knew in the first place."

"Too late, wiseass," Jonelle said. "You two are coming with me."

"Like hell," Shawn said. He turned and bolted toward thick bushes bordering the property, with Randy close behind screaming everything but her name.

"Yeah, whatever," she shouted at their retreating backs. She lowered the wooden handle. "I need to get one of these. Might come in handy." She flung the handle on the ground, reached inside the open driver's side door, cut off the engine, took the keys and threw them in the bushes. "They'll have to figure another way outta here."

She removed a penlight from her purse and checked the floor. Nothing but fast food wrappers and beer and soda cans. A quick search of the back behind the driver's seat yielded the same result. The unlocked glove compartment was filled with papers. Not wanting to stick around any longer in case the young receptionist alerted the cops, she shoved the papers in her bag. She picked up the broom handle and strolled back to her Jeep.

The receptionist stared from the safety of the lobby when Jonelle gave a thumbs up and placed the broom handle on the pavement near the entrance. Once inside her vehicle, she left the way she came, noting the faint *woop-woop* of sirens in the distance. Driving five miles above the speed limit, she kept a constant eye in her rearview mirror on the lookout for police until she reached the Maryland state line where she finally relaxed.

Back on familiar territory, Jonelle headed for the Westminster, Maryland IHOP, a place she'd frequented often. She parked beside the last handicap spot in front and trudged inside, chose a booth close to the exit, and sat facing the door. The large window gave her a good view of her Jeep. Stifling a yawn, she waved away the menu and ordered a ham and cheese omelet with home fries and coffee, no toast.

She settled in the tan-colored booth and pulled out the papers taken from the sedan. Before spreading them out, she tried rubbing the tiredness out of her eyes and succeeded only in making them ache. She stared at her reflection in the glass.

There she was, alone in the middle of the night, eating breakfast at a time when normal people returned home after a real dinner out with family and friends. Adrienne's harping on her not giving Burt a chance weighed on her. He was a good guy. Actually, he was better than that. The man had a great job he loved. A great personality coupled with an easy sense of humor made him more than attractive.

Jonelle sighed deeply and fingered the crumpled papers stolen from the two lowlifes. And then she remembered the picture on the fliers the kids made of four-year-old Lark. No matter how lonely she got sometimes, working a case beat delivering summonses by a wide margin any day. She thought back to the porn studio warehouse and the legitimate businesses there. All that room to make something out of nothing and with a break in taxes to boot. What if . . .

She worked the kinks out of her shoulders, hiking them up to her ears and down again, rotating each one in turn. The waitress came with the coffee, and she sipped thoughtfully while studying the sheets on the table. Most were receipts for car repairs, fast food restaurants, and drug stores. Jonelle noted with amusement that the drug store receipts were mostly for condoms. Two handwritten notes were signed "Lorraine."

On one note written in ink were the words, "Find R right away! He's not answering his phone. Can't find him at the WM!" No date, so she had no idea what the words meant. She pushed the unlined paper to one side. The other message read, "Pick up S at T's sis house. Need to regroup. Keep your damn phone on, can't be leaving no paper trail!" And the idiot didn't even throw these away. The initial R probably stood for Randy, but that didn't make sense. Or maybe Reggie? And the only S she knew was Shawn. What was Shawn doing at Tamora's sister's house?

She leaned against the booth and stared out the large window, once again gazing at her own reflection. She was no closer to finding the child than when she first started. Another look at the notes. This "R" sounded like he or she took matters into their own hands. What did "WM" stand for? Maxine? A friend's apartment? One of the stores at the strip mall?

The waitress arrived, toting her food. "Careful, it's hot," she said, setting the plate on the table. "Anything else I can get for you?" She topped off the coffee.

"I'm fine, thanks."

The waitress turned to go.

"Wait a minute. I'm stumped about something. These days people abbreviate everything. You ever hear anybody use 'WM' to refer to anything?"

"WM? The only person I've heard use that is my mother-in-law. That's what she calls Walmart. So, could be that, I guess."

"Thanks." Walmart? What the heck's going on at Walmart? She picked up her phone and searched for Walmart locations closest to the Pennsylvania line.

CHAPTER 47

Even at this late hour, crowds walked in and out of the massive store. She parked her Jeep and hurried toward the white on blue Walmart Supercenter entrance, her eyes searching the area for any sign of the familiar silver SUV.

Instead of going inside the overly bright store, Jonelle turned back, convinced there must be some mistake. No one would hide a child in a department store—Supercenter or not.

Her head pounded. She couldn't think straight. Driving through the lot might clear her head. Five mind-numbing minutes of going up and down rows and rows of vehicles led to one depressing thought: It seemed as though every owner of a silver car had errands to run at Walmart this time of night, and none matched Watkins' license plate.

On her last loop at the farthest end of the enormous lot on the left side of the property, a mini motorhome poked out, the back half in semidarkness. She drove closer. The white camper with brown stripes had running boards under the doors. No signs of life inside.

Few cars occupied spaces at this end. She settled her Jeep a few yards away in between a pickup truck and early model sedan and studied the motorhome. Several thoughts ran through her head, none of them good. If—and that was a big if—Lark was inside, then who was with her? She'd left Randy and Shawn in Pennsylvania somewhere around the interstate.

She grabbed her phone to call Burt, and immediately changed her mind. What if instead of a young African American child the camper held a retirement couple from Florida? She'd never live the mistake down. Only one way to know for sure. She settled the phone back in her bag and tucked the weapon in the small of her back.

A quick glance at her surroundings confirmed no one paid any attention to her. Jonelle strode up to the camper as if she belonged, and ambled around the motorhome. Blinds covered the windows on the right side of the approximately twenty-foot RV. Same for the other side so she walked to the back.

The license plate hung below the metal ladder and spare tire. She pulled out her phone and took a picture of the Maryland tag. That done, she strolled back to the side, and as her hand reached up to try the door handle, a man and woman passed, throwing her a curious look. What she needed to do didn't include appearing on someone's social media page for breaking into a motorhome.

The strangers passed with one last glance.

Jonelle pressed her ear against the door. A soft sound she couldn't identify came from inside. One more brief look around. She tiptoed to the window deepest in shadow and listened. A sneeze cut through the silence, a deeper sound than a small child would make.

Standing around suspiciously eyeing the RV wasn't getting her anywhere. She rushed over to the front of the store. A young woman in a blue vest stood at the edge of the sidewalk, smoking a cigarette.

"Excuse me?" Jonelle smiled. "This might sound weird, but I was wondering if I might borrow your work vest for a few minutes."

The young woman held the cigarette a few inches from her mouth. "Say again. You wanna do what?"

"I'm a private investigator, and I need some sort of, um, cover. Your vest might do the trick. I can pay you for your help. What I have to do shouldn't take long." She showed the woman her ID.

The employee studied Jonelle for several seconds. "How much?"

"Twenty?"

She held out her hand. Jonelle removed a twenty from her wallet and placed it in the young woman's palm.

She slipped out of the vest so fast Jonelle wondered if the woman would remain employed for very long. "I just started my dinner break, so I've got twenty-five more minutes. I'll need it back by then. Who you lookin' for, anyway?"

Jonelle pointed to where the mini RV stood like an abandoned cabin in the woods. "I have to check out that camper. You happen to know how long it's been parked over there?" Jonelle slipped on the thin vest. "Anything about who lives inside?"

"Some guy."

Jonelle waited for the young woman to say more and when nothing else was forthcoming, asked, "You see him with anyone else?"

"Once I saw him with a little girl. They was eating at the Mickey D's near the back of the store. When I went to get one of my co-workers to show them, they'd gone." The young woman squinted at Jonelle. "He do something wrong?"

"Not sure. Can you describe him?"

"Black dude about my complexion. Average height and weight, I guess. Wouldn't notice him unless you had a reason to look twice. Know what I mean?" She blew smoke out of the side of her mouth.

Jonelle thought back. Average weight didn't apply to the too skinny Jelani. And Randy's complexion was two shades lighter. What other males did she know who were involved with Tamora? Except for Vaughn Hanson, only one other person.

"Did you ever see him wearing any kind of uniform?"

The clerk threw the cigarette on the ground and used her foot to stamp it out. "Not me. One of my co-workers said he coulda sworn he saw him once wearin' a rent-a-cop uniform. You know, like security people wear."

"And he's not part of the security here?"

"Nope. And not only that, somebody else swears they saw that same camper parked at another Walmart."

Jonelle opened her mouth to say more but the sound of a racing motor stopped her. She stared in horror as the motorhome sped out of the lot.

She turned back to the clerk in a what-the-hell-was-that gesture

"Don't worry about it. He usually comes right back. Listen, I'm glad you're checking him out. A few of us was talking about it and were gonna call the cops. It's okay to park in the lot for a day or two, but he's been there way longer than that."

"I've got to find him. You said he comes back. Are we talking hours or days?"

"Hours. You want me to tell everybody to keep a look out?" The young woman's eye's shone. The eagerness displayed in them made Jonelle uncomfortable.

Ignoring the question, she handed the young woman a business card. "Please call if you see him."

The young woman studied the card. "You got a gun?"

Jonelle suppressed a sigh. "All I plan to do is talk to whoever's inside."

"This is way cool. Mind if I call my friend? Might wanna get this on my Instagram."

Afraid to comment any further for fear the woman would get even more excited and screw everything up, Jonelle waved goodbye and ran back to her Jeep.

Where would he go? He must've seen her. No way could she wait around for him to come back. That is, if he did in fact, return. Maybe . . .

Jonelle started her Jeep and headed for the exit. A left turn led to the main road, a right turn led to a neighborhood. She turned left and after several feet came to a stoplight. On the nearest corner sat a gas station and food mart. Across the street the red, white and green sign of a 7-Eleven glowed. She pulled into the gas station, parked in front and strode up to the cashier.

"Help you?" asked the man behind the counter.

"Hope you can. I'm a PI and was wondering if you have surveillance on the outside. If so, I'd like to take a look. I've got my license in here if—"

"Don't bother." He lowered his voice although as far as she could tell, the only other customer was nowhere near them. "It don't work. We only keep if for show."

Damn. "You know anything about the Seven-Eleven across the street?"

He shrugged. "Don't you need a warrant or something?"

She held his gaze.

"Okay, fine. I heard the manager of that place hardly lets his employees take a leak, so if I were you I wouldn't hold my breath on the off chance he'd let you look at his tapes—assuming he has any, that is."

She leaned against the counter as if needing the structure to keep from toppling over. "Okay. How about this? I'm interested in a white camper with brown stripes. Can't be too many of those around here. Have you noticed anything like that?"

A customer approached with several items. She waited to one side while the clerk bagged everything and handed the customer his receipt.

"Why didn't you say that before? Yeah, I seen it. Hard to miss something that big. But that was last week."

Weary from riding around all night and coming up empty-handed, she sat in her Jeep staring at all the cars coming and going on the busy road.

CHAPTER 48

Had to go back to my place for a little while. Went up the back way so nobody would see. She's safe there for a little while since that detective has everybody chasing their tails. Problem is the kid's getting twitchy. And more upset. And tired of the games we play.

Instead of napping after her snack, she started whining. Can't have that. Put some allergy medicine in her chocolate milk. As soon as she drifted off, I locked up and left to do my research.

The city's the best place to look. Got my pepper spray and a small knife handy if anybody tries anything. A few asked for money. Told 'em I wanted information first. Everybody obliged. Funny how no matter how hard life is, more people than you'd think would rather hold on to what they had. The easy ones to offer what I need are too old. They have too much attitude.

Once a kid gets used to the street, they already know too much. I'm looking for younger. The younger they are, the more they trust. I need innocent.

Heard about a shelter that only takes women with young kids. It's off the radar, though, 'cause it ain't licensed. Sounds perfect.

CHAPTER 49

O ne more thing. One more thing picked around the edges of her brain. If—and that "if" was huge—Reggie did keep Lark in the camper where would he go? No way could she search the parking lots of all the Walmarts in the area. Jonelle pulled out her notepad. And then she saw it. Of course. The man worked for security. Even at this late hour those agencies were 24/7. She found Reggie's name in her early notes. Reginald Tobias, followed by "Security" and the name of the company who employed him.

She searched for "Alpha and Omega Security" and dialed the number listed. After stating who she was and that she needed to reach Mr. Tobias on an important matter, the woman who answered put her on hold. Interspersed with details about the company was the loudest, most annoying hold music she'd heard in a long time. Why couldn't people be content with silence? She almost ended the call when at last the woman came back on the line.

"I'm sorry but Mr. Tobias is no longer with the firm," she said in a clipped voice.

"Was he fired or did he quit?"

"I can't divulge that information. Sorry."

"Wait a sec," Jonelle said, not wanting the woman to hang up. "Can you tell me how long ago he left?"

"Um. I don't know if I can . . . hold on."

She held the phone away from her ear.

"Hello, ma'am?"

"I'm still here."

"I can say that Mr. Tobias' last day was a week ago."

"Where was he last assigned?"

A long pause. "Guess there's no harm in telling you. He was one of three we had working rotating shifts at the City Mall." With that the woman clicked off. Jonelle stared at her phone. That was the same mall where she confronted Randy and Shawn.

The possibility that she might find the camper there provided her with an extra jolt of adrenaline. Less than a half hour later she pulled into the lot. At this time of night customers had long gone. Darkness shrouded the areas around buildings whose only source of illumination were inside security lights and the outside signage. She smiled at the sign for "Discount Shoes" now reading "Discount _hoes". Several other signs also had missing letters leading to the overall rundown feel of the place.

One working street lamp shone above a lone car parked in front of "Metro Liquors". She eased to a stop a few feet away. A man left the store and pulled down a metal security gate, the scraping sound harsh in the still night. He turned and stiffened at the sight of her Jeep.

"Excuse me, Mister. I'm uh, looking for someone. He drives a white and brown motorhome. One of those small ones. Have you noticed anything like that around here?"

He shook his head and scooted inside the sedan.

Oh no you don't, she thought. Not after the night I've had.

She pulled her Jeep behind him, blocking his exit, and leaned out the window.

"All I want is a little information. Honest. I'm a private investigator working a case."

He peered around at her. "PI, huh? Lemme see your ID."

The leather holster still hung at her waist. She left the Jeep where it was and slid up to the man, careful to avoid his car door in case he swung it open. She held her shield out to him.

He studied the case. "You don't look like any PI I've ever seen, don't care what that thing says. Get outta the way."

"No moving until you answer a few questions. Which, by the way, you coulda answered without all this drama and been on your way to the wife and kids."

He groaned. "As if that's a benefit. What you wanna know?"

"Okay. Have you seen a motorhome around here? Especially at night?"

"You mean one a them house on wheels? Naw. You can't fit those things in here."

"This one's smaller. About half the size of those big ones."

"Still ain't seen it."

"What d'you know about the security guard that worked here? Names Reggie . . . Reginald. Works for Alpha and Omega."

"That who you're lookin' for? Ain't seen him in a while. 'Course when he was here he wasn't, if you catch my drift. Now I gotta go." He poked his thumb behind him. "Move that thing."

"In a minute. You ever see him with anybody?"

The man shook his head then seemed to reconsider. "Oh yeah. One time I seen him talking to a real hot lookin' mama. Thought it mighta been his girlfriend the way they was arguin'. It was near closin' time and when I heard all this yelling I poked my head out. When they saw me the girl strutted off and hopped into a fancy SUV."

"Silver?"

"Coulda been. Or white. Light colored anyway. I don't know nothin' else. Now move."

She didn't care that the man was getting pissed. "One more thing."

"Oh, good God."

"Where's his replacement? I don't see anybody around. So if nobody's here late at night, anybody could come around and do whatever they wanted." She glanced at the storefronts. "Any outside surveillance?"

"We—me and the other tenants—was talkin' about that. The association's gonna look into it. It'll be a whole lot easier than hiring these rent-a-cops that don't show up half the time."

"Thanks for your help."

She returned to her Jeep, and backed away from his bumper. She expected him to peel rubber in his haste to leave, but he surprised her by waving good-bye.

Strip malls only allowed vehicle traffic in the lot so she parked her Jeep in the now vacant spot in front of the liquor store. She grabbed her flashlight from the glove compartment, exited her Jeep and engaged the security system. Open dark spaces never bothered her. Night time provided a sort of comfort. Kind of like a warm blanket on a cold night. The soles of her shoes scraped on the concrete sidewalk and echoed off the buildings. She followed along the stores in the front and a short way along the side. At that point the sidewalk ended.

She hesitated before entering the tight alley where three large dumpsters stood with maybe a foot between each one. "Could a camper squeeze in behind here?" She spoke out loud to hear her own voice—and to scare off whatever critters made those scurrying noises. Her legs tingled at the idea of one of those creatures sliding across her feet. She shone the flashlight in a large arc and entered the alley.

The space was surprisingly clean. A line of trees on the left side took up most of the back area. The branches were so close together that a tiny compact car couldn't fit around them, much less a twenty-foot camper. Dejected, Jonelle faced the fact she'd reached another deadend. She yawned and turned to go back to her Jeep. And stopped as she rounded the corner.

A gray sedan shone it's headlights into her Jeep. Had the liquor store owner come back? Why? Did he forget something? Couldn't be him, she thought, his sedan was darker. She couldn't see the driver and decided to wait and let the scene play out.

The car door opened on the driver's side. A figure slid out.

Jonelle's breath caught.

A woman emerged from the passenger side.

Both sauntered to the Jeep and peered in the window.

Jonelle almost laughed out loud with relief. She didn't recognize those people. No matter the reason for them being there she wanted them away from her vehicle.

"Help you?" She called out, standing next to the shoe store.

The young couple scurried back to their car and made a U-turn out of the mall.

Jonelle walked a few steps forward, and stopped. The only store that didn't have an iron grate was Discount _hoes. She hurried to the back. Sure enough, each business' door had their name stenciled on the outside.

Using her flashlight to examine the lock, she knew her picks wouldn't do the job in the short amount of time she wanted to spend. Of all the shops in the mall, the auto parts store might provide her with something substantial enough to use to break in.

She searched all around the trash bins and came up with nothing. Even with the ragtag appearance of the mall, the shopkeepers were strangely neat. Jonelle aimed her flashlight at the lock and noticed all the scratch marks where it looked as if several attempts at breaking in had already occurred. Figuring the place probably had reinforced the lock from the inside, she gave up. She rubbed her head in frustration, angry at herself for what she considered doing. *Couldn't hide a kid in there, anyway.*

Jonelle trudged back to the front, turned the air conditioning in the Jeep to full blast, found the loudest music she could and exceeded the speed limit on the way home. Better that than falling asleep at the wheel.

After letting herself in and checking to make sure Gracie's bowls were full, she threw a few of the catnip mice in the living room to make-up for the guilt she felt for ignoring the kitten. "Sorry, kiddo. I'll do better once this case is over. Promise."

Jonelle pulled herself into the bathroom for a quick shower and afterwards wrapped herself in her softest nightshirt. She sighed contentedly as her head hit the pillow. "So tired of everybody jerkin' me around. Wait'll tomorrow. Just you wait."

CHAPTER 50

E arly the next morning, right after she'd had her second cup of coffee, the "Hawaii Five-0" theme announced a call from Piper.

She hesitated. Burt was first on her agenda, so she let the call go to voicemail, and immediately felt guilty. She wanted to hear what the kids had to say, so decided on a compromise. Not wanting to speak to him right away she called the main number for Burt's division instead of his private number and left the name Reginald Tobias, his previous employment and telephone number, and added information about the Walmart RV. Before disconnecting she included the name of the strip mall and said she'd see him after she took care of another matter.

Not proud of the fact she deliberately omitted Maxine's name, she didn't feel guilty about it either. She wanted to deal with Lark's babysitter herself.

After listening to Piper's message, Jonelle drove to Tamora's building to speak to the kids in person. The young woman's message held a sense of urgency but didn't go into any details. On the drive over she wondered at the abductor's skill of keeping the upper hand, as if anticipating her every move. "That or my ham-handed approach is sending off warning bells," she grumbled to herself.

All three youngsters waited out front while she pulled into a visitor's spot. No sign of Watkins' car.

"How come you didn't answer?" Piper strode over to the Jeep and held out her phone for emphasis.

"Decided to come in person. What's up?"

"We think Mrs. Watkins quit."

Jonelle exited her Jeep. "What makes you think that?"

"'Cause she's missing in action," Fred said.

"Yeah. Vanished into thin air," Grayson said, not wanting to be left out. "Poof."

"When was the last time you guys saw Jelani around?"

The looked at each other then shook their heads in unison. "You think they're together?" Piper asked, then answered her own question. "I don't think so. She only kept him on because nobody else wanted the job."

"You don't know that for a fact," Grayson said.

"I know more than you." Piper placed her hands on her hips.

"You said you had something to tell me. That it was an emergency," Jonclle said, jumping in to avoid an argument. "Let's go around back and talk." Without further comment, she headed to where the playground equipment and benches were kept. All three youngsters trudged close behind.

She perched on a picnic bench with Piper and Grayson on either side while Fred snagged a swing and dangled her legs in front. "I'm the one with the news," Fred said. "I saw Lark yesterday."

"You what?"

"She's not really sure," Piper said. "Fred only thinks she saw Lark. There's lotsa little kids in here."

Jonelle stared at Fred who contentedly swung back and forth as if relishing her time in a spotlight that didn't often shine.

She waited for the redhead to say more. Instead, Fred kept swinging back and forth, higher and higher. Occasionally a giggle would emerge from her freckled face.

The urge to grab the swing and yell at the youngster to get on with it was almost a physical need. As if sensing her mood, the other two kept quiet.

After what seemed an eternity and with Jonelle's blood pressure increasing the higher Fred swung, the youngster finally stopped and pointed a grimy finger at Jonelle. "You're no fun. All right, I'll tell you. I know where Lark is." The youngster jumped off the swing, as if doing a gymnastic dismount. "Ta-da."

When no one responded, she continued. "Saw her last night. In the basement near the storage room. She was by herself, I think, so I almost said something. But then this guy came out of the janitor's office, so I hid around the corner. When I looked again, she was gone."

Jonelle didn't believe her but decided to play along. "Was it Jelani?"

Red Fred rolled her eyes. "If it was him, I'd 'a said so. Don't know this guy. Never seen him before."

"What time was this?"

"Don't know, but it must've been a little before midnight 'cause that's about when my mom passes out for the night."

Jonelle glanced over at Piper who shrugged.

"It's no big deal, okay? I get bored in that stupid apartment. So what?"

"Guess I should go check it out then," Jonelle said.

"She's not there," Fred said quickly. "I already looked this morning,"

Jonelle suspected that wandering around late at night wasn't the only odd thing about the redhead. She rubbed both hands over her face and mentally counted to five.

She leaned forward and peered into the youngster's eyes. "See, here's the thing, Fred. This isn't a game. Never has been and, if you think it is, well, you're wrong. I'm afraid for Lark. She's probably scared being away from her mother so long, and she may be with people who might make her do things a child should never have to do. If you know something, you need to tell me now. Please."

"I'm not playing games!" She glanced at her two friends, whose eyes studied the ground. Fred shoved her hands in the pockets of jeans frayed at the hem and worn through the knees. She, too, stared at the dirt on the ground. "I don't want anything to happen to Lark, either," she mumbled. "This morning, after my mom left, I went to the storage room, and nobody was in there."

"Okay. Back to the guy, can you describe him?"

"Not really. Average looking I guess."

"Black or white?"

"Black. I think. But coulda been mixed up like Grayson."

Jonelle wanted to throttle the twelve-year-old. "You think? What's that mean?"

Fred shrugged.

What the hell was going on?

"Are you screwin' around," Piper asked. "'Cause if you are—"

"I'm not," Fred shouted.

Jonelle held her head in her hands, aware of three sets of young eyes boring into her, waiting for her to take some action . . . to do something, anything. But all she could think of was getting back into Tamora's apartment where this whole mess began.

"Anybody know if Miss Maxine is home?"

"I knocked on her door a couple hours ago and didn't get an answer," Piper said.

"While we was waitin' for you, Ms. Wright came up and demanded to know where Miss Maxine was 'cause she promised to watch her kid while she went out," Grayson said.

Tired of ending up one step behind, Jonelle studied the trio. Somehow, they—whoever they were—were able to move Lark around without drawing attention to themselves. She didn't think Grayson would say anything, nor Piper.

But Fred. Fred craved attention. Was it possible the redheaded twelve-year-old bragged about what she knew and tipped off the perpetrators whenever Jonelle closed in on their hideout?

"Where's Lark?" Jonelle asked.

Fred shrugged, stepped back, and averted her eyes.

Quietly, but firmly, she repeated the question. "Where's Lark?"

With green eyes wandering around the small play area, Fred picked at her forearms so aggressively Jonelle became concerned the youngster would draw blood. But this wasn't about Fred.

"Tell me the truth. This has gone on long enough."

"What did you do?" Piper's voice sounded distant, even though she was only a few feet away. "If you know something about Lark, you've gotta tell Miss Jonelle."

Tears flowed down Fred's face. She hung her head. "I didn't . . . do anything. I saw . . . stuff. More than I said before." She sniffed. "I'm sorry."

She plopped down on the ground and buried her head in her arms, sobbing.

"We don't have time for your personal pity party," Jonelle said, harsher than she intended. "Tell me everything you know, without lies, without making stuff up. Got it?"

Several seconds passed before Fred nodded, head still buried in her arms.

"I know where to hide around this place," she said through hiccups. "Jelani never locked up like he was supposed to, so I can get in and out of rooms that no one else is supposed to go in. I hear stuff. Not only here. At the store across the street, too."

Jonelle reached inside her bag and handed Fred a tissue.

"Did you see who took Lark that night?"

"No," Fred yelled. "Honest. But I seen who put her in the storage room and when they took her right out again. They did that because of you . . . you poking around here. They said you screwed up the plan."

"Who was it?"

"Mrs. Watkins and some guy. Don't know his name."

"What?" Piper yelled.

"You never said," Grayson shouted.

Jonelle's chest tightened. "Did you hear what the plan was?"

Fred blew her nose and held out her hand for another tissue. "They said something about everybody staying together so as not to mess everything up."

She banged on Maxine's door. No answer. She went across the hall and pounded on Tamora's and got the same result. The lock picking tools lay at the bottom of her bag. It'd only take a few minutes to get inside both places. Before she could begin, her phone rang. She frowned at the unknown caller display and considered not answering. And answered anyway.

"Hey. Luther let me use his phone."

Jonelle groaned upon hearing the voice she'd come to dread.

"Been asking around about the creeps at that video place and thought you'd like to know what I heard."

"Thanks anyway, Riley, but—"

"Couple guys hang out there hoping somebody'd throw away something interesting," she said as if Jonelle hadn't spoken. "They stay around back, but they know who comes and goes in that place. One of 'em mentioned an older black lady."

"Yeah, I already know about Lorraine Watkins. Thanks anyway, but—"

"Hey! Hold on. It ain't that fat black lady. I met her and the description ain't the same. I said older. More like . . . well it's kinda hard to tell with you black people. You guys age really well."

Her finger hovered over the end call button. "You got something to say, say it." Damn. That woman could get under a person's skin faster than the roadrunner harrassing that coyote.

"All right. Keep your drawers on. If I had to guess from what he said, I suppose maybe mid-sixties. He paid attention because he'd seen her before. Claims she's trolling the streets looking for homeless kids. Little ones. At first he figured her for one of them do-gooders, wanna save all the poor unfortunates." Riley snorted. "Yeah, right."

"Go on." A thought bloomed in the back of Jonelle's skull. It would explain all the children's clothes in Maxine's apartment.

"But she wasn't handin' out anything. She wanted the kids to go with her. Promised their moms lots of money, she'd take care of 'em, give 'em nice clothes, plenty to eat. She'd be like another granny until they got back on their feet."

"Any mention of how she'd give them all this money?" Her stomach soured.

The excitement in Riley's voice came through the line. "Yeah. Pictures. She wanted to take a few pictures. Claimed she knew people who'd pay a lot of money for certain kind of pictures of kids. You catch my drift?"

Several seconds passed while Jonelle pondered everything. "You got a name for this guy?"

"Yeah."

A few more seconds ticked by.

"You gonna tell me or what?" Jonelle asked, her voice rising. One hand gripped the phone so tight she was afraid it would shatter in her hand.

"You oughta know names don't matter out here. I gotta show you where he's at. He did say the ole lady acted really nervous. Kept lookin' around, scared like somebody was gonna grab her." Riley chuckled. "My guess is you're probably the one who's got her spooked."

Not much traffic flowed around Luther's warehouse so Riley and Jonelle spotted each other at the same time. The woman had trainers on her feet, a different—and cleaner—cotton print top and jean shorts. Instead of the wild woman hairstyle, she looked as if she'd run a comb through the unruly locks. Riley waved for Jonelle to come closer. "I'm gonna kill her if this doesn't pay off," she muttered as the Jeep stopped at the curb.

As soon as Riley's butt hit the passenger seat Jonelle asked, "So where's this guy?"

"And a good day to you, too," Riley said. She turned in her seat. "Drive towards the harbor. Look. I know you got a problem with me, most people do. But . . . I really wanna find this kid before anything bad happens to her. That is, if it hasn't already. Truce?" She extended her hand.

Jonelle paused before grasping the offered hand. The grip was firm and dry. "Tell me something. Why'd you call? Not like we enjoy each other's company or anything."

Riley paused for so long Jonelle figured she wasn't going to answer. And then she did.

"Because." She looked out the window. Abandoned warehouses gave way to neat rowhomes. Several children played on the sidewalks and across the street a dirt covered playground sported a basketball court.

"When I was doing stuff for you the voices screaming in my head stopped . . . for awhile. The invisible bugs swarming up and down my body slowed down to almost nothing. I could fight off the urge to scratch until I bled. That good enough for you?"

Jonelle swallowed hard. "Where do I go?" she asked in a voice barely above a whisper.

Riley peered closely at Jonelle, opened her mouth to say something, then closed it again. "He hangs around the Camden station." She leaned against the seat and stared straight ahead.

Jonelle struggled with what to say. She didn't like the woman and knew the feeling was mutual. Yet they shared a common goal—finding Lark. Plus, Riley revealed something it must've been hard for her to admit. In spite of herself, Jonelle admired the woman's strength. "I'll cruise around, see if you spot him. You think he'd be, um, lucid enough to talk to me?"

"About as lucid as I am."

"Great. Something to look forward to."

Riley tipped her head back and laughed. "You might not believe this, but I kinda like you detective lady."

"You got a weird-ass way of showing it," Jonelle said.

Riley emitted a sound somewhere between a braying Mule and an agitated cow. She slapped one hand against the dashboard, mouth wide and revealing several missing teeth.

Jonelle tried, and failed, to keep from smiling.

They spent the rest of the way lost in their own thoughts. Jonelle drove around the front of the historic three-story red brick building with no results. "You wanna get out and see if he's on one of the platforms?" Jonelle asked.

"Naw. Even if he had the money he don't go there. If he ain't out front you gotta check the streets nearby. Turn on South Howard."

For a brief moment Jonelle considered if Riley was leading her on a wild goose chase. She turned where instructed. No one caught Riley's attention.

"Try Eutaw or Paca. He hangs around there sometimes."

Jonelle gripped the steering wheel. She decided to drive around for fifteen more minutes and if Riley didn't see—

"Hey! There he is. Hey, Silas. Over here. Silas! Don't pretend you don't hear me. It's Riley. I'm gonna cut you off if you don't get your skinny ass over here. Pronto."

The young man who turned at the sound of Riley's voice looked as if he regretted his decision to stop. Jonelle wondered about the "cutting him off" remark as she pulled down a tree-lined side street off of Paca and waited for Silas to approach.

Tall, skinny and dark complexioned the young man sported blond dreadlocks that instead of making him look tacky made him look as if he'd stepped out of a trendy fashion magazine. She must've stared at him a little too long because Riley cleared her throat.

"Yeah. Silas' got that effect on women. Too bad he swings the other way."

"Why you out here harassing people?" he asked, strolling up to the Jeep. "Ain't you still hangin' with Luther?"

"I am."

"So, what you want?" His eyes flitted to and then away from Jonelle.

"What I'd like," Jonelle replied, forcing him to focus his attention on her, "is information about an older woman seeking out little kids—say under ten-years-old. She claims she wants to help the family get back on their feet. To do that, she offers to take a few pictures and in return give them money, food, clothes, for the privilege."

"I don't know—"

"Yes you do," Riley said. She pointed a finger with the nail bitten down to the quick, at Jonelle. "She ain't a cop. Not a real one, anyway. Go on. Tell her what she wants to know."

"What's in it for me?" He smiled lop-sidedly and shoved his hands in jeans that hung below his waist.

"My eternal gratitude," Riley said with an edge in her voice.

The young man got the message. "Alls I know is some ole woman's been hangin' out at the shelter off MLK Boulevard. It's one of them small ones that only take women with kids and don't have much in the way of rules. Always full up, no matter what time 'a year. But you gotta know about it. There ain't a sign and I don't have no address." Instead, he rattled off the streets that ran around the place.

Riley snorted. "Heard about that one. That ain't a real shelter. People say it's run too loosey-goosey. And you gotta pay more to stay there."

"I thought mothers with children had better places to go," Jonelle said.

"They do. If they've been abused or runnin' away from somebody. But if all you want is a place for you and your kids until you get back on your feet, well, them places are harder to find and even harder to get into," he said. He smiled again, transforming his face from wary to cunning. No doubt about it, this kid could make big bucks staring out of the pages of a magazine.

Jonelle considered her options. She wanted to return Riley to the warehouse while she checked out the place to see if anyone knew Maxine and the young child who may be with her. And she intended to do it alone.

"Thanks, Silas. I'll see if I can find it." She reached inside her bag and pulled out a twenty.

He smiled that dazzling smile again as he shoved the bill in his pocket.

"You know . . . well, never mind," she said.

"You ain't the first one to think what you're thinkin'. It won't work 'cause he likes it on the streets. By the way, I'm comin' with you," Riley said, crossing her arms across her chest.

Silas turned away, chuckling and shaking his head. He'd only gone a few feet when he turned back around. "Hey, lady. Easier to let Riley's attitude play out. She gets ahold of somethin', she don't let go."

Neither do I, Jonelle thought.

They circled two blocks up and down one street and then the other before they found the building. With no sign out front, and no specific address from Silas, the only indication they had the right place was two women trudging up concrete stairs, heavy bags and small children in tow.

"Excuse me," Jonelle called. Both women turned. "Is this the shelter?"

"Who wants to know?" asked the first woman.

"Lookin' to help a friend and her little girl," Riley yelled before Jonelle could answer.

"Then you come to the right place." The woman turned, opened the door and slipped inside. The second one followed wordlessly behind.

"Weird it doesn't have security," Jonelle said. She squeezed her Jeep in a space a little too close to a fire hydrant.

"Ten to one this place ain't legal. That's why they don't advertise."

"So where do they get the money?" Jonelle asked.

"These ladies work. If I had to guess, I figure they must turn over a good bit of what they earn. How you wanna play this?"

Jonelle considered the three-story row home. The building sat in the middle of the block. Instead of the same light stone as the others, the dark gray façade sported blackened areas from bottom to top. The bowed window on the main level was angled, not rounded. The stone steps led to a bright blue door with a half moon of glass at the top.

Each rowhome exhibited a green hedge out front of varying heights and amounts of foliage. Every third home featured a shade tree near the street.

Her eyes drifted to the end of the block. On one corner, the ever present liquor store. Opposite and diagonally across the street stood a vegan restaurant, with a city bus stop out front.

"Hey. Did you hear me? Can't stay here all day with you sittin' here daydreamin'. We goin' in or what?"

Jonelle sighed, already regretting her decision to bring Riley along.

"Too late," Riley said, as if reading Jonelle's thoughts. "I'm seein' this through." She hopped out of the Jeep and was halfway up the steps by the time Jonelle caught up with her.

She elbowed Riley to one side and tried the doorknob. Locked. She hadn't noticed either woman using a key. Riley reached past and pounded on the door.

"Knock it off," Jonelle hissed. Before she could say anything else the door opened and they stood face-to-face with a pleasant-looking middle-aged woman. Short and with the face of a woman who smiled often, the woman said, "How can I help you ladies?"

While the words were pleasant, the woman's body blocked the door.

Jonelle had no idea what to say so she opted for part of the truth. "Afternoon. My name's Jonelle Sweet. I'm looking for Maxine. She's . . . an older woman with a young child. Lark. She's four." Jonelle reached in her bag and pulled out her private investigator's ID. "The child's mother asked me to find them. She and Maxine, uh, had a falling out and now she wants to make amends. Can I come in?"

"She means me too," Riley added. "I'm working with her on this."

The woman frowned at Riley's words.

"We don't want the police involved. Tamora only wants to know her daughter's safe," Jonelle said.

The woman squinted at Riley as if having trouble believing anyone would want the abrasive blond as their assistant. Before Jonelle could tell Riley to return to the Jeep, the woman moved to let them inside.

All three squeezed into a narrow corridor painted bright yellow with white trim. Doors opened on the left. "My name's Wanda," the woman said.

Jonelle's chest tightened in the close space. "Can we go someplace to sit down?"

Wanda led them up carpeted stairs to the second floor. She stood to one side. "Go inside that door there," she said, pointing to the right. "That's the office."

Jonelle and Riley stepped inside.

The small room's walls were painted the same bright yellow as downstairs and two long, narrow windows allowed a lot of natural light. Jonelle relaxed.

Wanda indicated two somewhat battered, slat-backed chairs. A small slit in the center of one chair cushion exposed foam rubber.

Jonelle took the one without the tear, ignoring Riley's grunt. She wanted to get right to the point but waited until the woman situated herself behind the cluttered desk. Next, Wanda rummaged through a small metal file cabinet and pulled out a manila folder.

For the first time since she began working on the case, Jonelle believed she was getting close to finding Lark. She didn't want anything—or anyone—to screw that up. She willed Riley to keep her mouth shut while Wanda frowned at the words in the file.

"Pretty sure this," she tapped the file, "is who you mean, since we don't get many women her age coming in here. She showed up a few days ago. Early that first day, she came alone. A few hours later, she left and came back with the young child. Didn't give her name as Maxine, though."

Jonelle leaned forward. "Can I take a look at that?" she asked, indicating the folder.

"Afraid not. This is confidential." She placed the file back in the cabinet.

"The county provides for the elderly. I'm not set up for that. Only reason I let her stay is she had the money and said she'd babysit for the mothers so they can go to work." Wanda's gaze shifted back and forth. "I like kids, but they get on my nerves sometimes. Claims she doesn't mind. Says she likes lots of kids. The more the merrier. So I agreed."

"Do you know how the mothers planned on paying her?" Jonelle asked. She kept her suspicions to herself.

Wanda shrugged. "I don't really know. That was up to them." Her gaze shifted from Jonelle to Riley and back again.

"Didn't you find it odd an older woman towed a little one around?"

Sad eyes focused at Jonelle. "No. A lot of children end up staying with their grandmothers. Know what I mean?"

Neither Jonelle nor Riley responded.

"I didn't know she'd taken her granddaughter." Wanda sat up straighter and smoothed out her blouse. "We don't allow crime in here."

"Does she have a room?" Jonelle asked.

"All we had left was on the top floor. It's real hot up there, so—"

Jonelle held her breath. "Are they upstairs now?"

Wanda shrugged. "Don't know. They spend a lot of time in the common room. We can check there first."

CHAPTER 51

I hear voices coming from downstairs. I sneak down a few steps and lean over the railing. I recognize a voice other than Wanda's. I can't believe it. How'd she find me? I climb the stairs as fast as my arthritis will allow. My eyes water from the pain. Damn knees. If I try to leave the front way, I'll have to pass where the voices are coming from. I open the door and she's sitting on the bed, eyes wide, thumb in her mouth. Butterfly puzzle, butterfly pictures spread all over the place. Damn butterflies. I hate all of that stuff now.

What to do? Hide!

Where? The closet.

No, can't do that. That's the first place she'll look. I grab the child's arm and yank her close to me as I circle the room. She starts crying. She does that a lot these days. I shake her to get her to stop. She cries louder.

The window. Maybe we can climb down the back way. Down the fire escape.

I open the window and lean out, but it's too far to go with the child. What good is she to me now? Everything's ruined. I'll leave her. Maybe I can make it if I don't have this little . . .

I hear footsteps.

What am I gonna do?

CHAPTER 52

A blaring television signaled their arrival to the common area. Children and toys filled the large room, but no sign of Lark or Maxine. Across the hall, the tiny kitchen was empty. "You stay down here," she told Riley. For once the woman obeyed, standing on the landing and watching as Jonelle climbed up to the next level.

Each step increased the temperature and Jonelle started sweating. At the top of the stairs she wiped her forehead with her bare hand. She faced three closed doors and the end of a short hall. She put her ear against the first door. Loud voices came from inside. She knocked, first softly then harder. Someone turned down the sound. A couple seconds later a young girl around Piper's age opened it with a "help you? My mom ain't here."

"Do you know which room Miss Maxine stays in?"

The girl frowned. "Who?"

"Older woman. Babysits the kids."

"Oh, yeah. Last one on the end." She closed the door before Jonelle could thank her.

A child's cries stopped Jonelle in her tracks. Her hand reached in her purse and closed around the pistol.

She tip-toed to the last door and listened. The crying rose in volume.

Instead of knocking, Jonelle slowly turned the doorknob.

A little girl sat in the middle of the bed, dressed in pink shorts and holding tight to a plush bunny. She stared at Jonelle with wide, wet eyes.

Finally. She nearly fell to the floor from relief.

"It's okay, Lark." She took her hand out of her bag and smiled. "I'm going to call your daddy. Would you like that?"

Lark nodded, setting in motion pink butterfly barrettes.

No sign of Maxine. Jonelle checked the one closet and under the bed. No one else was in the room. Curtains fluttered against the open window. She leaned over the sill and observed Maxine clanging her way down metal fire escape steps.

Jonelle ran out of the room and shouted to Riley. "She's going down the fire escape out the back. Stop her."

Riley sprinted down the stairs.

When Jonelle returned to the room, instead of calling Burt, whom she knew would have a million questions, she put in a call to Langford. It rang several times before the attorney picked up.

"Good thing your number shows on caller ID or I'd have let it go to voicemail," he said. "This is my day to catch up on paperwork. I was starting to wonder about you since you haven't been that great keeping me informed."

She ignored the comment. "I found Lark." She gave him the address. "Maxine was with her. We've got her cornered."

"Maxine? Who the hell's Maxine?" The attorney shouted.

"Babysitter. Remember?"

"Oh yeah. She's had her all this time? Are you kidding me?"

"Don't think so. I believe several people took turns moving Lark around. One of the guys who had her ran off in an RV, but I know who he is. I'm not sure, but I think Maxine decided to take matters into her own hands. The important thing right now is, Lark's safe."

The silence on the other end stretched for so long, Jonelle glanced at her phone to make sure they were still connected.

"Call the cops. I'm on my way."

She sighed. "I'd rather call her father first." Lark stopped crying and stared at Jonelle with wide eyes. Jonelle turned and lowered her voice. "I thought about something. If I call the cops they might put her in some kind of home until things get sorted and she needs to be with someone she knows . . . and trusts." She thought back to what Watkins, Tamora and now Maxine, had planned for the little one and couldn't stand the thought of the child being tossed around again.

"Tell you what," Langford said. "I'll call the cops and her father from my phone when I get there. Maybe they'll be more understanding with a relative there. You sure you've got Maxine?"

Jonelle thought about Riley and smiled. "Oh, yeah."

With Lark's hand grasped firmly in her own, Jonelle stepped very slowly down the stairs. Wanda kept ringing her hands, muttering over and over again, "I don't want no trouble" and "are you gonna call the police?"

"Don't have a choice," Riley said. "You was giving shelter to this one," she held up Maxine's arm gripped tight in her fist. "And she ain't going nowhere until the cops get here."

Maxine squirmed, trying to get away.

Riley held fast.

"Something told me you was gonna be trouble." Wanda pointed a finger inches from Maxine's face.

Riley hauled Maxine onto the sofa. Maxine shrank into the sofa cushions.

"Shoulda listened to myself and kept you outta here. That's what I get for pitying folks." Wanda leaned against the doorframe, folded her arms and glared.

"Listen, Wanda," Jonelle said. "I don't care what you do here. Fact is, looks like you provide a decent service. But Lark was kidnapped—"

"She weren't no such thing," Maxine screamed.

Lark hid behind Jonelle's legs.

"Tamora knew all along what we was doing. She was part of it," Maxine said.

"Save it for the cops, granny," Riley said.

"Nobody's calling the cops until Tamora's lawyer gets here. It'll be his call. Me? I'd rather Lark's daddy take her away from all this mess," Jonelle said. "In fact, if Langford's not here in a half hour, I'm calling Vaughn Hanson myself. But first, I've got a few questions for you." She stabbed her index finger at Maxine.

Wanda cleared her throat and managed to get herself together long enough to suggest the residents—lurking in the hall wondering about all the commotion—and their children stay in their rooms or maybe take a long walk for an hour or two, and they grudgingly obliged. Wanda mumbled something about fixing Lark a snack of milk and chocolate chip cookies. Jonelle almost felt sorry for her as Wanda led the child to the kitchen.

Jonelle sat on the other side of Maxine, turning sideways to face her. "I don't care what you do or do not tell the cops. I've some questions of my own and you're gonna answer them. You've jerked me around for the last time, old lady."

"If you don't wanna answer the detective lady's questions, I'm gonna do all I can to convince you that's not a good idea. Got it?" Riley squeezed Maxine's arm for emphasis.

Maxine yelped.

"Ease up a little, Riley."

Riley relaxed her grip.

"Okay, Maxine. First question: who took Lark from the apartment?" Jonelle asked.

At first she kept her mouth pressed tight.

Riley shifted on the sofa, tightening the space between the three of them.

All the air seemed to leave Maxine's body. "It was supposed to be Jelani," she said in a high-pitched voice. "Idiot didn't show so Lorraine told me to do it. I hid her in my apartment until Reggie showed up and took her away."

"Did she stay with Reggie the whole time?" Jonelle thought she knew the answer but wanted to hear it from Maxine.

"No. The plan was always to move her from one person to another so as to keep the cops off our trail." She snorted. "As if they were ever really on it. Only one who threatened to mess everything up was you. Poking around like you owned the place."

Riley leaned across Maxine. "Don't think she likes you," she told Jonelle.

"Yeah. Breaks my heart. So who planned this whole thing. Tamora?"

Maxine busied herself straightening her clothes.

Riley poked her. "Answer the question."

"I don't want her here," Maxine whined to Jonelle. "Make her leave me alone." She rubbed her hand against her side.

"Nope. I'll ask again. Did Tamora plan the kidnapping?"

She flinched when Riley got even closer. "Her and Lorraine. It was only gonna be until we could get the pictures out and then Lark was supposed to be left off at a church or somewhere for the cops to pick her up and return her to Tamora. That would prove Tamora's innocence. But everybody started getting nervous with you sticking your nose in. And . . . they were getting way more money than me. Wasn't fair. I took more risk than anybody."

"What kinda pictures?" Jonelle wanted to smack her upside the head for what she put Lark through.

"Ones of Lark and Tamora. Together."

"Naked?" Riley asked. "Lady I don't care how old you are I feel like wringing your scrawny neck."

"Lorraine said it's like what you see in an art museum. Nothing dirty."

Jonelle stood so fast, Riley jumped.

"This isn't the first time you guys have done this. Right?"

Maxine looked down at her hands.

"But I'm guessing this is the first time you hit so close to home." Jonelle shook her head over and over, afraid to speak for fear of losing her temper.

"Okay if I smack her now?" Riley asked.

Jonelle almost said yes. She breathed deeply. "I doubt the people who buy these pictures go to many museums. What happened?" Jonelle asked before she got sick. Let the cops determine the so-called art value of this whole mess. "Who was supposed to have her last?"

"Reggie. 'Cause that's how it worked before. He'd park that camper thing in Walmart parking lots. Nobody'd suspect anything. One day he was at the one I shopped at so I told him I'd watch her while he went in and got some stuff. When he left, I . . . took her."

"Why?" asked Riley, leaning forward.

At first it seemed as though Maxine wouldn't answer. Riley nudged her.

"Too many hands in the money pot, cutting in on my share. I'm an old woman. I ain't got a fancy pension. Things were easier when we didn't have a personal relationship with . . . the others. But Lorraine said this way was easier. Tamora already had a following, so involving Lark should be easy. All we had to do was wait until things blew over. People would lose interest in trying to find a black child. Didn't figure on you."

"You went back to your apartment?" Jonelle asked, her eyes warning Riley to keep quiet.

"For a little while. Sometimes. To pick up some things. I heard about this place so when the coast was clear, we left."

"What about Lorraine?"

Maxine shrugged. "She went to Pennsylvania and tried to get her mother to take Lark, figuring nobody would look for the child there. But her mother wasn't having it and Tamora started getting tired of the whole thing."

"Where's Tamora now?"

A loud banging on the front door startled everybody in the tight, overly warm room. Jonelle ran to answer it.

Langford wore a loud, Hawaiian print shirt under a navy, wrinkled sport coat.

"Where's the kid?" he asked.

Jonelle led him to the kitchen. A subdued Lark munched on a chocolate chip cookie. Wanda and Langford eyed each other. Instead of introducing them, Jonelle said, "Maxine's in the common room with Riley."

"Who's Riley?"

Good question, Jonelle thought.

"She, um, helped me out a few times. Anyway, let's step in the hall for a minute." She ignored the constriction blossoming in her chest. "Maxine says she took Lark and Tamora knew everything. Not only about the abduction, but the whole sordid plan."

Langford groaned.

"Thing is there are so many people involved at all different stages. What I know is when Reggie parked the camper at the Walmart the last time—"

"Walmart?"

"Yeah. The one near Westminster. Anyway, Maxine offered to watch Lark while he went shopping but decided to swipe her instead. Took her back to the apartment for a little while then brought her here. I've got a feeling Maxine'll finger everybody to save her butt."

"Where's Tamora?"

Jonelle shook her head. "No idea, but Maxine insists Tamora was involved from start to—well at least up to the point Maxine decided to go rogue."

Langford took a handkerchief out of his breast pocket and wiped his forehead. "Go on."

"Met Reggie once. I have his name and the company he used to work for, plus I took down the RV's tag, so he might not be hard to find. He does have another vehicle, but I didn't pay attention to the make or model, so not much help there. Sorry."

"Hell. You've got the kid. That's pretty damn good in my book. She seems okay, what little I saw."

"She's fine. For now, anyway. That's why I'd like to call her father."

"Sounds reasonable to me, but I've gotta call the cops first." He pulled out his phone. "I'm calling a friend of mine with the police. She's one of the best they have in dealing with kids."

Jonelle was shaking her head before he finished. "She should be with her daddy."

"He can accompany them down to the station, but we've got to make sure Lark wasn't physically harmed in any way."

Jonelle cringed at the word "physically."

While Langford called the cops, Jonelle rang Hanson. She cut off his questions by telling him he should get to the address as fast as possible and somebody'd fill him in later.

Jonelle approached Langford. She wanted to talk outside but didn't trust putting too much distance between herself and Lark.

"Going back to what we talked about. Gimme the names of everybody you know who's involved," he said.

"In addition to Tamora, Reggie, Maxine and Lorraine Watkins, there's Shawn Mowerby—Lorraine's son—Randy and Jelani. Oh, and Mary Burroughs in York, Pennsylvania is Watkins' mother. She has information too."

Langford swore under his breath. "This Watkins. She the ringleader?"

"Not so much that as coordinator. In this case, anyway. There's a lot more to unravel, but the cops need to do that. As far as Lark's abduction, Watkins couldn't control this many people. Why the hell she thought she could is beyond me," Jonelle said.

"Lucky for us she did," Lanford said. "'Course one of them's my client, so that sucks." He wiped his head again.

Langford stared at the open door where Maxine sat confined by Riley. "You know, it's not a problem with me if you wanna go on in there and ask Maxine a few questions before the cops get here."

"Uh. Already did that."

He lifted his eyebrows.

"She was willing to talk."

He considered Jonelle for several seconds, a slight smile on his face. "Doesn't surprise me." The grin morphed into a scowl. "This business about taking still photos of her child, completely naked or not, with and without the mother, is something that's not gonna help Tamora one bit, no matter if she thought that she could protect Lark from . . . whatever. Damn, I need a smoke."

He pulled a pack from his jacket pocket. Then stuffed it back in again. "So. How'd Maxine and Lark wind up here?"

"She knew about this place and offered to babysit the kids here while the mothers went to work. All she wanted in payment was the okay to take a few pictures. I'm pretty sure Wanda didn't know anything about what Maxine had in mind."

"And you know this, how?"

"A source."

"Damn." He pulled out the cigarettes again.

Emergency *whoop-whoops* signaled the arrival of the police.

Jonelle inhaled deeply. "Here goes."

Langford went to open the door. Behind two uniformed police officers strode an agitated Vaughn Hanson, followed closely by his fiancée Cheryl. One of the officers tried to hold them back.

"Excuse me," Jonelle said, "that's the child's father."

A vein in Vaughn's head pulsed, and his eyes shot daggers at the cop who tried to prevent him from entering the building. He yelled at the cop to get out of his way.

"Vaughn," Jonelle shouted. "Mr. Hanson, please calm down. Lark is okay. Come over here for a minute. Cheryl, I think it might help if you stayed outside. Please."

After a slight pause, Cheryl nodded and walked back out.

The young cop, pale and with acne eruptions on his face, visibly relaxed.

Jonelle led Vaughn over to the common room.

"What's she doing here?" he asked, pointing to Maxine. "And who's that?"

"Hiya," Riley said.

"It's complicated," Jonelle said. "Someone will explain everything to you in great detail, but for right now, the cops are gonna need to talk to Maxine first."

The elderly woman made a sound resembling a trapped rat at the mention of her name. She turned her head to avoid looking at Vaughn.

"The lawyer said I could see Lark," he said. "Where is she?"

"In the kitchen. I know her being so close and you not able to hold her is the worst part, but right now everyone's focus is making sure Lark's okay after her . . . ordeal."

Langford motioned for a blond policewoman to go down the hall.

Hanson made to follow, but Jonelle held him back. "Not yet," she said.

"Where's Tamora? She know what's going on?" Hanson asked.

"I'd rather her lawyer fill you in," Jonelle replied.

After what seemed ages, but was probably only a few minutes, the policewoman came back carrying Lark who sucked hard on her thumb. When she saw her father the thumb plopped out and she grinned from ear to ear.

"Daddy! It's my daddy," she said to the policewoman. "I gotta go." Lark wriggled out of the officer's arms and ran to her father who lifted her up and held on so tight, that for a moment Jonelle wondered if the little one could breathe.

The lead detective who'd arrived after the uniforms, spoke briefly to Langford in the hall, and motioned everyone into the common area.

Wanda approached the detective. "Officer, sir. I don't know nothin'—"

"Get to you in a minute, ma'am."

He nodded for Jonelle to take a seat. He had the eyes of someone who'd seen too much and wanted to work his last days before retirement with as little excitement as possible.

Too late, Jonelle thought.

"So," he said. "How'd you know the little girl was here?" He stared at a spot behind her with such intensity that it made her think the answer was written on the wall.

She decided to give him the CliffsNotes version and let Langford fill in the details. "I didn't. I, um, got a tip that an older woman and a child were staying here. Maxine lived across the hall from where Lark was abducted. Lorraine Watkins is the property manager and I believe that she and Maxine, along with several other people know who took Lark away, and how." She pointed to Maxine. "That one knows everything."

"What's your interest?" he asked.

"Mr. Langford, Tamora Phelps' attorney"—she motioned to Lanford, casually leaning against the wall—"hired me to assist in the case." The detective's eyebrows shot up. Finally a response, Jonelle thought. At least now he's interested.

"And you're saying you don't know where the mother's at now. That right?"

"No idea."

"Bet this one here knows," Riley said, again poking Maxine in the ribs.

"Hey," Maxine shouted. "Stop that. Somebody get her away from me."

The detective settled his gaze on Riley. "And you are . . . ?"

"A concerned citizen," Riley said, staring hard at the detective until he looked away.

Jonelle jumped in before the detective's attention shifted back to Riley. "She heard about a tip that led us to this place. Not sure how long it would've taken to find Lark without her help."

"Uh-huh," he said, not at all convinced. "You look familiar," he said, turning to Jonelle. "Have we met before?"

Riley grunted.

They both ignored her.

"I've worked with the police in the past," Jonelle said. "Do you know a detective Burton? Thelonius Burton?"

One corner of his mouth turned up in what could've been the trace of a smile. "You know Burt? He and I used to ride patrol way back in the day."

Good ole Burt. She'd have to tell him that once again his name was an ice breaker. "Yes. He's a personal friend."

The detective's tone went from accusatory to almost friendly. "Tell me everything. Don't leave anything out."

Langford interjected before Jonelle could comply. "Are you asking her for a formal statement?"

The frown returned. "Nothing official, counselor. Call it a conversation. I want to know what I'm dealing with here."

Langford raised his hand in a stop gesture. "Tell you what, detective. We've got the child with her father. She seems okay and happy. Plus, you've got the lady who brought her here—you can ask her whatever you want. After she and I talk, Ms. Sweet will be happy to come down to the station later to make a formal statement. That okay with everybody?"

The adrenaline rush that coursed through her earlier quickly evaporated. "Fine with me," Jonelle said.

Before the detective could reply, Langford's phone rang. "Gotta take this. Don't say anything until I get back," he said.

"Lawyers," the detective grumbled.

315

No one said a word while Langford talked on the phone. His face looked ashen when he came back.

"What's wrong?" Jonelle asked.

"Got a call from Mercy Medical Center. Tamora's in the emergency room."

CHAPTER 53

J onelle stared long and hard at Langford. "What happened?" she asked. Before he could respond, she added, "And why call you? Seems like she'd call her sister."

"I don't know the answer to any of those questions. Yet. Gotta get to the hospital." He made to go past her but she stepped in his way.

"What?" he asked.

"Do I need to demand to see her? To see for myself what happened?"

"I can fill you in later."

"Nope," she said, still blocking his path.

He sighed. "Fine."

Hanson declined Langford's offer to meet at the hospital, wanting only to take his daughter home. Once Jonelle and Langford vouched for Hanson, he left with Lark clinging tightly to his neck. Jonelle smiled. "I'd like to see someone try to take her away from him."

A quick check of the common room found the detective questioning an agitated Maxine.

One person remained for Jonelle to deal with: Riley.

Left sitting on the sofa, Riley didn't utter a sound while the cops sorted everything out. Every now and then Jonelle caught her running rough hands up and down her arms, as if she was freezing and needed to warm up.

Once, Jonelle caught Riley picking at the skin on her arms and face. Riley stopped, embarrassed. For a brief moment the woman's face softened, then almost immediately hardened up again. Her mouth formed a tight line as if waiting for an argument, an accusation, a criticism.

"I need to take you back to the warehouse," Jonelle said, striding over to the sofa. "Tamora's at the ER and her lawyer's letting me see her. You ready? Or do you wanna be dropped off somewhere else?"

"What if I said I ain't leavin'?" She crossed her legs and swung the top one up and down.

Jonelle sighed. She was too damn hot and tired to argue. "That's up to you. But I'm going. So you can stay here as long as you want and help Wanda sort all this out with the cops, or you can walk to . . . wherever. Up to you."

Riley turned away from Jonelle.

"Listen. You've been a great help. Really. And I appreciate it. I can arrange some type of compensation if you—"

She swung back around. "Compensation? That what you think I want, detective lady?" Riley's leg swung faster and faster. Her fingers dug into her forearms.

"Fine. What do you want?"

"Gave you a bigass hint on the way over here. You don't remember, that's on you. I can find my own way back." With that, she bolted from the sofa and stomped out the front door.

"Hey!" One of the cops called out.

"Let her go," Langford said. "We know how to find her if you need to ask more questions." His eyebrows shot up at Jonelle. "Right?"

"Yeah," she said. A couple minutes earlier, she was pumped up, ready for anything. Now her entire body felt as if someone pulled the plug on her soul. She knew what Riley wanted. She also didn't want to pay that price.

For the past several days she'd broken her promise to her uncle not to neglect her duties at the agency, got kids involved and hooked up with a homeless woman who couldn't stand her—and the feeling was mutual—all because she went further than Langford had asked her to go. Worse, she didn't miss going to the agency.

At the ER the doctors made Langford and Jonelle wait until positive Tamora remained stabilized. A uniformed police officer stood outside the examination room.

For a while neither Langford nor Jonelle spoke. She broke the silence first. "Guess I owe you a complete report. Sorry I didn't check in as much as you wanted, but when things got going, I didn't want to break the momentum."

"Yeah. I thought so. Also figured you went above and beyond the initial request to verify her alibi. That right?"

She leaned against the cool wall in the ER and closed her eyes, trying not to inhale too much sickness and antiseptic smell. She struggled to form the correct words to say to try and make him understand her obsession with finding out what happened to an innocent four-year-old. When she opened them again the lawyer still stared at her, but the worry lines had faded.

"I knew the alibi was a lie when I talked to Reggie at the convenience store. It didn't matter to me if the surveillance video was off or not. I wanted to know what really happened."

Instead of angry words aimed at her, the lawyer chuckled. "Can't say I didn't get my money's worth, but now I've gotta think of a new way to defend her. That is, if she wants me to. Don't mean to sound crass, but its people like Tamora Phelps doing stupid shit that ensure folks like me have job security. I thank God that little girl is safe. This could've turned out a whole lot worse."

After Tamora's X-ray's showed no broken bones, the doctor informed Langford over twenty stitches ran from her upper arm down to the elbow on her left side. Only a few sutures were required on her face. Langford gave the doctor Evelyn Clifton's name and number as next of kin and was allowed a few minutes to talk to his client before they wheeled her to a room.

"I'm gonna see if the cops'll let her stay in the hospital to recover, rather than sending her to jail." He allowed Jonelle to sit in with the caution to not say anything.

Tamora's arm was bandaged, and an IV drip flowed into the other one. Gazing down at the self-absorbed woman willing to jeopardize her daughter's safety, Jonelle wanted to shake the silly creature and shout at her for being so stupid.

"Did you tell the police who attacked you?" Langford asked.

"Yes," Tamora whispered, eyes half-closed. "Lorraine did this. With a screwdriver."

"Why?" Jonelle asked.

"Ms. Sweet. What did I say?" His tone warned her to keep quiet.

Tamora answered as if she hadn't heard her lawyer. "Told her everything was going to hell and I wanted out. I thought at first the whole idea was no big deal. But, I couldn't do . . . what they wanted me to do with Lark. Then Maxine went crazy, going out on her own, not telling anybody where she was, and I got scared she'd hurt Lark and I wouldn't get my baby back." A tear flowed from the corner of her eye and down the side of her face.

"Why didn't you think about Lark in the first place?" Jonelle asked.

Langford shot Jonelle an angry look, but didn't interrupt.

"I did this for my child," Tamora said. "I needed the money. Everyone said she wouldn't get hurt. It'd be like a holiday, like some sort of game we'd all play with her. That's what Lorraine promised. She lied. And then things got worse with Maxine."

"Where's Watkins?" Langford asked.

"Don't you understand? I had to defend myself." Her eyes pleaded with Jonelle.

Jonelle kept quiet.

Tamora sighed deeply. "She keeps some of the apartment building's tools in her car. She started screaming that everything bad happened because of me being so stupid, and she was leaving Maryland and I'd get the blame for this whole mess. I grabbed a hammer from the back. Only as a threat. That's all, I swear. Anyway, she attacked me and started stabbing me with that screwdriver." She closed her eyes. "I had to defend myself or she would've killed me."

Jonelle repeated Langford's question. "Where's Watkins?"

When Tamora opened her eyes, they were filled with tears. "Left her near Reggie's motor home. He parks it in the Westminster Walmart parking lot."

"Reggie split in the RV. Try again," Jonelle said.

Langford sighed. Jonelle imagined he wished he'd never met Tamora. "It's over," he said. "You either tell the truth or get yourself another lawyer."

Tamora's eyes started to lose focus. "I . . . the fight happened at her place. In the garage. I left her there. A cop stopped me when I ran a red light, saw all the blood and brought me here."

"Was Watkins alive when you left?" Langford asked.

"Yes. At least I think so."

"Where does she live?" Langford asked.

Tamora mumbled the address.

Considering Tamora's condition, Jonelle wasn't sure about Watkins. Tamora was younger and didn't carry around as much weight. Still, Watkins looked like the type of woman a person wouldn't want to meet in a dark alley—especially if threatened.

Langford headed for the door.

"Where're you going?" Jonelle asked.

"I've gotta tell the cops where to find Watkins." He turned toward the body on the hospital bed. "I hope for your sake she's still alive."

Tamora responded by closing her eyes.

"What about Playcat?" Jonelle asked when Langford left. "Are they involved in this?"

Tamora shook her head. Her mouth and eyes remained closed.

Before she could ask another question, an ER nurse came and insisted Jonelle leave. Langford was on the phone when Jonelle met him in front of the nurse's station. He ended the call and mirrored her weary eyes. "A fine mess this is, huh?" He tried, and failed, to smile at her.

"Got that right. I'm beat but I've gotta tell you before I talk to the cops what happened in York."

He rubbed the top of his head and motioned for her to follow. "I know where the cafeteria is in this hospital. Follow me. We should be able to get a cup of coffee."

She didn't want coffee but matched his step out of the ER.

Instead of the strong-smelling brew, she selected a cup of tea, took a few sips, and threw the colored water in the trash. They sat at a table near the back. "I'm not good at chatting, and I can tell you're not in the mood, either," Jonelle said, as Langford's butt hit the chair.

He gave her a lopsided grin. "Just the facts, ma'am, or I guess in my case, sir. Am I right?"

She nodded.

"Okay. Tell me what you're gonna tell the cops."

She told him everything, including the twelve-year-olds and quickly added they were only extra eyes, nothing more.

He rubbed his face and stared off in the distance for several seconds. "I wanna know something," he said. "How'd you get from verifying my client's alibi, to discovering drugs and an alleged mugging in a porn studio, going across state lines, harassing two lowlifes—"

"Four if you count Shawn and Reggie," she interrupted.

"Okay. Four. Considering all you've told me, why put yourself in harm's way? Most of the detectives we've used in the past follow my instructions to the letter. They do what I ask. Period. Full stop. Grab the money and run. You take going the extra mile to the extreme, you know that?"

"I'll take that as a compliment. I go where the evidence takes me."

"And then some," he agreed.

After promising to arrive on time for her appointment with the Baltimore police department, she left Langford nursing his coffee and pulling out his phone to make another call. The last twenty-four hours, while exhilarating, taxed her to the limits of her resolve.

All she wanted now was to go inside her building, and if Hamilton was rehearsing on his cello, maybe sit on the steps for a while and listen. Afterwords, she'd enter her apartment, play a bit with Gracie, listen to smooth jazz, and sip a glass of wine.

And maybe, if she wasn't too tired, give Burt a call.

ACKNOWLEDGMENTS

A big thank-you as always to my DreamWeaversINK critique partners, Kim Hamilton, L. R. Trovillion, Karen Neary Smithson, Missy Burke, Mike Sage and P. J. O'Dwyer for their thoughtful insights and comments.

I'm also grateful to editor Amy Harke-Moore for her expertise and truly appreciate the feedback from beta readers Shirley Pratt and Kevin Lowery. Your fresh eyes kept me on track.

ABOUT THE AUTHOR

R. Lanier Clemons was born in Vermillion Parish, Louisiana and was employed as a corporate journalist for many years. She lives in Maryland with good friends Lucy the cat and Ramsey the wonder horse.

If you've enjoyed the book, a brief review on Amazon's website will be greatly appreciated. And if you'd like to know more about the character Riley, check out her own Amazon short read entitled, "Who's Riley? A JSM Short Read: Book 1." Note: JSM stands for Jonelle Sweet Mystery. Thank you.